THE ROAD TO YALTA

Books by Louis Fischer

The Road to Yalta

Russia's Road from Peace to War

The Life of Lenin

The Essential Gandhi *(Editor)*

Russia, America, and the World

The Story of Indonesia

Russia Revisited

This Is Our World

The Life and Death of Stalin

The Life of Mahatma Gandhi

The God That Failed *(Co-author)*

Thirteen Who Fled *(Editor)*

Gandhi and Stalin

The Great Challenge

Empire

A Week with Gandhi

Dawn of Victory

Men and Politics *(An Autobiography)*

Stalin and Hitler

The War in Spain

Soviet Journey

Machines and Men in Russia

Why Recognize Russia?

The Soviets in World Affairs *(2 volumes)*

Oil Imperialism

LOUIS FISCHER
1896-1970

THE ROAD TO YALTA

Soviet Foreign Relations 1941–1945

By LOUIS FISCHER

1817

HARPER & ROW, PUBLISHERS

NEW YORK, EVANSTON, SAN FRANCISCO,
LONDON

FIRST EDITION

STANDARD BOOK NUMBER: 06-011262-x

LIBRARY OF CONGRESS CATALOG CARD NUMBER: 69-15306

CONTENTS

PUBLISHER'S NOTE

The present volume is unfinished. It ends where Louis Fischer stopped writing before his death on January 15, 1970. The book was planned as the second volume of Louis Fischer's history of Soviet foreign affairs from the birth of the Bolshevik revolution to the present. The first volume, *Russia's Road from Peace to War: Soviet Foreign Relations, 1917–1941,* was published in 1969. Two sections of that volume, A Note to the Reader and Acknowledgments, throw some light on how the author saw and prepared the work as a whole.

For the present volume, Louis Fischer had completed an initial revision of the manuscript. *The Road to Yalta* is published from the manuscript as he left it.

FOREWORD

By George F. Kennan

> *Speech at Memorial Service,*
> *Auditorium of Woodrow Wilson School,*
> *of Public and International Affairs,*
> *Princeton University,*
> *Princeton, New Jersey,*
> *January 23, 1970*

My purpose here is simply to say some things about Louis Fischer as a historian, and particularly a historian in a field in which both of us had an active scholarly interest, an interest not shared with very many other people: the history of Soviet power, and particularly of Soviet foreign policy.

I know that what I may say will be inadequate. No one can do justice to the fullness of a man's life and work, even in so limited a field, and particularly not to the life and work of so unusual a man as Louis. His interest and knowledge in this field were poured out in literally thousands of written and spoken efforts—not just books, but articles, lectures, seminars, informal discussions, and, above all, conversations. Louis was the precise opposite of the lonely scholar. For him, scholarship was a process of human communication—a process in which he was constantly giving as well as receiving. No earthly tongue—no earthly pen—will ever record the totality of what he gave. I myself, when I think back on the influence he has had on me, do not know what to attribute to his written works and what to his talk.

I first met Louis in Moscow in 1933, and our acquaintance was pursued in that city for nearly four years thereafter. We were very different people. Louis was already very much the cosmopolitan, free-wheeling, free-lance journalist, a man always on the move, enjoying a host of acquaintanceships in Russia and elsewhere. I was still very much the faithful, correct foreign service officer, narrowly confined in the cocoon of my own official obligations and associations, unknown outside the Embassy, and almost the opposite of Louis in my shyness toward strange people. I had at that time had a training in Russian language and history more thorough than Louis', but narrow and bookish. I knew something about the Soviet economy and about earlier Russian history; but he knew vastly more than I did about the Soviet Union generally, and particularly about the immediate historical background of the heyday of Stalinism, into which we were then moving.

We took, as one can imagine, entirely divergent views of the Russian Revolution and the Soviet regime. Mine was a skeptical, theoretical, governmental view, dominated by what seemed to me to be the monumental impropriety of the world revolutionary aims and efforts of the Soviet leaders, as well as by a profound distaste for their habits of polemic exaggeration and falsehood. Louis' view, while even then by no means uncritical, was tempered by his greater sympathies for the underdog, by a more receptive understanding for socialist outlooks generally, and above all by his wide range of personal acquaintance with the earlier generation of Soviet leaders. He had known well a number of these people and viewed some of them with sympathy and admiration. He had been exposed, after all, over the course of several years, as I had not, to what one might call the enormous initial charm and appeal of the Russian Revolution. The excitment, the drama, the idealism, and stupendous hopes, all of which surrounded the Soviet experiment in the Leninist period and its immediate aftermath, often picked up Western visitors and residents, even ones who had never considered themselves Communists, and swept them along emotionally in their powerful currents. This great intoxicating fog of enthusiasm—this benevolent miasma—was just in process of fading when I arrived in Russia. But I remember being caught up in it once, myself, when I attended the play of *Intervention* at the Vakhtangov Theatre. I came out of the theatre, my head swimming with this contagious excitement, feeling that for a brief hour I had shared the belief that all of mankind was being in some way redeemed in this great purifying revolutionary effort. But this was, for me, a brief and unusual experience.

Louis, on the other hand, had been exposed to this excitement for years, and in its most heady forms. It had given him a view of Soviet realities —and above all a sense of participation, of being himself a part of the scene, an actor as well as an observer, which we diplomats, isolated as we were from Soviet society by the relentless suspicion and hostility of the Soviet secret police, were never normally permitted to feel.

In these circumstances, our mutual relations in those years, while pleasant and I think respectful on both sides, were never close. It took the discipline of the decade of horror and suffering that was to follow—the nightmares of Hitlerism, Stalinism and the Second World War—to temper our respective illusions and prejudices. It took common schooling in the phenomenon of tragedy to enlarge our capacity for charity along with our skepticism for all political causes and pretensions, and to bring us together to a point where we could see things, and particularly Russian things, very much alike and collaborate happily together as we finally did (to my great profit) in the analysis of them.

Louis, when I first met him, was already a well-known writer. Only three years before he had published the first, and in many ways still the most important, of all his contributions to the history of Soviet diplomacy: *The Soviets in World Affairs*.

Now, there were two personalities in Louis' intellectual make-up: the journalist and the scholar. Neither was ever wholly absent from his creative activity; but it was the journalist that developed first and dominated the earlier years of his mature activity, whereas the scholar, I think, really came into his own later—primarily, in fact, during his years in Princeton. *The Soviets in World Affairs* was thus a book that bore strongly the imprint of the journalistic experiences out of which it had arisen. It was a bubbling, colorful book, free and easy in style and organization, based very largely on Louis' own observations and interviews with a host of people. It was colored by the pro-Soviet sympathies which were then in the air he breathed, sympathies to which he confessed with characteristic candor when he wrote the foreword to the new edition of the book, put out twenty-one years later by the Princeton University Press.

But I don't think that any more valuable contribution has ever been made, or ever will be made, to the history of that early period in the relations between revolutionary Russia and the outside world than this early work of Louis'. It is quite unique. A great quantity of interesting and significant facts were here brought to light and made a matter of record which would probably otherwise never have been known to posterity. Russians themselves, now barred by the policies of a timorous political leadership from scrutinizing with any objectivity this chapter of Russian history, will some day be grateful to Louis Fischer for the great service to Russian historiography which this book represents.

This was, of course, only the first of Louis' major contributions in this field. The ones that followed are too numerous to list. Of the later major ones, written in Princeton, two must be particularly mentioned. One was the life of Lenin, which was probably Louis' greatest and most mature work. The other was the summary history of Soviet diplomacy from 1917 to 1941 which he published only a year before his death.

Let me add a word or two about Louis' style and approach as a historian. They were like those of no one else. They were entirely his own. The journalist in him never wholly disappeared. For him the history he wrote was largely a matter of his own experience. Historical evidence and personal experience were for him inseparable. He saw history in terms of great people and of great events. He knew most of the people. He had experienced, in one way or another, most of the events. He treated them all with a broad brush. He had, if anyone ever had, the large view —not large in the sense of sweeping theoretical generalization; quite the contrary—large, rather, in the sense of a persistent concentration on the people and events that seemed to him to be important and a refusal to be deterred or sidetracked by trivia. Not for him were the intracacies of detailed chronology, the complexities of diplomatic correspondence, the complicated processes of governmental bureaucracies. His interests were well summed up in the title of his autobiographical work: *Men and Politics.* The "Men," you will note, was quite properly put first.

To the treatment of these two subjects—men and politics—he brought, as I scarcely need to tell you, qualities that were also uniquely his own. I can mention only a few.

Louis was very much an American, and yet he was a citizen of the world. To him, national differences were never essential. All men, in his view, shared the same vital problems and dilemmas. The same great moral principles were applicable for all. He could identify, therefore, with all men in whom he detected a measure of idealism—from Lenin to Gandhi, from Gandhi to F.D.R.

Louis had a wide-ranging curiosity and a highly developed sense of the interrelatedness of all political phenomena on this crowded planet. His mind knew no tidy separate compartments. All things were connected. There was, in his make-up, a most rare and appealing combination of tolerance and compassion and understanding for the outlooks of others, together with a firm personal commitment to certain moral and ethical principles. There was a relaxed detachment and judiciousness in the appraisal of both men and events. There was an unshakable sociability and interest in people, combined with really exceptional talent as an interviewer. Doors once opened to him were seldom ever again closed. Armed with these qualities, Louis was able, in his own peculiar way, to take the firsthand observations and experiences of a talented journalist and to mold them, objectively, conscientiously, and with enormous thoughtfulness, into the stuff of scholarship. And of these extraordinary qualities we who surrounded him as colleagues, as friends, or as students, in his final years were only the nearest, and the most immediate, of a host of beneficiaries.

Louis Fischer was a child, and a distinguished bearer, of the great liberal idealism of the early part of this century. It is perhaps a merciful circumstance that he did not live to see any more than he was obliged to see of the erosion of these ideals under the many disillusionments and bewilderments of this second half of the century. It would not have been easy for him.

But there are some of us who believe that nothing which had value, and stands recorded, is ever wholly lost in the mysterious progression of human ideas and institutions. There will come another day, I am sure, when lessons will again be sought in the great events of the early part of this century of which Louis was the witness and the interpreter, and in which, emotionally and intellectually, he had his being. When that day comes, it is both to his observations and to his analyses that students are going to have to turn. Only then will the full value of his life and work become completely visible. The students of that distant day will pay to Louis, no doubt, another sort of recognition than we are able to pay today. What they will never know is the warmth and color of his personality and the sorrow, for his friends, of his passing.

THE ROAD TO YALTA

PROLOGUE: THE BIRTH
OF A SUPERPOWER

The collapse of German and Japanese military strength and the weakness of Great Britain and France following the second world war left the field open for the emergence of two superpowers: the U.S.A. and the U.S.S.R.

That the United States, incompletely isolationist after the first world war, should have become an active superpower after the second is a startling enough fact. But America, her territory unscathed, her sacrifices sad yet few, had the industrial, financial, and military might (including the atomic bomb) for a new interventionist role in world affairs. Russia, however, was depleted by the war. She paid a price, unprecedented in the history of nations, for victory over Germany. In the Stalin period the Kremlin admitted to 7 million battlefield dead. In 1957 in Yalta Chairman Nikita S. Khrushchev told Mrs. Eleanor Roosevelt the Soviet Union had suffered about 12 million fatalities. More recently Soviet sources speak of "twenty million" dead, and foreign analysts of the 1959 Soviet census, taking the previous (prewar) census and adding the average annual increase of births over deaths, find that 40 million persons are missing: 30 million military and civilians killed, most of them in their prime, and 10 million unborn because the men had gone to the front. Material losses were no less staggering. Soviet territory temporarily occupied by Hitler's armies "accounted for 45% of the population" of the country, "33% of the gross output of industry, 47% of the sown area, 45% of the livestock (in terms of cattle), and 55% of the length of the railway lines."[1]

1. Nikolai A. Voznesensky, *The Economy of the U.S.S.R. During World War II,* p. 85. Voznesensky was a member of the Soviet Communist Party's Politburo,

The Nazis killed or carried off 7 million of a total of 11.6 million horses in the occupied territories, 20 million of a total of 23.6 million hogs, 17 million of a total of 31 million cattle, and 27 million of 43 million sheep and goats. They destroyed 137,000 tractors, 40,000 combines, 46,000 tractor grain seeders, 35,000 complex and semicomplex threshing machines, 285,000 barns, 505,000 hectares of fruit orchards, and 135,000 hectares of vineyards. They ruined thousands of industrial plants, railway terminals, post offices, telegraph and telephone stations, as well as 6,000 hospitals, 43,000 public libraries, and approximately 85,000 schools.[2]

The most harrowing aspect of this devastation was its suddenness. In the first four months of the German invasion of Russia—from June through October, 1941—Soviet industrial output was reduced by one half. In that brief period the Nazis occupied territory inhabited by 40 percent of the U.S.S.R.'s population which had produced 63 percent of its coal, 68 percent of its pig iron, 58 percent of its steel, 60 percent of its aluminum, 38 percent of its grain, and 84 percent of its sugar.[3]

By the first week of December, 1941, Leningrad was surrounded and under pounding siege and the Nazis were 40 miles from Moscow. Kiev, the country's third city, had fallen to German forces on September 17. At the end of 1941 Russia counted hundreds of thousands killed; more were wounded and taken prisoner. The military and political outlook was black, victory prospects nil. Panic reigned in Moscow, Alexander Poskrobyshev, Stalin's first secretary, wrote in *Pravda* of December 21, 1949. The Soviet press exhorted soldiers not to throw away their rifles.

Nevertheless, Britain, having long stood alone under German bombs and communist barbs, welcomed Russia's involuntary entry into the war. Immediately Churchill heard of the Nazi attack he decided to address the nation and promise aid to the U.S.S.R. How could he, the arch-anticommunist, his private secretary chided, "bow down in the House of Rimmon?"—make obeisances to the pagan god of Stalinist totalitarianism? "I have only one purpose, the destruction of Hitler, and my life is much simplified thereby," Churchill replied. "If Hitler invaded Hell I would make at least a favourable reference to the Devil in the House of Commons."[4]

Churchill accordingly took to the wireless at 9 P.M. on June 22, 1941. He did not compromise. "The Nazi regime," he said, "is indistinguishable from the worst features of Communism. . . . No one has been a more

---

Deputy Premier of the Soviet government, and Chairman of the State Planning Commission. According to the *Biennial Report of the Chief of Staff of the United States Army to the Secretary of War, July 1, 1943, to June 30, 1945,* p. 107, U.S. losses throughout the second world war were 201,367 deaths and 570,783 wounded.

2. *Ibid.,* p. 86.
3. *Ibid.,* p. 22.
4. Winston S. Churchill, *The Second World War. The Grand Alliance,* p. 370.

consistent opponent of Communism than I have for the last twenty-five years. I will unsay no word that I have spoken about it. But all this fades away before the spectacle which is now unfolding. The past, with its crimes, its follies, its tragedies, flashes away.... We have but one aim and one single, irrevocable purpose. We are resolved to destroy Hitler and every vestige of the Nazi regime. From this nothing will turn us—nothing. We will never parley, we will never negotiate with Hitler or any of his gang. We shall fight him by land, we shall fight him by sea, we shall fight him in the air, until, with God's help, we have rid the earth of his shadow and liberated its peoples from his yoke. Any man or state who marches against Nazidom will have our aid . . . we shall give whatever help we can to Russia and the Russian people. . . .

"This is no class war. . . ."

Earlier in the day Churchill said Hitler, by invading communist Russia, "was counting on enlisting capitalist and Right Wing sympathies in this country and the U.S.A." In his broadcast Churchill asserted: "if Hitler imagines that his attack on Soviet Russia will cause the slightest divergence of aims or slackening of effort in the great democracies who are resolved upon his doom, he is woefully mistaken."

Yet Churchill could not forbear from one comment on the Soviet-Nazi pact and protocol. "This is no time," he declared, "to moralise on the follies of countries and Governments which have allowed themselves to be struck down one by one, when by united action they could have saved themselves and saved the world from this catastrophe." (The same criticism applied to British and French appeasers.) But aid to Russia, Churchill stressed, was aid to Britain: Hitler "wishes to destroy the Russian power because he hopes that if he succeeds in this he will be able to bring back the main strength of his army and air force from the East and hurl it upon this island. . . . His invasion of Russia is no more than a prelude to an attempted invasion of the British Isles." The argument won England's approbation.

Churchill had another arrow in his quiver. His supreme desire was to bring America to his side. He therefore warned, in a peroration, that if Britain fell to Hitler "the scene will be clear for the final act, without which all his conquests would be in vain—namely, the subjugation of the Western Hemisphere. . . . The Russian danger is, therefore, our danger, and the danger of the United States."[5]

The United States waited upon the pleasure of Japan before entering the war. It is difficult for a nation at peace, particularly one remote from the conflagration, to take a running broad jump into deadly flames. President Franklin D. Roosevelt had, in his October 5, 1937, "quarantine the

5. *Ibid.,* pp. 371–373.

aggressor" speech at Chicago, advocated war-prevention measures. The American people said no. For F.D.R. it was a searing experience. Apropos a suggestion for another war-prevention move, Mrs. Roosevelt wrote me on February 28, 1938, "the President . . . feels that we could not get the people to change this point of view without a period of education and perhaps from experiences which they have not as yet had."[6]

The American public's education was advanced by the early course of the second world war; in thinly disguised ways the United States helped Britain fight. And when Russia was attacked President Roosevelt went to her aid. The alternative of joining capitalist Nazi Germany to destroy communism was never considered, much less adopted by anticommunist America or anticommunist Britain. Those two "citadels of capitalism" put national interest above class and ideology.

Harry S. Truman, the senator from Missouri and President-to-be, though he could not yet have dreamed it, took a Maverick-Machiavellian stance. "If we see that Germany is winning we ought to help Russia and if Russia is winning we ought to help Germany and that way let them kill as many as possible, although I don't want to see Hitler victorious in any circumstances. Neither of them thinks anything of their pledged word." The second Democratic senator from Missouri, Bennett C. Clark, went further. "Stalin," he declared, "is as bloody handed as Hitler. I don't think we should help either one." But Acting Secretary of State Sumner Welles, speaking for President Roosevelt and with Secretary of State Cordell Hull's approval, condemned the Nazi attack on Russia, warned against the German plan of "universal conquest," and by stating that "Hitler's armies are today the chief dangers of the Americas," implied that the United States would help the Soviet Union.[7] Soon a heavy river of arms, food, and factories flowed from America into Russia, and before long the overwhelming friendly public sentiment for atheistic, communistic Russia shaped wartime and postwar policies.

In 1941 it occurred to no American or Briton that Russia would emerge from the second world war as a superpower. The only concern was to keep the Soviets in the war as long as possible, for after Stalin's June, 1937, massacre of Red Army officers and the Soviet debacle in the 1939–1940 winter war with Finland, western estimates of Russian fighting capacity were extremely low. ". . . most of the British experts, like the German," reads an official British history of the war, "believed that the campaign in European Russia would be over in a few months if not weeks."[8]

6. Louis Fischer, *Men and Politics,* Rev. ed., Appendix, p. 643.
7. *New York Times,* June 24, 1941.
8. J. R. M. Butler (Ed.), *History of the Second World War.* United Kingdom Military Series. *Grand Strategy.* Vol. II: *September 1939-June 1941,* p. 544. "The

U.S. military opinion was equally pessimistic: Russia would be defeated, the question was when. On hearing of the Nazi invasion of the U.S.S.R., Secretary of War Henry L. Stimson "spent today in conference," as he wrote the President, "with the Chief of Staff and the men in the War Plans Division of the General staff. . . . *First.* Here is their estimate of controlling facts. 1. Germany will be thoroughly occupied in beating Russia for a minimum of a month and a possible maximum of three months."[9]

Given these glum transatlantic predictions, every day Russia held out was a day gained for Britain. So Churchill felt. So Stimson thought. Roosevelt hesitated. He was not sure of Congressional and public support. But he quickly won both constituencies. By the end of 1941 Russia in effect had joined in an East-West alliance with the United States and the United Kingdom. Russia paid most for it. Stalin extracted most from it. The Soviet Union became a superpower. The biggest investment brought the largest dividend—an empire. In perspective, Russia's rise from wreck to raj is a fantastic historical phenomenon.

* * *

Imperial expansion has a dynamism all its own. The British, seeking trade in India, muddled into political possession and, having achieved it, gradually conceived a consuming interest in much that lay between Gibraltar and Suez and between Suez and Bombay. With the Soviet communists it was a more deliberate process. First they coveted the former regions of the Tsar. Then they sought a tier of satellites or colonies in eastern Europe to cordon off those regions. The next step took them into the Mediterranean because, in the words of *Pravda* of November 27, 1968, "the Soviet Union, a Black Sea power and in that sense a Mediterranean power, is intimately connected with all the problems affecting the peoples of that part of Europe, Africa, and Asia. It is directly interested in safeguarding the security of its southern frontiers." So a Soviet fleet sails the Mediterranean as far west as Algeria ostensibly to defend the Caucasus and the Ukraine. The U.S. Sixth Fleet roams the Mediterranean, the Seventh the western Pacific, and U.S. land forces are scattered around the globe for the stated reason of protecting America's national interests. These ingredients have sparked the confrontations and crises between the two superpowers since 1945. In fact, the crises began during the second world war.

---

authors of the Military Histories," reads a prefaced note to this multivolume series, "have been given access to official documents."

9. Robert E. Sherwood, *Roosevelt and Hopkins. An Intimate History,* pp. 303–304.

I STALIN, THE GEORGIAN GREAT RUSSIAN

In the first weeks of the war the Red Army resisted the mighty Nazi onslaught when quick withdrawal would have saved lives. But the generals feared to order a retreat, they were not trained to take the initiative, the initiative could come only from Stalin, and Stalin had suffered a breakdown, locked himself in a room, and saw nobody. "Stalin," Khrushchev said in his secret speech of February 24-25, 1956, "for a long time actually did not direct the military operations and ceased to do anything whatever. . . . He returned to active leadership," Khrushchev continued, "only when some members of the Politburo visited him and told him that it was necessary to take certain steps immediately"—presumably permit voluntary retreat—"in order to improve the situation at the front. Therefore, the threatening danger which hung over our Fatherland in the first period of the war was largely due to the faulty methods of directing the nation and the party by Stalin himself."[1]

Soviet Ambassador Maisky records in his memoirs that "Churchill was somewhat put out by the fact that Stalin did not in any way respond to his broadcast of June 22." On the first day of the war Foreign Commissar Vyacheslav M. Molotov spoke to the Soviet people on the radio. Maisky, listening in London, thought to himself, "Why Molotov? Why not Stalin? On such an occasion a speech by the head of State was necessary." Stalin was Chairman of the Soviet government as well as chief of the Soviet Communist Party. He remained in silent seclusion. ". . . it was precisely in the first weeks of the German-Soviet war," writes Maisky, "that my

1. Nikita S. Khrushchev, *The Crimes of the Stalin Era. Special Report to the 20th Congress of the Communist Party of the Soviet Union.* Annotated especially for this edition by Boris I. Nicolaevsky, p. 40.

doubts about the statesmanship of Stalin, which first appeared in the days of the Soviet-Finnish war, began to grow stronger."

Maisky's judgment of Stalin mingled objectivity with personal venom. The despot, in a crescendo of anti-Semitism toward the end of his life that took many victims, had banished Maisky to a concentration camp from which the ex-ambassador returned only after March 5, 1953. The balm of membership in the Academy of Sciences notwithstanding, such a hurt lingers on to cloud the mind. Stalin retained the capacity for his kind of leadership; he recovered from the initial shock. Yet Maisky correctly sensed at the time that something in Stalin had snapped. Not until July 3, twelve days after the Nazi invasion, was he able to face the microphone and his people. "Stalin spoke in a toneless, slow voice, with a strong Georgian accent," writes Konstantin Simonov in his novel, *The Living and the Dead.* "His voice was low and soft, and might have seemed perfectly calm but for the heavy, tired breathing, and that water he kept drinking during his speech."[2] Maisky made similar observations in London: "Stalin spoke with a kind of toneless and colorless voice, stopped often and breathed heavily; once or twice the glass from which he drank clinked. It seemed that Stalin was ill and was making an effort beyond his strength. This could not raise morale or arouse the enthusiasm of his listeners."[3]

Stalin's collapse into the total passivity of which Khrushchev spoke followed the collapse of his policy. He had striven to keep his country out of war. It was at war. He had trusted Hitler as he had trusted no other foreign leader, and perhaps as he had trusted nobody anywhere. Hitler had betrayed that trust. Germany attacked, Molotov complained on June 22, without making any demands. Stalin had expected to have a chance to bargain, to compromise, to buy off Hitler. The Nazi leader had disappointed him. Stalin had disappointed the Soviet people and he knew it. He had been warned of the coming catastrophe and refused to listen. The all-enveloping illusion that he was master of the situation had crumbled. He was faced with reality. He tried to shut it out. He shut himself in. When he gave the first public sign of life his voice, breathing, and words suggested tensions. He wanted to ingratiate himself, he addressed his listeners with the unprecedented "Brothers and Sisters." He wanted to justify himself. "One might ask," he said, "how was it possible for the Soviet government to sign a non-aggression pact with such inhuman scoundrels as Hitler and Ribbentrop? Had not a serious mistake been made? Of course not. A non-aggression pact is a peace pact between two states, and that was the pact proposed to us by Germany in 1939. No

2. Cited by Alexander Werth in *Russia at War 1941–1945,* p. 166.
3. *Novy Mir,* December, 1964, p. 165. This passage is omitted from Maisky's 1965 book of memoirs in Russian and from the 1967 English translation.

peace-loving state could have rejected such a pact with another country even if scoundrels like Hitler and Ribbentrop stood at its head. All the more so since this pact did not in any way violate the territorial integrity, independence, or honor of our country." No mention of the secret protocol, attached to the pact, which started Moscow on the road to empire. Nor did Stalin allude to the Soviet demands on Bulgaria and Turkey, which precipitated Hitler's decision to launch the long-planned attack on Russia.

"Inhuman scoundrels" was a belated discovery. "Once we trusted this man," Stalin, referring to Hitler, said to Harry Hopkins, President Roosevelt's special envoy, in July, 1941. He trusted the chief inhuman scoundrel. He entertained another—Ribbentrop—in cordial fashion, and when the Nazi Foreign Minister wired Stalin congratulations December 21, 1939, on his sixtieth birthday, the communist dictator replied, "The friendship of the peoples of Germany and the Soviet Union, cemented in blood, has every reason to be lasting and firm."

In Stalin's July 3 broadcast the word "treacherous" occurs five times. The Nazi invasion was "treacherous." The invasion, Hopkins wrote after seeing Stalin, "was regarded in Moscow as the treachery of a partner who had suddenly revealed himself a rabid dog."[4] "Suddenly" Stalin's "partner" had revealed himself. Since he loved himself Stalin had not thought badly of Hitler, had not understood his evil nature.

Nor had Stalin understood the international situation. "The President told me," Ambassador Joseph E. Davies writes, "that he told [Soviet] Ambassador Oumansky, when he was leaving to go to Moscow, to tell Stalin that if his government signed with Hitler"—the F.D.R.-Davies conversation took place on July 18, 1939—"it was certain as night followed the day that as soon as Hitler conquered France he would turn on Russia."[5] This logic escaped Stalin.

Five days after his own broadcast Stalin permitted Litvinov to speak on the radio, but only in English and on a wavelength beamed to foreign countries. Litvinov said, "No agreement or treaties, no undertaking signed by Hitler and his henchmen, no promises or assurances on their part, no declarations of neutrality, no relations with them whatsoever can provide a guarantee against a sudden unprovoked attack.

"In his diabolical plans for attacking other countries in order to fulfill his dream of world domination, Hitler has always been ruled by the principle of 'divide and attack.' He uses the most insidious means to prevent the intended victims from organizing common resistance, taking special pains to avoid war on two fronts against the most powerful European states. His strategy is to mark down his victims and strike them one

4. *American* magazine, December, 1941.
5. *Mission to Moscow*, p. 450.

by one in the order prompted by circumstances." Hitler "intended first to deal with the western states so as to be free to fall upon the Soviet Union. There was a hitch somewhere. Hitler lacks the training as yet for a Channel swimmer. And so another plan matured in his brain. Believing that he had secured himself a de facto truce in the West, he decided to have a 'blitzkrieg,' a lightning war, in the East."

This was a condemnation of Stalin's foreign policy and of the Soviet-Nazi partnership in particular. Stalin permitted it—perhaps he was not yet himself—to indicate that he had reverted to the pro-western policy of collective security. Except for top officials and high military officers with short-wave sets, Soviet citizens did not hear Litvinov's criticism, they heard only Stalin's defense.

The leader's July 3 broadcast created an unfavorable impression on discerning intellectuals. The general impact was good; Stalin was back. A country accustomed for centuries to look to the autocrat for guidance and, in the last twelve years, to Stalin as the source of all wisdom, could assimilate setbacks and losses provided it knew that the captain sat firmly at the wheel of the bulldozer of state. The people needed Stalin. And for the first time Stalin behaved as if he realized he needed the people. The war began so disastrously that everything depended on morale—at the front, immediately behind the front where Stalin, on the radio, urged partisan guerrillas to harass the invaders, and at the rear in factories, on collective farms, among potential recruits, and especially among the women left behind.

Repression is no morale builder. The terror abated though it did not disappear. The masses had to have a faith to sustain them in war's long ordeal. One of the Kremlin's first measures was to discontinue the *Bezbozhnik* (The Atheist) magazine which mocked all religions. Stalin ostentatiously received leading churchmen. Soviet newspapers, periodicals, and radio no longer stressed communist slogans and goals. Georgi Dimitrov, head of the Third International, who enjoyed a tremendous reputation in Germany after his defiance of Air Marshal Goering at the Leipzig Reichstag fire trial, remained silent. He had denounced Britain and France as aggressors in 1939 and 1940 during the Soviet-Nazi honeymoon. He did not denounce Hitler now. No proclamation or manifesto came from the Third International's Moscow headquarters. No congress of the Third International was convened.

The Kremlin did convene a Slav congress—on August 10 and 11, 1941. It was addressed by Alexei N. Tolstoy, author of a novel on Peter the Great. He called Moscow "the heart of Slavdom." The September, 1941, session of the Soviet Academy of Sciences history division affirmed that "the whole history of the Slav peoples has passed under the sign of a stubborn war for freedom and independence from the Teutons. . . . The destruction of Hitlerism will lead to the national, political, and cultural renaissance of the Slav nations." Professor Nikolai S. Derzhavin, a member of the Academy of Sciences, stated on October 3, 1941, that "Fascism is the worst foe of Slavism." A new magazine appeared in Moscow called *Slavyane* (Slavs), its cover resembling traditional Russian embroidery, its contents devoted to the glory of the Slav race. During the war Stalin received a Yugoslav delegation. He "spoke very little or not at all about [communist] Parties, Communism, Marxism, but very much about the Slavs."[6]

To Stalin as to Churchill this was no class war. It was not a war of communism against fascism, of socialism against capitalist imperialism, of working class against the bourgeoisie. It was a war of Russians against Germans, of Slavs against Teutons. Stalin adopted the past, he built bridges to the heritage of tsarism. In 1942 a coveted military decoration was established in the name of General Alexander V. Suvorov, the eighteenth-century Tsarist general who fought the revolutionary French in Italy and Switzerland; another in the name of Prince Mikhail I. Kutuzov, commander of Russian armies that resisted Napoleon; a third in the name of Bogdan M. Khmelnitsky, a Ukrainian hetman known for his wars on the Poles and his pogroms on Jews and especially appreciated in Red Moscow because he brought the Ukraine into a political union with Russia.

Such racial nationalism and sentimental tsarism prepared the Soviet subconscious for postwar Soviet imperialism. When Milovan Djilas explained to Stalin that the Albanians were not Slavs, Stalin "winked roguishly" and said, "I had hoped that the Albanians were at least a little Slavic."[7] The better to swallow them. Stalin was not a discriminating eater.

The Soviet leader had realized that socialism, communism, Marxism, and kindred ideologies conduced neither to national cohesion nor to patriotic emotions. After watching Hitler whip Germany into a chauvinistic frenzy, Stalin began, in 1934, to cultivate Russian and Ukrainian nationalism and Soviet patriotism. It was then that the word "Rodina," or fatherland, first appeared in communist print. With the fatherland in danger beginning in 1941, nationalistic and racial propaganda filled all ears and touched many hearts. Stalin, the Georgian, was functionally, politically, a Great Russian who believed in a Great Russia.

6. Milovan Djilas, *Conversations with Stalin,* p. 95.
7. *Ibid.,* p. 79.

II THE FUTURE IS PRESENT

Hitler made Russia Britain's ally. On July 12, 1941, in Moscow, Foreign Commissar Molotov and Sir Stafford Cripps signed an agreement of mutual military assistance. It also provided that "during this war" the two governments "will neither negotiate nor conclude an armistice or treaty of peace except by mutual agreement."[1] This reflected mutual suspicion. (The U.S. and Britain had no such agreement.)

Soviet Ambassador Maisky received instructions to negotiate similar agreements with the Czechoslovak and Polish governments in exile in London. The treaty signed on July 18 by Czechoslovak Foreign Minister Jan Masaryk and Ambassador Maisky presented no difficulty. The treaty with Poland did.

Maisky, Polish Premier Wladyslaw Sikorski, and Foreign Minister August Zaleski conferred in the British Foreign Office where the Ambassador proposed a mutual assistance pact. He "added that the U.S.S.R. undertook in the future to facilitate the re-establishment of the Polish State in its national frontiers.

"Sikorski and Zaleski met my words without great enthusiasm and Zaleski immediately asked how they were to understand the formula 'the Polish State in its national frontiers.'

"I explained that as we saw it the future Polish State should only consist of Poles, and should cover those territories which were inhabited by Poles."[2]

This meant that Moscow claimed the Polish territories inhabited by Ukrainians and Byelorussians and occupied by Moscow under the Soviet-Nazi pact and secret protocol of August 23, 1939, and the supplementary secret Soviet-German treaty of September 28, 1939. It meant that Russia could have national minorities, Poland could not. Sikorski rejected the pretense for annexation. With Britain's help he prevailed. The treaty signed on July 30 by Sikorski and Maisky in the presence of Churchill and Eden stated that the "Soviet-German treaties of 1939 regarding territorial changes in Poland were considered to have lost their validity."[3]

1. Ivan Maisky, *Memoirs,* p. 166.
2. *Ibid.,* p. 173.
3. *Ibid.,* p. 174. All documents and details of the Soviet-Polish negotiations and

Thereby the Soviets, for the first time, acknowledged the existence of the secret treaties and protocol which demarcated those changes, but which they have never seen fit to publish. Unless otherwise agreed, accordingly, postwar Poland would have the same boundaries as prewar Poland; it would include the Ukrainians and Byelorussians of its eastern half. The problem of Poland's future nevertheless plagued Anglo-American-Soviet relations until Germany's defeat and after.

In the same month of July Harry Hopkins, heavy with the weariness of a long, circuitous flight from Scotland via Archangel, flew into Moscow for extended talks with Stalin about American military aid. The United States, not yet at war, officially neutral, was committed to the defense of Britain and the defeat of Hitler, hence to the defense of Russia. "I expressed to him"—Stalin—"the President's belief," Hopkins reported, "that the most important thing to be done in the world today was to defeat Hitler and Hitlerism." Stalin reciprocated with a lofty abstraction. Nations could not coexist, he declared, without "a minimum moral standard. . . . The Germans were a people, he said, who without a second's thought would sign a treaty today, break it tomorrow and sign a second one the following day. Nations must fulfill their treaty obligations, he said, or international society could not exist." Stalin thus identified the German people with the Nazi government which signed and broke treaties. Hopkins, speaking for Roosevelt, had not done that.

After these preliminaries the two men got down to business.

Stalin was meticulously briefed. He gave the visitor a carefully balanced synopsis of the to-and-fro of battle involving millions of Soviet and enemy men. Then he turned to Russia's arms deficiency—after years of preparation. "He stated he needed one million or more" American rifles. "We have plenty" of ammunition for them. More pressing was the need of medium-caliber and antiaircraft guns, "approximately 20,000 pieces," as well as "large size machine guns for the defense of the cities." The antiaircraft guns would "immediately release nearly 2,000 pursuit ships which are today required for the protection of military objectives behind the Soviet lines." For a long-range war Stalin asked high-octane aviation gasoline and aluminum for the construction of airplanes. "Give us antiaircraft guns and the aluminum," Stalin suddenly exclaimed, "and we can fight for three or four years." Hopkins informed Stalin that American 200 Curtis P-40 fighter planes were already on their way to Russia.[4]

That evening, with Stalin's approval, Hopkins met General of the Artillery M. P. Yakovlev. Hopkins learned a lesson in Stalin autocracy. Stalin

---

of Eden's interventions in General Sikorski Historical Institute, *Documents on Polish-Soviet Relations 1939–1945*, Vol. I: *1939–1943*, pp. 113–145.

4. This and the further substance of Hopkins' Moscow talks from Robert E. Sherwood, *Roosevelt and Hopkins. An Intimate History.* Revised edition, pp. 323–347. Sherwood had access to Hopkins' papers.

was the only free man in the Soviet Union. He spoke with Hopkins and others as freely as he wished. Not so Molotov or Yakovlev or any Soviet subject. Hopkins suggested to Yakovlev the desirability of sending a technical military mission to Washington. "Yakovlev refused to comment on the suggestion saying it should be taken up with Stalin." Hopkins asked Yakovlev whether they required war materials other than those discussed with Stalin. Yakovlev said he could think of nothing else. Did they not need tanks and antitank guns? Hopkins wondered. "I think we have enough," Yakovlev replied. "I am not empowered to say whether we do or do not need tanks or antitank guns," he added. Hopkins inquired about the weight of Russia's heaviest tank. "It is a good tank," the general explained.

The next evening—July 31—Hopkins had a second conference with Stalin. It lasted three hours. Litvinov interpreted.

Hopkins said President Roosevelt was eager to have Stalin's appreciation of the Soviet-German war. At the end of forty days of fighting, according to Stalin, the German troops "are tired" and "have no stomach for offensive." Stalin repeatedly expressed "his confidence that the Russian lines would hold within 100 kilometers [approximately 63 miles] of their present position." The front "would be solidified not later than October 1." He felt certain that "the line during the winter months would be in front of Moscow, Kiev and Leningrad."

This was a gross underestimate of German power. Before the winter was out the Germans advanced hundreds of kilometers from "their present position." But if Stalin wanted munitions that would take months to manufacture and deliver, or many weeks to transport from U.S. warehouses to the Soviet front line, he had to create the impression of relative military stability. He succeeded. Hopkins felt, Robert E. Sherwood writes, that "A man who feared immediate defeat would not have put aluminum so high on his list of priorities."

Nevertheless, Stalin did not conceal the gravity of his problems. Though the Red Army's morale was excellent, much would depend on the early arrival of American supplies, including tanks. Stalin "believes," Hopkins reported by coded telegram to the President, "that his largest tanks are better than" the German tanks. "He stated that the two largest Russian tanks were of 48 and 52 tons respectively, with 75 mm. armour and 85 mm. guns. They have approximately 4,000 of these tanks at present. The Russian medium tank of just over 30 tons has 45 mm. armour and 75 mm. guns. The infantry tank is 13 tons and has 37 mm. armour and 45 mm. guns. They have approximately 8,000 medium (30-ton) tanks at present and 12,000 light (13-ton) tanks. . . . He stated that they would be short of steel for tank manufacture and urged that orders for this steel be placed at once. He later said it would be much better if his tanks could be manufactured in the United States . . . the aid of the

United States in supplying steel and tanks is essential. He would like to send a tank expert to the United States."

Hopkins' mission was limited to questions of supply. But Stalin gave him a message for Roosevelt on a broader matter: The German army and German people, whose morale "is already pretty low, would be demoralized by an announcement that the United States is going to join in the war against Hitler. . . . He said that the one thing that could defeat Hitler, and perhaps without ever firing a shot, would be the announcement that the United States was going to war with Germany." Stalin believed "it was inevitable that we," Hopkins telegraphed, "should finally come to grips with Hitler on some battlefield." Why not the Russian battlefield? "He wanted me to tell the President that he would welcome the American troops on any part of the Russian front under the complete command of the American Army."

Hopkins was skeptical.

Since it is known how zealously Stalin barred even single American and British military observers from the front during the subsequent course of hostilities, one can imagine his desperation on July 31 when he offered nonbelligerent America a share of the war in Russia. He had already sent a similar distress call to Britain.

Stalin had not thanked Churchill for his June 22 broadcast offer of aid to Russia or replied to the Prime Minister's personal messages dated July 8 and July 10, 1941. On July 18, however, he acknowledged both telegrams: "Now, as you have quite rightly stated it, the Soviet Union and Great Britain have become fighting allies in the struggle against Hitlerite Germany. I do not doubt that our countries will, in spite of all the difficulties, find sufficient strength to smash our common enemy." But he immediately diluted this confidence with harsh realism. "Perhaps," Stalin said, "it will not be superfluous to inform you that the situation of the Soviet armies at the front continues to be strained." Here Stalin interpolated another defense of the Soviet-Nazi pact, for he sensed that his close relation with Hitler Germany between August, 1939, and June, 1941, weakened the force of the appeal he was about to make. "It seems to me . . ." the appeal read, "that the military position of the Soviet Union, as well as that of Great Britain, would be significantly improved if a front against Hitler were established in the West (Northern France) and in the North (the Arctic).

"The front in Northern France could not only draw Hitler troops away from the East, it would also make a Hitlerite invasion of England impossible. . . . It would be easier still to create a front in the North. Here only British naval and air forces are required, without a landing of infantry, without the landing of artillery. Soviet land, naval, and air forces would participate in this operation." Stalin, in his last sentence, suggested the

use too of "one or more light divisions of Norwegian volunteers."[5]
Therewith began the lengthy, bitter debate about the second front.

* * *

When Germany invaded Poland on September 1, 1939, and England and France went to war two days later, the British and French communists opposed their governments and sabotaged the war effort. The French communists thus contributed to the fall of France and hence to the invasion of Russia. If Stalin, in joining Hitler, had acted merely from expediency, he would have instructed foreign communists to hurt Germany. Instead, foreign communists hurt the enemies of Germany. Stalin did not see Hitler as his ultimate foe. Faith in an unbreakable friendship made him deaf to all warnings of an impending Nazi invasion.

Stalin served German strategy. The Soviet-Nazi pact, *Pravda* wrote on August 23, 1940, the treaty's first anniversary, "has guaranteed Germany undisturbed security in the East." Germany was thereby guaranteed freedom to disturb the security of the West. But the communist mind zestfully shifts blame to others. "If in Berlin," reads a book published in 1964 under the imprint of the Soviet Academy of Sciences, "they had not based their hopes on American neutrality and on the hope that the Congress would now defend to the end the neutrality of the U.S., the Germans would hardly have rushed so impetuously into the hurricane of war."[6]

No word about the Soviet Union's less than neutral collusion with Hitler under the pact and protocol signed nine days before Germany rushed headlong into war. If the United States and the Soviet Union had indicated that they would support Britain and France when Hitler attacked Poland he might indeed have been deterred. American abstention and the assurance of Russian collaboration no doubt bear much, perhaps all, of the responsibility for the outbreak of the second world war and for the West's incapacity to build in northern France the front the communists were now demanding of Churchill.

The moment Hitler invaded totalitarian Russia the second world war became, for the earth's communists, a war for democracy. Forthwith

5. U.S.S.R., Ministry of External Affairs. *Perepiska Predsedatelia Sovieta Ministrov SSSR S Presidentami SSHA I Premier-Ministrami Velikobritanii Vo Vremia Velikoi Otchestvenoi Voiny 1941–1945. Tom Pervii, Perepiska s U. Cherchillem i K. Ettli (Iul 1941–Noyabr 1945).* (Correspondence of the Chairman of the Council of Ministers of the U.S.S.R. with the Presidents of the U.S.A. and the Prime Ministers of Great Britain during the Great Fatherland War, 1941–1945. Vol. I: Correspondence with W. Churchill and C. Attlee [July 1941-November 1945], hereafter referred to as *Perepiska*), Vol. I, pp. 10–11.

6. V. I. Lan, *SSHA V Voennie I Poslesvoennie Godi (1940–1960)* (The U.S.A. in the War and Postwar Years 1940–1960), p. 11.

they launched a raucous propaganda campaign for a second front. Churchill wasted a minimum of scorn on them: "The British Communists, who had hitherto done their worst, which was not much, in our factories, had denounced the 'capitalist and imperialist war,' turned once again overnight and began to scrawl the slogan, 'Second Front Now' on our walls and hoardings. . . . We did not allow these somewhat sorry and ignominious facts to disturb our thought."[7]

The calls from Moscow for a second front could not, however, be dismissed with the same airy contempt. There was always the fear that Russia's defenses might crumple or that Stalin, in the absence of a second front, would sign a second pact with Hitler and retire from the fight. The Kremlin's awareness of this fear and Russia's heavy bleeding, which centered all thought and feeling on self, closed Moscow's mind to argument. Churchill tried to pry it open.

"The Chiefs of Staff," he informed Stalin on July 20, 1941, "do not see any way of doing anything on a scale likely to be of the slightest use to you. The Germans have forty divisions in France alone, and the whole coast has been fortified with German diligence for more than a year, and bristles with cannon, wire, pillboxes, and beach-mines. The only part where we could have even temporary air superiority and air-fighter protection is from Dunkirk to Boulogne. This is one mass of fortifications, with scores of heavy guns commanding the sea approaches, many of which can fire right across the Straits. There is less than five hours' darkness, and even then the whole area is illuminated by searchlights. To attempt a landing in force would be to encounter a bloody repulse, and petty raids would only lead to fiascos doing more harm than good for both of us. It would be over without their having to move or before they could move a single unit from your front.

"You must remember that we have been fighting alone for more than a year." Action in the Arctic was being planned, Churchill added, but "There is no Norwegian Light Division in existence."[8]

No reply from Stalin.

Five days later Churchill told Stalin in a personal message that the War Cabinet had "decided, in spite of the fact that this will seriously deplete our fighter aircraft resources, to send to Russia as soon as possible two hundred Tomahawk fighter airplanes." Churchill also promised "up to two to three million pairs of ankle boots. . . . We are arranging to provide during the present year large quantities of rubber, tin, wool and woolen cloth, jute, lead, and shellac. . . .

"We are watching with admiration and emotion Russia's magnificent fight, and all our information shows the heaviest losses and concern of

7. Winston S. Churchill, *The Second World War. The Grand Alliance*, p. 379.
8. *Ibid.*, pp. 384–385.

the enemy. Our air attack on Germany will continue with increasing strength."[9]

Ten thousand tons of rubber were ready for dispatch on July 31 from Britain to Russia's northern ports, Churchill notified Stalin. No reply from Stalin.

"I tried my best," Churchill moans, "to build up by frequent personal telegrams the same kind of happy relations which I had developed with President Roosevelt. In this long Moscow series I received many rebuffs and only rarely a kind word. In many cases the telegrams were left unanswered altogether or for many days.

"The Soviet Government had the impression that they were conferring a great favour on us by fighting in their own country for their own lives."[10]

It was difficult or next to impossible to build up happy relations with Stalin. Churchill was not dealing with a Roosevelt or with anybody the likes of whom he had ever encountered in person, in history books, or in fiction. Secretary of the Soviet government Abel Yenukidze, Deputy Foreign Commissar Leo Karakhan, Politburo member Sergo Orjonekidze, and Commissar of Foreign Trade Anastas I. Mikoyan, all natives, like Stalin, of the Caucasus, all Stalin's buddies, came to his apartment often for a midnight supper. He had Yenukidze and Karakhan shot without trial and without known cause; he drove Orjonekidze to suicide; Mikoyan told me in Moscow in the summer of 1956 that he too contemplated suicide and that he had been on a list of those to be executed, but at the last moment, for no known reason, Stalin scratched off his name. Stalin killed his own wife. He ordered the execution of members of her family. Kindness was not a component of Stalin's character. Nor did he understand the meaning of giving. What others gave him he regarded not as generosity, that would have been too alien to his nature to comprehend, but as his due. This was the man who led Russia in the most sanguine war of all time and simultaneously conducted another war on the diplomatic front in which his allies were treated as enemies. He had trusted Hitler. Now he distrusted friendly democratic helpers. His name was steel, his banner hatred, his personal history hostility.

9. *Ibid.*, pp. 386–387.
10. *Ibid.*, p. 388.

III THE CHURCHILL-STALIN DEBATE

Early in September, 1941, "every senior German officer regarded the war against Russia as won. It was not 'whether,' but 'how?' "[1] Stalin was desperate. He thanked Churchill for the gift of 200 Tomahawk planes and for 200 Hurricane fighters promised subsequently. But these, Stalin mourned, would come too late to alter conditions at the front. ". . . in the last three weeks," he wired Churchill on September 3, "the situation of the Soviet forces has significantly deteriorated in such important regions as the Ukraine and Leningrad." The Germans had thrown into battle 30–34 infantry divisions, an enormous number of tanks and planes, and 20 Finnish and 26 Rumanian divisions. The "relative stability at the front achieved three weeks ago has crumbled." Hitler was transferring troops "with impunity" from the West to the Russian front. "The Germans believe it is entirely possible to defeat their enemies one by one: first the Russians, then the British."

This recalls the Litvinov logic of collective security which Stalin rejected in 1939.

Stalin elaborated on the latest setbacks. Russia faced "mortal danger." There is only "one way out of such a situation: to create a second front this year somewhere in the Balkans or France . . . and at the same time supply the Soviet Union by October of this year with 30 thousand tons of aluminum and a *monthly* minimum assistance of 400 planes and 500 (small or medium) tanks. Without these two forms of aid the Soviet Union will either suffer defeat or will be so weakened as to lose for a long time the capacity to help its allies by active efforts in the struggle against Hitlerism."[2]

Stalin's gloom was justified. In September, 1941, Germany came within a hair of winning the war. Yet such was the magnitude of events in the East and the speed with which they unfolded that by the end of December, 1941, it was almost certain that Hitler could never win.

Each side made enormous blunders which swayed the scales of battle violently. Foremost were the Soviet blunders. ". . . in the middle of May 1941," five weeks before the Nazis attacked, writes Alan Clark, "there

1. Alan Clark, *Barbarossa. The Russian-German Conflict, 1941–45,* p. 124.
2. *Perepiska,* Vol. I, pp. 18–19.

were nearly 170 [Soviet] divisions or over five sevenths of the country's armed strength, outside the 1939 frontiers."[3] That is, outside a fortified line of defense. In that indefensible theater Stalin's strategy of "attack the invader whenever and wherever he is encountered" spelled murder, especially since "In the first two days the Russians lost over 2,000 aircraft —a casualty rate without precedent. The (numerically) strongest air force in the world had been virtually eliminated in forty-eight hours."[4] The Russian army, thus deprived of sight, harried by the Luftwaffe and mangled by the Panzers, was no match for the experienced Wehrmacht. Minsk, the capital of Byelorussia and well within the old pre-September, 1939, frontier, fell to the Germans on June 28, the seventh day of the war. The 200-mile wide East Polish region annexed by Moscow in 1939 had proved worthless as a shield for the Byelorussian Republic. Presided over by military bungling in Moscow, the area became the cemetery of mountains of equipment and masses of Red Army soldiers. Soviet Communist Party Chief Leonid I. Brezhnev declared in Minsk on December 28, 1968, that one fourth of the inhabitants of Byelorussia were killed in the Great Fatherland War.[5] (The republic's population in 1939 was officially estimated at 8,910,000.)[6]

Calamity visited the three Baltic countries as well. "Only too swiftly did it become apparent," writes Harrison Salisbury, "that the glacis which the Soviets had hoped to create in the Baltic States as a defensive zone and protection to Leningrad was a deadly trap."[7] Kaunas, the former Kovno, capital of Lithuania, fell to the Germans on June 25; Riga, capital of Latvia, on July 1. Tallinn, the capital of Estonia and a naval base, was defended by the big guns of a large Soviet fleet. The Nazis cut off the city on August 8 and began their final assault August 13. The Soviet problem now was not to hold Tallinn, everybody recognized that as impossible. The problem was to evacuate the defenders, including the wounded, and above all to save the fleet. The operation developed into what Salisbury calls "the Russian Dunkirk."

The fleet sailed without air cover from Tallinn to the safety of Kronstadt. It had to dodge German mines, elude German submarines, and take Luftwaffe bombs. During the 220-mile odyssey under fire the Germans hit many targets. First, the troop transport *Ella* went down with part of its human cargo; the others were fished out of the sea by escort craft. Then the larger transport *Virona* came under air attack. Bombs cracked her deck and sides. She began to sink. The rescue ship *Saturn* ap-

3. Clark, p. 40.
4. *Ibid.,* p. 50.
5. *Pravda,* December 29, 1968.
6. *SSSR V Tsifrakh V 1960 godu* (The U.S.S.R. in Figures for 1960), p. 64.
7. Harrison E. Salisbury, *The 900 Days, The Siege of Leningrad,* p. 155.

proached. It struck a mine and went to the bottom followed by the *Virona* followed by the *Alev* and two more transports. Now the icebreaker *Voldemars,* which had been picking up *Virona* survivors, sank with them. The mine layer *Gordy* was blown up by a German mine; moments later another mine layer, the *Yakov Sverdlov,* stopped a torpedo. In the evening a submarine guarding the 7,000-ton cruiser *Kirov* was pierced by a German mine. A mine exploded near the hull of the destroyer *Minsk.* She took on 650 tons of water but remained afloat. Later in the evening the Soviet mine layers *Sneg, Tsiklon, Artem,* and *Volodarsky,* and the transports, *Kalinin, Luga, Everitis,* and *Yarvamaa* were added to the list of the day's fatalities. The transport *Ivan Papanin* with 3,000 troops, the *Vtoraya Pyatiletka* with an equal number, the *Luga* with 300 wounded, and the *Balkash* and *Tobol* with several hundred fighting men sank before midnight. Altogether 13 ships of the navy and 34 transports were lost. Deaths numbered at least 10,000. The white night, the calm summer sea helped save thousands of stalwart young soldiers and sailors who swam to rescue vessels and held on until they were lifted on board. Nobody was able to keep exact count of survivors or victims during that harrowing flight from Tallinn or to do any exact arithmetic when the wounded convoy crept into Kronstadt.

The Soviet disaster in the Baltic countries flowed from Stalin's foreign policy in 1939 and 1940. Lithuania, Latvia, and Estonia, ethnically non-Slav and historically anti-Russian, had, with British or German aid, wrenched themselves loose from Lenin's weakened realm. Moscow recognized them as sovereign states and concluded nonaggression treaties with them. In 1940 Stalin annexed them. They resented the loss of independence and the terror that followed. Russians came to rule in place of native officials sent by cattle car into Siberian exile. Baltic businessmen traveled by similar conveyances to a similar fate. Repression bred an armed underground movement which surfaced the moment war began. Soviet administrators were assassinated, Russian soldiers ambushed. When the Wehrmacht arrived it found some of its work done. Kaunas, for instance, was seized by Lithuanian insurgents on June 24. The Red Army fled. Moscow ordered it back and it went—to be massacred. Had the Lithuanians, Letts, and Estonians not been robbed of their independence they might have fought to defend it and summoned the British fleet and air force to help. Instead they facilitated Hitler's conquests.

Stalin was Stalin again. His nerves quieter, his megalomania once more in high gear, he resumed the purge of the military. After nearly completing three five-year plans directed, in large measure, to the production of armaments, Russia was deficient in tanks, antitank guns, antiaircraft guns, machine guns, and even rifles; Stalin had not believed war imminent; the country consequently was unprepared for the Nazi blow. Her armed forces took severe punishment. Lest a scintilla of blame attach to Stalin, somebody else had to be blamed. This principle guided most of the purges of the 1930's (except the purges of the military and of prominent communists—those were spawned by Stalin's sick fears, furious hates, unbridled jealousies, and pathological inferiorities). It was now applied to generals at the front:

The day war dawned General Dmitri G. Pavlov, commander of the western front, received reports of German attacks all along the line. He passed the reports to Moscow. "Comrade Stalin," Defense Commissar Semyon K. Timoshenko telephoned Pavlov, "has forbidden opening artillery fire against the Germans." Pavlov knew he would be shot unless he bowed to this insanity. He bowed. Battles were lost. Territory and men were lost. On June 30 Pavlov, a veteran of the Spanish Civil War, together with his chief of staff, General V. Y. Klimovsky, and his chief of operations, General V. Y. Semenov, were flown to Moscow and shot the day after their arrival. This form of atrocity, used often during the war, boomeranged: generals, intelligence agents, and top communists like Voroshilov, who was charged with the defense of Leningrad, were afraid to report defeats. As a result Stalin remained misinformed at some crucial moments.

Lieutenant General K. P. Pyadyshev, another veteran of the Spanish Civil War, had, without awaiting Moscow instructions, built the Luga Line where, for a time, he blocked the Nazi avalanche tumbling toward Leningrad. He was removed on July 23, 1941, and executed. After the 1956 Twentieth Soviet Communist Party Congress he was rehabilitated as innocent.[8] His case is not unique. On being assigned to the command of a front near Leningrad in July, 1941, Major General M. P. Petrov, for instance, exclaimed, "So now they are going to shoot me too."

Major General Andrei E. Fedyunin, in command of a guards' division on the Leningrad front, mounted an offensive in July and pushed back Field Marshal Erich von Manstein's motorized force—a rare feat in the early months of the war. The Germans counterattacked and crushed Fedyunin's unit. His dead body was brought out by retreating Russian soldiers. The official announcement said he was killed in combat. He in fact committed suicide to avoid capture. Stalin had established the rule —it claimed many victims—that anyone taken prisoner must have surrendered and was therefore a traitor.

The purges in the Red Army command hastened the dissolution of the Soviet defenses on the western front. The roads to Leningrad, the Ukraine, and Moscow lay open.

8. *Ibid.*, p. 190.

Now the Germans began to blunder. The notion of a harmonious German High Command automatically doing Hitler's bidding is fiction. Dissension flared with the false dawn of victory. From the very first Field Marshal Walther von Brauchitsch, commander in chief of the Wehrmacht, urged a one-prong thrust to Moscow. Military and political considerations spoke in its favor. Moscow was more to the Soviet Union than London is to Britain or Paris to France or Rome to Italy. Moscow was the heart and brain of a thoroughly centralized country where all power and initiative rested in the hands of one man. Stalin, to be sure, could have moved to the Volga or the Urals. But anybody with any experience of the U.S.S.R. can imagine the resulting panic and chaos. The fact that Stalin bravely stayed in Moscow when the Germans reached it is credited by Soviet historians—correctly for once—with having saved the city.

A Wehrmacht offensive aimed at Moscow only might well have succeeded. But Hitler vetoed the Brauchitsch plan. Did he fear the fate of Napoleon? There were enough one-story wooden houses of the kind the French Emperor saw to make a crackling fire. Or did Hitler hope to enter Moscow in climactic triumph over a prostrate Russia that had sued for peace? Cautiously he ordered Leningrad seized first. Simultaneously he directed a massive assault on the Ukraine. Leningrad, population a million and a quarter, was encircled September 8. A colossal catastrophe overtook the Ukraine. Stalin had given orders to hold Kiev, the ancient capital of the Ukraine, come what may, and appointed Marshal Budenny to command the Ukrainian front. Simeon M. Budenny had been a sergeant major in the Tsar's cavalry. Despite all his military and political promotions and a broad breast hung with decorations he remained a cavalry sergeant major whose limited brains matched his unlimited loyalty to Stalin. To this safe incompetent Stalin committed the lives of a million soldiers and the fate of the Ukraine, the largest Soviet minority republic, population some 35 million.

Budenny's host faced a large Nazi army under Field Marshal Gerd von Rundstedt, perhaps the finest German strategist of the second world war. To reinforce Rundstedt Colonel General Heinz Guderian descended from the north with his dread Panzer army. The result was a holocaust. Stalin's order to stand fast invited encirclement. The Red Army of the Ukraine would have done better to withdraw eastward, away from the Nazi crunch. Soviet generals advocated this course, but Budenny knew Stalin's mind and threw more and more divisions into the steel ring being forged by Rundstedt. Moscow denies the German claim of 665,000 Soviet prisoners taken in the August-September, 1941, battle for the Ukraine. It puts the figure much lower. But ultimately all of the Ukraine was occupied and, later, the Crimea as well. "Nearly one third of the

Soviet Army, as it had been at the outbreak of war, was eliminated."[9]

The Ukraine, fertile agriculturally, is fertile politically too. Nikita S. Khrushchev said in his secret speech of February 24–25, 1956, that during the war "whole nations, together with all communists and Komsomols [young communists] without any exception" were deported "from their native places." The Chairman listed the Karachai, the Kalmyks, the Chechen, the Ingushi, the Kabardinians, and the Balkari, and left out the Tartars of the Crimea. Stalin, Khrushchev declared, was "the initiator" of these "monstrous acts." Stalin suspected the exiled national minorities of disloyalty to Bolshevism and sympathy for their Nazi conquerors. "The Ukrainians," Khrushchev added, "avoided meeting this fate only because there were too many of them and there was no place to which to deport them. Otherwise he would have deported them also."

Many Ukrainians, communist, noncommunist, and anticommunist, had been avidly nationalistic, some eagerly separatistic. Stalin purged Ukrainian nationalists throughout the 1930's. Nationalistic or not, top communists in the Ukraine, whether Russian or Ukrainian, received the special attention of Stalin's terror apparatus. Pavel P. Postyshev, named secretary of the Ukrainian Communist Party in 1933, Stanislav V. Kossior, a member of the Politburo and General Secretary of the Ukrainian Communist Party, and Vlas Y. Chubar, Chairman of the Ukrainian government, and scores of their close coworkers were executed on Stalin's orders in 1938. Stalin abhorred any nucleus of power that pretended or might pretend to influence or popularity. In the Ukraine and in Leningrad Stalin was little loved and much disliked by the average citizen and by communists. In the winter of 1931–32 the Ukraine was ravaged by a man-made famine directly attributable to Stalin's policy of ruthless collectivization. It is said that one or two or three million died. (Individuals, especially foreigners, cannot obtain exact data on such tragedies and the Soviet government does not publish them.) In the 1950's the memory of that famine was still alive.

Small wonder Stalin feared subversion in the Ukraine. In numerous small towns and villages elders met the Nazi intruders with bread and salt—the traditional Slav welcome. Some wished to curry favor with their conquerors. But to no negligible extent these friendly gestures were a reaction to the horrors communism had visited upon them. Here Hitler missed a great opportunity not because he was stupid or ill-informed but because whom God would destroy He first makes racist. As soon as the Germans occupied Soviet territory they drew up plans for colonizing Germans on the new Lebensraum; the natives were to be exterminated or at best employed as slave laborers. Nor did Hitler have the sagacity to

9. Clark, p. 143.

disperse the collectives, the bane of the Ukrainian peasants' existence. He kept the collectives for the very reason Stalin had introduced them and the villagers hated them: they facilitated the confiscation of farm produce. Poor politics reduced the value of Germany's military gains in the Ukraine.

The war in the Ukraine also had remote repercussions on Soviet politics. Khrushchev became First Secretary of the Ukrainian Communist Party in succession to Kossior in 1938. As such he was the chief communist political officer in the Ukraine when war came. He witnessed the chaos and loss caused by Stalin's strange strategy. "When there developed an exceptionally serious situation for our army in 1942 in the Kharkov region we had correctly decided to drop an operation whose objective was to encircle Kharkov, because the real situation at that time would have threatened our army with fatal consequences if this operation were continued.

"We communicated this to Stalin," Khrushchev revealed in his secret speech.

"Contrary to common sense, Stalin rejected our suggestion and issued an order to continue the operation aimed at the encirclement of Kharkov, despite the fact that at this time many army concentrations were themselves actually threatened with encirclement and liquidation."

From the Ukrainian front Khrushchev telephoned Stalin in Moscow. Malenkov came to the phone. Khrushchev explained the problem to Malenkov and once more asked to talk with Stalin. "But Stalin did not consider it convenient to raise the phone and again stated that I should speak to him through Malenkov, although he was only a few steps from the telephone.

"After 'listening' in this manner to our plea, Stalin said: 'Let everything remain as it is.'

"And what was the result of this? The worst that we had expected. The Germans surrounded our army concentrations and consequently we lost hundreds of thousands of our soldiers."

A communist too is heir to all the weaknesses of the flesh. Stalin's wartime follies and his insulting treatment of Khrushchev rankled until the victim, in 1956, acquired the power to pull Stalin from his pedestal and later from the Lenin mausoleum, thus creating a crisis of faith in communism that continues to this day.

The Nazi envelopment of a large Russian army at Kiev and the encirclement of Leningrad were almost complete and their completion foreseeable on September 3, 1941, when Stalin telegraphed Churchill about the Soviet Union's "mortal danger" and the urgency of a second front. Churchill's reply is dated September 4. The Prime Minister obviously wished to reassure Stalin without delay. "The information at my disposal," he told Stalin, "gives me the impression that the culminating violence of the German invasion is already over, and that winter will give your heroic armies a breathing-space. This, however," he added for realism, "is a personal opinion." The opinion erred on the side of optimism but was not altogether mistaken.

As to supplies, "we are now prepared to send you *from British production,* one-half of the monthly total for which you ask in aircraft and tanks. We hope the United States will supply you with the other half of your requirements." Churchill explained that he was wiring President Roosevelt to expedite the arrival in London of W. Averell Harriman and would try, in consultation with him, before his departure for Moscow, "to tell you the numbers of aircraft and tanks we can jointly promise to send you each month, together with supplies of rubber, aluminum, cloth, etc."

On the question of the second front Churchill was restrained: "Whether British armies will be strong enough to invade the mainland of Europe during 1942 must depend on unforeseeable events. It may be possible, however, to assist you in the extreme North when there is more darkness."

Finally Churchill corrected Stalin's understanding of British and American aid. The dictator had asked the two western countries to "sell" Russia additional airplanes. "We . . . have never thought of payment," Churchill explained. "Any assistance we can give you would better be upon the same basis of comradeship as the American Lend-Lease Bill, of which no formal account is kept in money."[10]

"I can only repeat," Stalin replied on September 13, "that the absence of a second front is water on the mill of our common enemies." If the British government felt it could not at present open a second front in the West, "It seems to me that England could, without risk, land 25–30 divisions in Archangel or transport them through Iran to the southern regions of the Soviet Union for military collaboration with Soviet armies on Soviet territory. . . . That would be a great help."[11]

Stalin's invitation to Churchill, a leading sponsor of British intervention against Soviet Russia in 1918–19, to put a large foreign force on Soviet territory was either an attempt at an alibi ("I did all I could") in case European Russia fell to the Nazis or, more likely, an act of desperation. For with the Ukraine succumbing to German rule and Leningrad besieged, Hitler could reduce the number of troops on those fronts to garrison strength and hurl the bulk of the Wehrmacht against Moscow. When in mid-September the front around Leningrad was relatively stabilized and Germany consequently planned to kill the city by bombs, shells, and famine, Stalin began to rob "Peter," as older Russians still

10. Winston S. Churchill, *The Second World War. The Grand Alliance,* pp. 458–459.

11. *Perepiska,* Vol. I, pp. 22–23. Here and elsewhere, my translation from Stalin's Russian.

called Leningrad, to save Moscow. Much of Leningrad's arms output at that stage was flown out to the central front where the Nazis, it appeared, would soon make a supreme effort to capture the Soviet capital.

But Hitler was late. He had hoped to take Leningrad and the Ukraine and then throw an armed ring around Moscow and force Stalin to capitulate. Between 1936 and 1939, however, Madrid had demonstrated how difficult it is for an enemy to enter a big city. The Germans were superior to the Russians in everything from military tactics to techniques to equipment. Leningrad's defenders, despite the lesson of the 1939–40 Winter War against Finland, had no skis, for instance. The Germans had them. Yet by an almost superhuman effort Leningrad held the Nazis at bay.[12] But the German High Command, eager to punish Leningrad's defiance, gave Field Marshal Ritter von Leeb the additional arms and, what was infinitely more precious, the additional time to capture Leningrad. Von Leeb, a proud Prussian and a major military figure, insisted not only on victory at Leningrad but on a prominent role in the expected victory at Moscow. As the month of September, 1941, ebbed it was clear that he would not win victory at Leningrad. Some of his Panzer units were accordingly shifted to the central front for the assault on Moscow.

The battle for Moscow, the most decisive defensive battle of the 1941–1945 Soviet-Nazi war, loomed. Churchill clearly wished to encourage the Russians. He laid little stress in his message of September 17 on the question of the second front via Iran or Archangel because, as he writes in *The Grand Alliance,* "It is almost incredible that the head of the Russian Government with all the advice of their military experts could have committed himself to such absurdities. It seemed hopeless to argue with a man thinking in terms of utter unreality." (It is doubtful that Stalin asked any advice, or, if he did, that his military experts would say anything except what they knew he wanted to hear.) Instead Churchill dwelt on supplies. Harriman, accompanied by Lord Beaverbrook, could be expected in Moscow, the Prime Minister informed Stalin, "on the 25th of this month." They will "work out with you a definite program of monthly delivery by every possible route." The route he preferred was "the through route from the Persian Gulf to the Caspian, not only by railway, but by a great motor road in the making of which we hope to enlist American energies and organization. . . . We shall go on with you till victory."

Knowing Stalin's preoccupation with the problem of a second front, Churchill did say that Britain "had neither the force nor the shipping" to establish a front in Norway or anywhere else in the north. His hopes for a southern front rested on the Turks. ". . . if Turkey can be gained

12. The detailed story is told in Harrison E. Salisbury, *The 900 Days. The Siege of Leningrad.*

another powerful army will be available. Turkey would like to come in with us, but is afraid, not without reason."[13] Churchill did not elaborate. The Turks feared German punishment and, not without reason, Russian aggrandizement.

Beaverbrook left Britain with Harriman on September 21 by the cruiser *London*. Churchill gave him a letter for Stalin. It contained a few words that went obliquely and ever so lightly to the heart of the second-front matter. The British Isles, Churchill wrote, had a population of 44 million. "We can never hope to have an army or army munitions industries comparable to those of the great Continental military powers."[14] A nation, like a person, is held in the grip of an automatic urge for self-preservation. British manpower losses in the first world war created a trauma deeply embedded in the national psyche. Between 1914 and 1918 a whole generation of British young men, potential leaders among them, left their lives in the rat- and lice-infested trenches of France and Flanders. In subsequent decades British politics, economics, and art showed the effects of this tragic bloodletting. The British people recoiled from a second such experience. Biologically the nation could not afford it. This factor was never explicitly introduced into the long Moscow-London debate on the second front. Yet it may have been the decisive influence in Churchill's reluctance to send a British army once again across the English Channel.

The debate rolled on, but the second front which Stalin wanted was not established until the Soviet Union had been saved by its own valiant efforts. The greatest of these efforts, the turning point of the war and the cold beginning of the end of Hitler's design to subjugate Russia, was the battle of Moscow from October to December, 1941.

IV MIRACLE AT MOSCOW

Toward the end of September Moscow days grow shorter, the nights colder. The sun does not shine after 4 P.M. Outdoor tennis has ended. The brief but delightful summer is gone. October rains are likely to surround the big city with a sea of mud. In one or two months the sea will be a vast white expanse of snow and ice.

13. Churchill, pp. 463–464.
14. *Ibid.*, p. 466.

It was no time to launch a major offensive. Field Marshal Gerd von Rundstedt counseled against it. But Hitler wanted his crowning triumph and Stalin's scalp. To withdraw on the central front until spring and rest on their laurels, as Rundstedt advised, was contrary to Hitler's temperament and the Nazi generals' ambitions. In fact, Guderian believed his tank corps alone could take Moscow.

Despite the oncoming winter, despite the magnitude of the task, the Nazis almost succeeded in performing a miracle at Moscow. The capital of communism seemed to hang by a thread ready to fall into Hitler's hands in mid-October, 1941. Then by a heroic endeavor Stalin, his generals, Red Army soldiers, and civilian men and women snatched away the prize.

W. Averell Harriman and Lord Beaverbrook, angels from Western cornucopia, were in Moscow on September 30 when the Nazi offensive started. They conferred intensively with Stalin from September 29 to October 1. Stalin was pleased with their "speedy and effective" talks and thanked Churchill and Roosevelt "sincerely" for sending "such authoritative representatives." This message was written on October 3, yet already Stalin asked the British and United States governments to increase the monthly quotas fixed with Harriman and Beaverbrook and to expedite the arrival of supplies agreed upon "because the Hitlerites will try to use the months before winter to exert maximum pressure on the U.S.S.R."

Although Nazi forces were converging rapidly on Moscow, Stalin concluded this letter with a flourish of optimism. He did not wish his allies to abandon him. "As to the prospects of our common cause in the struggle against the Hitlerite bandits who rest in the center of Europe," he wrote, "I too am certain that, all difficulties notwithstanding, we shall achieve the destruction of Hitler in the interests of our freedom-loving peoples."[1]

Beaverbrook, a shrewd observer, remained in Moscow to survey the scene. "I do not regard the military situation here as safe for the winter months," he wired Churchill on October 4. But the agreement to give Russia more supplies had improved morale, delivery of those supplies would maintain morale, and "morale might make [the situation] safe."[2]

Churchill informed Stalin by code on October 6 that Britain intended to send an arms convoy to Russia every ten days. Twenty heavy tanks and 193 fighter planes were to arrive in Archangel on October 12; 140 heavy tanks, 100 Hurricane fighters, 200 Bren gun carriers, 200 antitank rifles with ammunition, and 50 two-pounder guns with ammunition would leave England October 12 and arrive in Archangel October 29. "Following will sail October 22: 200 fighters; 120 heavy tanks." Twenty tanks

1. *Perepiska*, Vol. I, pp. 27–28.
2. Winston S. Churchill, *The Second World War. The Grand Alliance*, p. 470.

were going via Persia and 15 "are about to be shipped from Canada via Vladivostok." These totals "do not take into account supplies from the United States." Churchill hoped that arms shipped to Archangel would reach the front expeditiously.[3] He knew about Russian inefficiency in the first world war. Stalin had asked, in addition, for 3,000 trucks. Churchill replied on October 12 that this request "would be met immediately" and delivery must not interfere with the stream of tanks and planes.[4]

These arms shipments strained Britain's industrial resources and denuded her own defenses but could not fill the gaping holes made by the Nazi invaders in Russia. In October, 1941, A. S. Shcherbakov, an alternate member of the Politburo of the Soviet Communist Party, admitted the destruction of 5,000 Soviet planes. The Red Army's tank forces, once its pride, had been shattered with astronomical loss. It had also lost a large proportion of its guns and gun crews. "Since huge ammunition dumps had been placed dangerously close to the frontier areas, these had been lost together with many of the means of producing ammunition."[5] According to German statistics marked Top Secret for use only by the German General Staff, the Nazis on November 1, 1941, had taken 2,053,000 Soviet prisoners,[6] an average of half a million a month.

In this depleted state Moscow met the Nazi onslaught.

Hitler's directive for the launching of Operation Barbarossa defined its primary purpose as the destruction of the Soviet armed forces. In part, this had been accomplished. But now, for political reasons, the Wehrmacht allowed itself to become bogged down in attacks on Russia's leading cities: Leningrad and Moscow.

Stalin seems to have understood, in the life-and-death crisis of the capital and perhaps therefore of the communist regime, that he was not the greatest military genius. The marshals and generals came to the center of the stage. When Leningrad appeared lost, Stalin sent Georgi K. Zhukov, a noncommissioned officer in the Tsar's army and commander of the Russian forces that defeated the Japanese on the Manchurian frontier in 1939, to stem the Nazi tide. Zhukov succeeded. Now Stalin put Zhukov in charge of the defense of Moscow and appointed Boris M. Shaposhnikov, a graduate of the Tsarist military academy, as his chief of staff. General Konstantin K. Rokossovsky, another Tsarist soldier, sent to a concentration camp in 1937, was given command of one of the armies fighting to rescue Moscow from encirclement. Politics had taken a back seat. Political marshals, notably Voroshilov and Budenny, went into total

3. *Ibid.,* p. 471.
4. *Perepiska,* Vol. I, p. 29.
5. John Erickson, *The Soviet High Command, A Military-Political History 1918–1941,* p. 625.
6. George Fischer, *Soviet Opposition to Stalin, A Case Study in World War II,* p. 3.

eclipse. The NKVD and army commissars, "the eyes and ears of the communist party," still badgered the military and punished "cowards" who retreated when overwhelmed. But in the cyclone of battle the gnats lost their sting.

Germany boasted 207 divisions in Russia—more than on June 22. Rumanian, Hungarian, Italian, Spanish, and Finnish reinforcements, less eager than Germans to die for Hitler, outnumbered Nazi losses. German control of the air was complete, German arms plentiful and superior. But the German tanks were the worse for wear, and the Germans, though willing, were tired and aghast at the stubborn resistance of small isolated Red Army units. If there was one hero in the Soviet-Nazi war he is the Soviet soldier. A hard life and hard work under Bolshevik rule had toughened his body. He could force march 20 miles a day, day after day, on a pound of black bread and a sour pickle. His fatalism matched his endurance. He had a soldier's highest qualification: he knew how to die. If he tried to avoid death, the NKVD would shoot him down without asking a question.

"After three and a half months of fighting," read Hitler's order of the day to the Wehrmacht on the eve of the Moscow offensive, "you have created the necessary conditions for the last vigorous blows which should break the enemy on the threshold of winter." The horror of a Moscow winter haunted him. On October 2, the third day of the offensive, Guderian, coming up from the Ukraine with repaired Panzers, erupted into Orel, 245 miles from Moscow. The streetcars were running, men and women were shopping as usual. He took the town by surprise. However, Tula, approximately halfway between Orel and Moscow, was stoutly defended. He bypassed it and headed for the main target. General Erich Hoeppner had led his tanks down from the Leningrad siege line. Zhukov threw in his reserves. Wherever the Germans met determined resistance they detoured and moved on. Time was of the essence. The Russian front had already been pierced and cut into segments with no easy communications. On October 8 *Red Star,* the Red Army daily, said, "the very existence of the Soviet state is in danger." *Pravda* on October 9 warned against "careless complacency," and on October 12 it admitted that a "terrible danger" threatened the entire country. The Germans continued to advance. On October 13 A. S. Shcherbakov, addressing a meeting of the Moscow Communist Party organization, exclaimed, "Let us not shut our eyes. Moscow is in danger." The same day it was decided to evacuate the capital to Kuibyshev, the former Samara, on the Volga. Most government offices and the diplomatic corps left. Stalin stayed.

"During the night of October 14–15," read the Soviet official communiqué of October 16, "the position on the western front deteriorated. The German-Fascists hurled large numbers of tanks and motorized infantry against our troops, and in one sector broke through our defenses." Panic gripped Moscow. Russians had grown accustomed to reading between the lines. "One sector" might mean several sectors or all sectors.

Konstantin Simonov, a Soviet author, in his wartime novel, *The Living and the Dead,* gives an eyewitness report of Moscow on October 16 and the days immediately following: stampedes at railway stations, officials fleeing in their cars without permits, communist battalions and guerrillas shuffling rather than marching, smoking but not singing (Soviet soldiers sing as they defile through city streets), the smell and smoke of burning archives, air raids and dog fights "in which Russian airmen often suicidally ram enemy planes," and "the demoralization of the majority and the grim determination of the minority to hang on to Moscow, and to fight, if necessary, inside the city."[7]

"By the end of October over two million people had been officially evacuated from Moscow; in addition, there were many others who had fled unofficially."[8] Residents of the outskirts moved into the center and took over empty apartments. Peasants, driving their cattle before them, came into the city to escape the bombs, shells, and death of the battlefield. Looters made hay in the chaos. Moscow throbbed with fear and rumor.

Presently the German offensive became mired in mud. While the Wehrmacht marked time for the ground to freeze, a bright sun rose out of the east in the shape of fresh, battle-tried Soviet reinforcements from Siberia.

Richard Sorge, born in Baku to a Russian mother and a German father who worked as an engineer in the Baku oil fields, joined the Soviet Communist Party, then for cover joined the Nazi Party in Germany and, disguised as a Nazi journalist, went to Tokyo where, after establishing friendly relations with the German Ambassador and well-placed Japanese, he sent Moscow by radio and courier authentic information which altered history. From Sorge the Kremlin knew in the spring of 1939 that Hitler would invade Poland on September 1—knowledge that bore fruit in the summer's Soviet-Nazi pact. From Sorge the Kremlin learned by radio on May 15, 1941, that Hitler would attack on June 22. This was one of the many precise warnings Stalin ignored.

After June 22, 1941, it was a matter of life or death for Moscow to learn whether Japan would take advantage of the German invasion to intervene in the Soviet Far East. A double blow might wreck the communist regime. The Japanese government had ordered large-scale mobilization. Would its armed forces go north into the U.S.S.R. or south into the French, Dutch, and British colonies rich in oil, rubber, rice, tin, and other necessities of war? Berlin was interested in the answer to the same ques-

7. Paraphrased by Alexander Werth, *Russia at War,* pp. 237–238.
8. *Ibid.,* p. 241.

tion, and so Nazi Ambassador Eugen Ott and his friend and Soviet spy, Richard Sorge, pooled their resourcefulness.

The answer both were seeking depended in large measure on Japanese-American relations. On July 24, 1941, Japanese forces entered French Indochina. Washington reacted two days later by freezing Japanese assets in the U.S. This seemed to indicate that Tokyo's primary preoccupation would be America rather than Russia. But diverse interests played on the highest Japanese decision makers. The army contended that the German eruption into Russia offered Japan a unique opportunity to wrest from Russia the vast region between Lake Baikal and the Pacific. The navy, on the other hand, favored a southern push for bases and the sinews of war.

The unraveling of the mystery of Japan's future course was obstructed by conflicting information. Of the newly mobilized troops, 300,000 were conveyed to Manchukuo, the puppet state in Manchuria. Later some units were returned to the Japanese islands. Light summer uniforms were distributed to a number of divisions. An Imperial Conference held in the presence of the Emperor on July 2, 1941, had decided that Japan would remain neutral toward both Russia and Germany. The decision, however, might be annulled by developments, by the German capture of Moscow, for instance. The Germans would never want to stretch out as far as the Pacific; the Russian Far East could be seized by Japan.

Sorge and Ott and their collaborators floundered in this welter of contradictory facts. Late in September and early in October, 1941, the German Embassy and Sorge agreed, and Sorge notified Moscow, that "the [Japanese] offensive against the Soviet Union has been suspended for the time being."[9]

"For the time being" meant at least until after the early winter months of 1942. At about the same time Sorge radioed Moscow that Japanese officials expected war with the United States in October or November.

This was clarity enough. The Kremlin had transferred small formations of the battle-hardened Far Eastern army to the western front beginning June, 1941. In October and November a quarter of a million of these troops, with 1,700 tanks and 1,500 aircraft, were shifted to the Moscow front, and it may be said that this force, dressed for below-zero fighting and inured to Siberia's climate, saved Moscow. (In 1944 the Japanese arrested and executed Sorge. The Soviet government, publicly acknowledging his services, awarded him posthumously its highest honor: Hero of the Soviet Union.)

"In November Stalin was grievously short of men as well as munitions and weapons. It was at this time that the strength of the Red Army forces

9. F. W. Deakin and G. R. Storry, *The Case of Richard Sorge,* p. 241.

on all European fronts fell to 2,300,000, the lowest they ever reached throughout the whole of the Soviet-German war."[10] The injection at Moscow of a quarter of a million men and their armaments spelled more power and better morale. The same effect was achieved by the introduction of the new heavy T-34 tank, which the Germans acknowledged as superior to any they had, and of the Katyusha rapid-firing, multiple-rocket mortars. In October, moreover, rain descended in torrents. The Germans had ringed Moscow; the ring was 40 miles or less in some places from the city streets. But now, due to the new circumstances, the offensive halted for re-equipment and reassessment. The Luftwaffe continued to harass the citizens of the capital.

In this state of suspended fate the Bolshevik revolution met its 24th anniversary. Traditionally the celebration begins on the evening of November 6 with a gala assembly in the Bolshoi Theater, where a communist leader, designated by Stalin in the years of his reign, delivers a programmatic speech. On November 6, 1941, the meeting was held in the all-steel Mayakovsky Square Metro station, some 120 feet underground, whose ornate platform, lit by its permanent crystal chandeliers and decorated with flowers, seated 2,000 of Russia's foremost party officials and military officers. This year, for reasons of morale, Stalin himself delivered the address.

The morning *Pravda*'s front-page editorial entitled "Death to Hitlerism, the Piratical Imperialism," began, "Our fatherland meets the twenty-fourth anniversary of the Great October in a threateningly grim situation. The Soviet people are engaged in a death struggle with a rabid, treacherous enemy. This is a struggle for the very existence of our country." Stalin struck the same note underground: "I must emphasize that after four months of war the danger has not grown less, but on the contrary has even increased. The enemy . . . is threatening our glorious capital, Moscow . . . he is straining all his efforts to capture Leningrad and Moscow before the end of winter, because he knows that winter bodes him no good."

Here Stalin offered his audience—the entire Soviet Union—the balm of manipulated arithmetic. He divided Soviet casualties and multiplied Nazi losses: "In four months of war," he said, "we have lost 350,000 killed and 378,000 missing, and our wounded number 1,102,000. In the same period the enemy has lost in killed, wounded, and prisoners more than four and a half million men." Had this been true the Red Army could have walked to Berlin. Hitler crashed into Russia with 3,050,000 German troops, half a million Finns who did little fighting, and 250,000 Rumanians. If one adds Italians, Spaniards, and other camp followers the total

10. Cited by Erickson, p. 631, from a Wehrmacht source.

would probably come to four and a half million. According to Stalin, all had been eliminated.

Further to reassure the Soviet public Stalin asserted that Hitler had failed to align the capitalist powers on his side. Britain and America were "in one camp with the U.S.S.R." Russia's "temporary reverses" were due to Germany's production of "considerably more tanks" and aircraft than the Soviets and to the absence of a second front in Europe. "But . . . there can be no doubt that the appearance of a second front on the European continent—and it must unquestionably appear in the near future ["Loud applause" reads the record]—will essentially ease the situation of our army to the detriment of the German army."

The task now, Stalin asserted, was to produce more weapons of all kinds, tanks in particular, "and to construct more antitank trenches and every other kind of antitank obstacles." He expected to fight the Wehrmacht in the outskirts of Moscow and in the city streets.

Suddenly, without a transition, Stalin shifted from the military situation to theory. The Hitlerites, as he always preferred to call them, "obstinately continue to call themselves 'National Socialist.' . . . What can there be in common between socialism and the bestial Hitlerite invaders who are plundering and oppressing the nations of Europe? Can the Hitlerites be regarded as nationalists? No, they cannot. Actually, the Hitlerites are now not nationalists but imperialists."

The "now" was explained as follows: "As long as the Hitlerites were engaged in assembling the German lands and reuniting the Rhine district, Austria, etc., it was possible with a certain amount of foundation to call them nationalists. But after they seized foreign territories and enslaved European nations—the Czechs, Slovaks, Poles, Norwegians, Danes, Dutch, Belgians, French"—all this occurred while Stalin was Hitler's applauding ally—"Serbs, Greeks, Ukrainians, Byelorussians, the inhabitants of the Baltic countries, et cetera—and began to reach out for world domination, the Hitlerite party ceased to be a nationalist party, because from that moment it became an imperialist party, a party of annexation and oppression."

Stalin was not an academic and the subterranean audience was not an academic audience. Stalin was not striving for a scientific definition. The possibility that the two totalitarianisms at war might be regarded as identical is what troubled him. For he had nurtured Soviet nationalism, Russian and Ukrainian nationalisms especially, and he regarded the Soviet system as socialist. That would make Russia a nationalist-socialist state. The Nazis called themselves nationalist-socialists; "Nazi" stands for national socialist. So eager was Stalin to differentiate the Soviet from the German political order that Soviet Ambassador Maisky was instructed to request the British Broadcasting Corporation to substitute

"Hitlerite" for "Nazi." Churchill refused. He was too fond of his repugnance-crammed pronunciation of "Naahzi." Actually, a state can wrap itself in xenophobia at home yet annex colonies abroad. Nationalism married to power has usually been the mother of imperialism. And the Soviet system, an unwithered, caste-ridden state conducting an economy based on money, piece wages, exploitation, and profit is socialist by no stretch of the imagination or of Marx.

Stalin hated the Nazis. He hated the Germans. "The German invaders want a war of extermination with the peoples of the U.S.S.R.," he said in conclusion. "Well, if the Germans want to have a war of extermination, they will get it. . . . No mercy to the German invaders! Death to the German invaders."[11]

Tradition called for a military parade on the Red Square the morning of November 7. Stalin did not intend to allow the Germans to prevent any part of the annual celebration. To avoid becoming a Luftwaffe target the parade was held before dawn.

None of these morale builders seems to have lifted Stalin's spirit. He was in an ugly mood on November 8. A communication from Churchill, dated November 4, had arrived the previous day and Stalin answered it immediately in a tone he might have used, in one of his more polite moments, toward a Soviet colleague. He was irritated, no doubt, by Churchill's opening proposal: "In order to clear things up and to plan for the future I am ready to send you General [A. P.] Wavell, Commander-in-Chief in India, Persia, and Iraq," and General Bernard Paget, "our new Commander-in-Chief" for the Far East "who has been in the centre of things here. . . . These officers will be able to tell you exactly how we stand, what is possible and what we think is wise."[12]

This could only have riled Stalin, for the two generals would obviously try to explain why Britain thought it impossible and unwise to launch a second front in France. "I agree with you," Stalin therefore replied, "that it is necessary to introduce clarity, which does not now exist, in the relations between the U.S.S.R. and Great Britain. This lack of clarity is the consequence of two circumstances: first—there exists no definite agreement between our two nations on war aims and on plans for the organization of the affairs of peace after the war; and second—there exists no agreement between the U.S.S.R. and Great Britain on mutual military assistance in Europe against Hitler. As long as there is no agreement on these two main questions there will not only be no clarity in Anglo-Soviet relations but, to speak quite frankly, even mutual trust is

11. Marshal Stalin, *On the Great Patriotic War of the Soviet Union. Speeches, Orders of the Day, and Answers to Foreign Press Correspondents.* In English, pp. 10–14.
12. Churchill, pp. 527–528.

not guaranteed. Of course the existing agreement on military supplies has great positive significance, but it does not settle matters and is far from exhausting the mutual relations between our two countries."

Now if Wavell and Paget were coming to discuss these subjects Stalin was ready to receive them in Moscow, but, he added disdainfully, if their concern was information or matters of secondary importance, "I do not see the necessity of tearing generals away from their work and I myself could not assign time for such conversations."

In several messages Stalin had urged Churchill to declare war on Finland, Hungary, and Rumania, whose troops were arrayed against the Russian army. Churchill harbored doubts: Finland had many friends in the United States; Hungary and Rumania had been "overpowered" by Hitler, but "if fortune turns against that ruffian they might easily come back to our side." Stalin was furious. "It seems to me an intolerable situation has been created." The Soviet proposal of a declaration of war against the three countries by Great Britain had been made in secret. Nonetheless it was being discussed in the press "pro and con at random." And the British government, "after all that, announces its negative attitude to our proposal. Why is all this being done? Can it be in order to demonstrate the discord between the U.S.S.R. and Great Britain?"

Finally Stalin showed his resentment of Churchill's remark in an earlier communication suggesting the speedy removal of British arms from the docks at Archangel and the terminals in Iran. "You can rest assured" on this score. "It is impossible, however," Stalin said in a last sentence, "not to assert, though this is a minor matter, that tanks, artillery and planes arrive in poor packing, that parts of artillery arrive on different ships, and that planes are so poorly packed that they arrive in a broken condition."[13]

"Even Stalin"—a perceptive two-word profile of the Soviet despot— "Even Stalin seems to have felt," Churchill comments, "that he had gone too far in the tone of this communication." Churchill did not answer it. "The silence," he says with justifiable self-satisfaction, "was impressive." Stalin made a half-apology. The monster bully may often have had regrets but was able to suppress them. In this case it was not politic to suppress them. Neither did he wish to put them on paper. Ambassador Maisky was accordingly ordered to speak with Foreign Secretary Eden, who recorded the conversation in a note to Sir Stafford Cripps in Kuibyshev. Maisky said, "It had certainly not been M. Stalin's intention to cause any offence to any member of the Government, and least of all to the

13. *Perepiska,* Vol. I, pp. 31–32. I have made the translation from the Russian because the translations in Churchill's *The Grand Alliance* are somewhat inexact in several places. In the last sentence, for instance, Churchill's translation reads "parts of the same vehicle," the Russian reads "otdelnie chasti artillerii."

Prime Minister. M. Stalin was very busy with affairs at the front, and had virtually no chance to think of anything else but affairs at the front."

This is a remarkable excuse. If one has no time to think it is best not to write.

The questions of wartime military assistance to Russia and postwar arrangements were "very important," Maisky continued, speaking from a precise brief, "and it was very undesirable to complicate them by any personal misunderstandings or feelings." What had apparently aroused Stalin's ire was Churchill's reluctance to declare war on Finland. (Churchill refers to "The almost hysterical note of Stalin's message about Finland.") Maisky told Eden that "the Finnish business had greatly hurt [Stalin] and the whole of the Soviet Union." (The whole of the Soviet Union was sunk in other concerns, chiefly bread and death.) "My Fatherland, said M. Stalin," Maisky continued, quoting Stalin directly, "finds itself in a humiliating position. Our request was made secretly. Then the whole thing was published, and also the fact that His Majesty's Government did not consider it possible to accept the Soviet request. This has put my country in a humiliated position, and has had a depressing effect on the minds of my people." Despite Stalin's hurt, Maisky concluded, Stalin still aimed at an agreement on military assistance and the postwar peace.[14]

Ninety-nine and a half percent of the Soviet population knew nothing about "the Finnish business" and the remainder would not have cared or shared Stalin's "hurt," for unlike him they were accustomed to having their requests rejected.

The Churchill-Stalin exchange took place against deafening background noises of cannonading and bombing; the Nazis were preparing to renew their offensive against Moscow. In any other case this would be accepted as a mitigating circumstance for Stalin's insulting message to the Prime Minister. But insulting people was an ingrained and purposeful habit with Stalin; he even insulted Lenin's wife, Krupskaya; Lenin broke off personal relations with him. Churchill could not break with Stalin. He thought it best to "smooth out relations" by sending Eden to Moscow again. Stalin accepted the offer.

Hitler's generals had had "the nose full," as the German goes, of fighting the Red Army in wintertime. They wanted to await the spring. Hitler denied them a respite. And he was right, for the ground was already frozen, there was no possibility of digging in, and all buildings had been burned in battle or deliberately destroyed in accordance with Stalin's announced "scorched earth" policy. The Wehrmacht could only rest

14. Churchill, pp. 530–531.

if it retreated hundreds of miles. Hitler would not contemplate that. He ordered an advance on Moscow. The new offensive began November 15. Guderian wrote his wife, on November 28, "Only he who saw the endless expanse of Russian snow during this winter of our misery, and felt the icy wind that blew across it, burying in snow every object in its path; who drove for hour after hour through that no man's land only to find too thin shelter, with insufficiently clothed half-starved men; and who also saw by contrast the well-fed, warmly-clad and fresh Siberians, fully equipped for winter fighting; only a man who knew all that can truly judge the events which now occurred."

The events that occurred are summed up in a few words: Guderian and his Panzers and all other German armies on the offensive were checked by the Russians, the Siberians, the cold, the shortage of food, and the almost-complete absence of winter clothing for the freezing Germans.

Further events followed rapidly. The gambler in his "Wolf's Lair" ordered another offensive. With Moscow only 40 miles away, he could not resist another throw of the Wehrmacht. The offensive opened on December 2. It was blocked 48 hours later and "burned out" completely on the 6th. On December 8 Hitler issued Directive Number 39: "The severe winter weather which has come surprisingly early in the East, and the consequent difficulties in bringing up supplies, compel us to abandon all major offensive operations and go over to the defensive."[15]

Stalin and Zhukov had not waited for Hitler. On the night of December 4–5 the Russians launched their offensive along the entire Moscow front. The Nazi condition beggars ordinary description. The Wehrmacht forces were hacked into segments which lost contact with one another. Small units "fought a thousand combats . . . in isolation . . . with unusable vehicles, small arms frozen solid (the grenade was the only weapon which maintained its efficiency), half-drunk on schnapps, frostbitten, and riddled with dysentery.

"The 'intestinal disorders' . . . were now rampant throughout the army; yet on days like 10th December, when Guderian recorded the temperature as falling to minus 63 degrees, it was death to squat in the open and 'many men died while performing their natural functions as a result of the congelation of the anus.' . . . There was no escape from this purgatory —save death itself. For that old soldier's standby, the self-inflicted wound, besides being a capital offence, could only mean a slow death from exposure and gas gangrene. Some men took their own lives with a hand grenade held against the stomach. . . . Under the double impact of the blizzards and the ubiquity of the Russian attack, the perils of the Army Group Centre mounted hourly . . . hundreds of tanks were aban-

15. H. R. Trevor-Roper (Ed.), *Blitzkrieg and Defeat. Hitler's War Directives 1939–1945*, p. 107.

doned in the drifting snow." Frostbite required amputation on the spot.[16]

The Germans had captured Rostov-on-Don in the North Caucasus on November 21. Six days later the Red Army recaptured it. This was the first big Soviet victory of the war. A bigger victory was in the making at Moscow—a victory and a miracle. Field Marshal Walther von Brauchitsch, commander in chief of the Wehrmacht, in conflict with Hitler over the Moscow battle, resigned. Hitler took over supreme command. Nothing helped. "In the period from 6th-25th December, the Red Army operations against Army Group Centre had liquidated the threat to Moscow," writes John Erickson, "although not until 22nd January 1942, was Moscow oblast [region] cleared of the enemy."

The German army had conquered the European continent from Norway to Greece, from the coast of France to Rumania's Black Sea beaches. It was well on its way to victory over Russia. At Moscow it met its first great reverse on land. The tide had turned. The miracle at Moscow proved that Hitler was not invincible. Stalin's authority was re-established. His self-confidence returned. Soviet morale bounced back. The war could be won. German morale at home slumped. After the war German men and women spoke with a shudder of horror of the Moscow ordeal.

Germany's defeat at Moscow was on a grander scale than Napoleon's. Both are so deeply engraved on mankind's historical memory that there is never likely to be another invasion of Russia from the west.

On December 7, 1941, while the Moscow battle raged in cold fury, the Japanese struck Pearl Harbor.[17] It hastened the dawn of victory for Russia. The day, however, would be long and the sacrifices many.

16. Alan Clark, *Barbarossa*, pp. 180–181.
17. Maxim Litvinov, flying the Pacific to take up his new post as Soviet ambassador in Washington, D.C., stopped in Honolulu two days before the Japanese assault on Pearl Harbor. Entertained by the highest American army and navy officials, he told them about the unexpectedness of the Nazi blow against Russia. He said a country at peace cannot get accustomed to the idea that it may soon be attacked and so it is caught unawares. At this very moment, he stated, the Japanese may be planning war on the United States; they might strike Honolulu. Litvinov advised the American officers to be vigilant day and night.

V A ROOSEVELT–STALIN QUARREL

British Foreign Secretary Anthony Eden, in Moscow from December 15 to 28, 1941, witnessed the Kremlin elation after the German defeat outside the capital. Yet the military situation remained grim. And the diplomatic horizon was black.

During September, October, and November, 1941, Marshal Stalin had indicated "the desirability of entering into negotiations for a political agreement with Great Britain." The Churchill Cabinet did not respond. As a result "Stalin displayed a spirit of bad temper."[1] Hence Eden's December, 1941, mission to Moscow.

British diplomacy was intimately coordinated with America's through a constant exchange of information and advice and by American obstructions. The State Department "had been in no doubt at the time" of Stalin's first inquiries about a political agreement that its purpose was to win British sanction "for certain territorial claims" and "certain territorial adjustments," which would, Hull told Roosevelt, "make the Soviet Union the dominating power in Eastern Europe if not of the whole continent." On December 5, 1941, therefore, before Eden flew to Moscow, Hull sent John G. Winant, U.S. Ambassador in London, a telegram "approved by the President" instructing him to tell Eden that the United States opposed any commitments by Russia, Britain, or America "regarding specific terms of the post-war settlement." Furthermore, Hull urged, "there must be no secret accords." Hull was an unusual diplomat. He had principles.

Winant, a tall Lincolnesque figure vastly popular in war-torn Britain, showed Eden Hull's telegram. Eden said he agreed.

Eden arrived in Moscow late on the evening of December 15 and conferred with Stalin the next day. The Soviet leader gave him the drafts of two documents: one, a treaty of alliance; two, an agreement on postwar cooperation that contained "a secret protocol dealing in some detail with European frontiers," Eden writes in his memoirs.[2]

1. From a memorandum, a history of the Eden mission and its aftermath, which Secretary of State Hull gave President Roosevelt on February 4, 1942, printed in *Foreign Relations of the United States. Diplomatic Papers. 1942.* Vol. III: *Europe,* pp. 504–512.

2. Anthony Eden, *The Memoirs of Anthony Eden, Earl of Avon. The Reckoning,*

"I suppose you will not object if we add a small protocol to our agreement on post-war reconstruction," Ivan M. Maisky, Soviet Ambassador in London who was present, quotes Stalin as saying.[3] Maisky, however, refrains from using the embarrassing word "secret." For in form and content the secret protocol Stalin offered Eden resembles the secret protocol attached to the innocuous Ribbentrop-Molotov pact of August 23, 1939. Resembles yet transcends it. Neither Eden in his book nor Maisky in his records the full extent of Stalin's aspirations. Eden did, on his return to London, report them to Winant, and they appear in Hull's February 4, 1942, memo to Roosevelt.

Stalin's secret "small protocol" on Russia's big appetite provided for British recognition of Russia's annexation in 1939 and 1940 of part of Poland and of Finland and of all of Estonia, Latvia, and Lithuania, Bessarabia and Moldavia; Soviet bases in Finland and Rumania; the restoration of Austrian independence; the independence of Bavaria; the detachment of the Rhineland from Prussia; the transfer of East Prussia to Poland and of the Sudetenland to Czechoslovakia; and the transfer to Turkey of the Dodecanese Islands and of certain districts of Bulgaria and Syria.

The independence of Austria and Bavaria was designed to weaken postwar Germany. Polish annexation of East Prussia would weaken Germany and make Poland dependent on Moscow. Stalin's generosity to Turkey at the expense of Bulgaria, Greece, and Syria seemed to be conceived as compensation for territory Russia intended to take from the Turks in accordance with a 1939 preview. Finland and Rumania would become Russian puppet states. The entire scheme represented a Soviet lurch for empire in confirmation of the Soviet-Nazi secret protocol attached to the pact of August 23, 1939, and of subsequent secret Soviet-German agreements.

But the foreign lands annexed by Moscow under the Soviet-Nazi pact and protocol proved no barrier to the German invasion of 1941. They added no iota to Russia's national security, nor was that their purpose. Stalin wanted them for his regime's internal security: to bring him the

---

p. 335. On February 4, 1942, Secretary of State Hull sent President Roosevelt a memorandum, based on dispatches from Ambassador Winant in London, on the Stalin-Eden talks. See *Foreign Relations of the United States. Diplomatic Papers 1942.* Vol. III: *Europe,* pp. 504–512. A copy of the typed memorandum, 16 pages long, seen in the Franklin D. Roosevelt Library in Hyde Park, was passed to Harry Hopkins on February 9 with the President's notation: "For your information and comment if any."

3. Ivan Maisky, *Memoirs of a Soviet Ambassador. The War 1939–1943,* p. 231. The original is entitled *Vospominania Sovietskovo Posla. Voina 1939–1943.* The translator, Andrew F. Rothstein, renders Stalin's word "ustroistvo" as "reconstruction," whereas the correct and revealing translation would be "order" or "arrangement."

support, the inadequacy of which the communists had felt since November 7, 1917, of the Russian and Ukrainian peoples. For Bolshevism's effect was divisive. It set the peasantry against the state (especially after collectivization in 1929), alienated Ukrainians resentful of Muscovite domination, and failed to rally the Great Russians who saw their motherland shrivel. Stalin tried to mend the situation by persuading Germany to grant the Soviets all Ukrainian-inhabited regions in eastern Europe and all former Russian-ruled territories. He pursued the same end with Eden.

On hearing Stalin's demands Eden declared that he had promised the U.S. government not to enter into such commitments. Moreover, he himself had no authority to accept them. This was not a summit conference. He would have to consult the Cabinet and the Cabinet would have to consult the Dominions and the United States. Stalin disliked such democratic inconclusiveness. He grunted and glowered at the Foreign Secretary. He stalked out of the room. But since Eden was constitutionally hobbled, the Kremlin leader relented and tendered his very important visitor the customary convivial toast-filled banquet.

Back in London, Eden repeated to Ambassador Winant snatches of his talks with Stalin. Eden had referred to the Atlantic Charter which Roosevelt and Churchill drafted in Placentia Bay, Newfoundland, and signed there on August 12, 1941. It begins: "Their countries seek no aggrandizement, territorial or other." Point two of the octalogue reads: "They desire no territorial changes that do not accord with the freely expressed wishes of the peoples concerned."[4]

Stalin: "I thought that the Atlantic Charter was directed against those people who are trying to establish world dominion. It now looks as if the Atlantic Charter was directed against the U.S.S.R."

Eden: "No, that is not so. It is merely a question . . . of my not being able to give you an immediate reply and asking you to allow me time to get an answer."

Stalin: "Why does the restoration of our frontiers come into conflict with the Atlantic Charter?"

Eden: "I never said it did."[5]

It did. It proposed to curb the appetites of the anti-German coalition. Germany would be dealt with separately. But Eden's replies indicate that a confrontation with Stalin was a grisly experience. The Foreign Secretary clearly hoped to give as little offense as possible and to limit his own irritation. This is borne out by another conversation when Stalin referred to the plebiscites conducted in the Baltic countries which resulted, according to Soviet announcements, in a large majority for incorporation

4. Winston S. Churchill, *The Second World War. The Grand Alliance*, p. 443.
5. *Foreign Relations of the United States (FRUS). 1942*. Vol. III: *Europe*, p. 502.

in the Soviet Union. Eden did not argue. But in London he stated that his exchanges with Stalin "on this aspect of the subject would have been even less profitable than they were if I had suggested that these 'plebiscites' were faked."[6]

Nevertheless, as Winant telegraphed Hull, Eden had been impressed by Stalin's case for annexations, and from London he wired Churchill, staying at the White House, that he "thought Stalin's wishes should be met." Churchill, under the influence perhaps of the spirit then pervading the Roosevelt home and the State Department, "replied to Mr. Eden in a rather stiff telegram expressing indignant disapprobation."[7] "We have never recognized the 1941 frontiers of Russia," the Prime Minister telegraphed his Foreign Secretary on January 8, 1942, "except *de facto*. They were acquired by acts of aggression in shameful collusion with Hitler. The transfer of the peoples of the Baltic States against their will would be contrary to all the principles for which we are fighting this war and would dishonour our cause. This also applies to Bessarabia and Northern Bukovina.... I regard our sincerity to be involved in the maintenance of the principles of the Atlantic Charter, to which Stalin has subscribed." (In the midst of the controversy the Soviet government signed the Atlantic Charter on January 1, 1942.) "On this also," Churchill added, "we depend for our association with the United States."

It seems the Prime Minister believed he and Roosevelt could permanently frustrate Stalin's territorial wishes, for he appended a paragraph to the same dispatch to Eden forecasting mistakenly that after the war "the United States and the British Empire, far from being exhausted, will be the most powerfully armed and economic bloc the world has ever seen, and that the Soviet Union will need our aid for reconstruction far more than we shall then need theirs."[8]

Economic determinism from the pen of a Tory statesman! Stalin would teach him, and Roosevelt, an expensive lesson: that politics often takes precedence over economics, that he could wrench a favorable decision from them during the war, and, above all, that wartime diplomacy is determined by who has how many divisions where.

If candor and congruity were among the requirements of politicians, Stalin's lust for empire would have put Churchill in a quandary, for he himself loved empire. "I have not become the King's First Minister," he told the Lord Mayor's Day luncheon on November 10, 1942, "in order to preside at the liquidation of the British Empire." He was the only prominent Englishman who refused to receive Mahatma Gandhi in England in 1931. How, then, could he oppose Stalin's wish to absorb eastern

6. *Ibid.*, p. 515.
7. *Ibid.*, p. 513.
8. Churchill, pp. 695–696.

Europe? But the statesman-historian remembered the century-old enmity between the lion and the bear. He was loath to open the gates to Russian expansion that might jeopardize British security. Nor did he dare to alienate Roosevelt, whose anti-imperialist stance, as embodied in his brainchild, the Atlantic Charter, was in the spirit that hovered over America's cradle (and was occasionally violated when the baby grew up).

Roosevelt wanted freedom for India, and on February 25, 1942, wrote a letter to Churchill urging some steps toward Indian self-government. "I wonder," he said, "whether there is sufficient spirit to fight among the Indian people." It would help Indians to forget hard feelings, to become more loyal to the British Empire, and to see the advantages of peaceful evolution over chaotic revolution if, the President advised, India were given Dominion status under a temporary government consisting of not more than thirty or forty persons of different parties, castes, regions, and occupations. "For the love of heaven," Roosevelt added, "don't bring me into this. It's none of my business except insofar as it is part and parcel of the successful fight you and I are making." But having written this, he decided it really was none of his business, and the letter was filed and never sent.[9] Roosevelt knew Churchill's sentiments. The Prime Minister favored freedom for Latvia and Lithuania, not for India.

F.D.R. also wanted independence for Indochina. France, he told Lord Halifax, British Ambassador in Washington, had held Indochina "for nearly a hundred years, and the people are worse off than they were at the beginning. As a matter of interest, I am wholeheartedly supported in this view by Generalissimo Chiang Kai-shek and Marshal Stalin."[10]

Stalin favored freedom for Indochina, and India, but not for Estonia and Latvia. One does not look for consistency in politics, only for interests.

The British government oscillated, without benefit of guiding principle, between its two new allies: the United States, uncompromisingly opposed to wartime territorial "adjustments," Stalin insisting on them. In this dilemma political opinions diverged. Sir Stafford Cripps, His Majesty's Ambassador to the Soviet Union, addressed a private meeting in the House of Commons advocating recognition of Russia's June 22, 1941, frontiers. Lord Halifax, His Majesty's Ambassador in Washington, who, in a previous incarnation as Lord Irwin, was Viceroy of India, took issue vehemently with Churchill. In an angry letter to his Prime Minister, Halifax stated that during the 1939 Anglo-French-Soviet negotiations when he, as Foreign Secretary, was largely responsible for their course,

9. Copied at the Franklin D. Roosevelt Library in Hyde Park. Box I (Classified), *Political-Military Messages, Roosevelt to Churchill, 1939 to October, 1942.*
10. Cordell Hull, *Memoirs of Cordell Hull,* Vol. II, pp. 1596–1597.

England's attitude toward the Baltic countries "had been one of the prime reasons" for the Soviet-Nazi pact. He clearly feared a repetition of the same if Stalin was resisted. Although much polluted Thames River water had flowed past the House of Lords since 1939, Halifax still did not yet understand what had happened to him in that fateful summer. Moscow signed with the Nazis, not with the Anglo-French, because Stalin had always intended, and said so as far back as 1925, to postpone belligerency as long as possible, and because after the military-industrial purges of 1937–1938 Russia could not risk going to war and inviting the full fury of Hitler's Wehrmacht. The Baltic States were a minor issue magnified.[11]

Although Halifax erred in his interpretation of events in 1939, he correctly reflected considerable British sentiment. There was fear approaching panic that Stalin would again make a separate peace with Hitler. However mistaken this mood might have been, it was a political reality. Eden reckoned with it when, in a telegraphed reply to Halifax's letter, he said, "I am apprehensive of the effect [on Stalin] of a flat negative." He continued: "If the United States Government feel that it is impossible to grant his full demands . . . I would hint two possible suggestions." Britain might consent to Russia's establishing military bases in areas it wished to annex without precluding annexation after the war. Or Britain could give Russia assurances of full support at the postwar peace conference for Russian control of the Baltic States. Eden said he preferred the first alternative. So did Halifax; it was a transparent disguise for immediate annexation.

Halifax showed Eden's telegram to Under Secretary Sumner Welles on February 18, 1942. Welles rejected both alternatives. The Soviet Union, he told the Ambassador, was entitled to security but not at the expense of peoples "bitterly opposed to Russian overlordship. . . . I could not conceive of this war being fought in order to undertake once more the shoddy, inherently vicious kind of patchwork world order which the European powers had attempted to construct during the years between 1919 and 1939."[12]

The next day Welles showed the President the copy of Eden's telegram to Halifax and repeated what Halifax had said. Roosevelt asked Welles to tell Halifax that after considering all this the "only word" that came to his mind was "provincial."

Halifax was shocked when Welles carried out F.D.R.'s instructions. "After Lord Halifax had recovered," Welles observed, "I went on to say" that the President stood by the Atlantic Charter which, in addition to proscribing aggression, provided for the disarmament of Germany—

11. For a detailed treatment of Soviet policy, see Louis Fischer, *Russia's Road from Peace to War,* pp. 240–243 and pp. 303–377.
12. *FRUS, 1942.* Vol. III: *Europe,* pp. 512–521.

security enough for Russia. Moreover, Roosevelt proposed to discuss the entire matter directly with Stalin.[13]

This offended the British government, which preferred three-power talks. Halifax asked to see Roosevelt. The President refused. He was hewing to the Hull line. Hull's hostility to Soviet territorial claims emerged from his political philosophy: he abhorred old-style spheres of influence and the diplomacy that gave them birth. Specifically, as he contended in his February 14, 1942, memorandum to Roosevelt, he believed wartime boundary deals would create "mutual suspicion" among the powers fighting Germany and Japan, and breed "intrigue in order to obtain commitments with regard to territory at the expense of other members" of the United Nations. If Britain, "with the tacit or expressed approval of this Government," agreed to Stalin's demands she would be unable to resist further demands "whenever the Soviet Government would find itself in a favorable bargaining position." Hull recognized that Moscow thwarted had an arsenal of weapons. It might threaten to sign a separate peace with the enemy. It might unloose foreign communist parties to bring pressure on Washington and London to yield to Kremlin desires. But should the British and American governments "succumb to pressure" of this type, relations with Moscow would improve only temporarily. Once the principle of no territorial aggrandizement had been breached, a scramble for annexations would follow. Chaos was sure to result. Roosevelt and Churchill would be charged with insincerity. "It would be extremely unfortunate if the manner in which the Soviet Union invaded the Baltic States and conducted the ensuing plebiscites should be accepted as the mode of ascertaining the wishes of the people with regard to their future."

It ill became nations purportedly fighting aggressors to be aggressors themselves. But Stalin could overlook this discrepancy. He had committed aggression in 1939 and 1940. That he was defending his country against the Nazi aggressor did not preclude Russia's engaging in aggression.

For Great Britain, however, this was a time of trial; attention was riveted on troubles which eclipsed ethical and theoretical considerations. In January, 1942, Field Marshal Erwin Rommel inflicted a grave defeat on a British army in North Africa. In February Nazi U-boats sank 384,000 tons of British shipping, "the highest rate" thus far in the war, Churchill noted. The great naval base at Singapore fell to the Japanese on February 15. Japan occupied the Dutch East Indies and Burma in March, and moved toward India.

In the midst of these catastrophes Churchill telegraphed Stalin on March 12: "I have sent a message to President Roosevelt urging him to

13. *Ibid.,* pp. 521–524.

approve our signing agreements with you about the frontiers of Russia at the end of the war."[14] In the darkness of defeat Churchill had abandoned the idealistic Atlantic Charter position he took while staying at the White House and informed F.D.R. that Stalin, not satisfied with the "draft texts" of the proposed boundary agreements, was sending Molotov to London to renegotiate them. Roosevelt indicated displeasure. But Churchill replied that Molotov "may even be already on his way."

Molotov accordingly came to No. 10, Downing Street and Washington.

VI   THE ROOSEVELT VICTORY

Chief executives like to meet chief executives. Lloyd George had hoped to meet Lenin at the Genoa Conference in 1922. Roosevelt wanted to meet Stalin. Soviet Ambassador Ivan Maisky writes that the President would have preferred to see Stalin alone—without Churchill. Roosevelt in fact said in a personal message to Stalin dated April 12, 1942, "Perhaps if things go as well as we hope, you and I can spend a few days together next summer near our common frontier off Alaska."[1] But Stalin never flew, and it would have taken him two weeks to reach that rendezvous by express train and ship. Nor did his suspicious mind allow him to leave Moscow. The military and political situations were too tense in 1942 and he could never know what generals with troops fighting under them might do when he was away.

So Stalin sent Molotov to Washington as his substitute. The Foreign Commissar traveled by plane from Moscow to Scotland where the royal train met him and took him down to London on May 20. After eight days in the British capital he went by the same Soviet plane to the United States. He was the President's guest at the White House.

"One of the White House valets," writes Mrs. Roosevelt, "was astounded when he unpacked Mr. Molotov's bag to find inside a large chunk of black bread, a roll of sausage and a pistol. The Secret Service men did not like visitors with pistols, but on this occasion nothing was said. Mr. Molotov evidently thought he might have to defend himself, and also that he might be hungry."[2]

Similar behavior had astonished his British hosts. Since London might

14. *Correspondence*, Vol. I, p. 40; *Perepiska*, Vol. I, p. 38. Churchill, *The Second World War. The Hinge of Fate*, p. 328.

1. *Correspondence*, Vol. II, pp. 22–23.

2. Eleanor Roosevelt, *The Autobiography of Eleanor Roosevelt*, p. 235.

be bombed, Molotov's mission chose to stay in the country, and Churchill placed the Prime Minister's official resthouse in Chequers at their disposal. "On arrival they had asked at once for keys to all the bedrooms," Churchill noted in his memoirs. "These were provided with some difficulty and thereafter our guests always kept their doors locked. When the staff at Chequers succeeded in getting in to make the beds they were disturbed to find pistols under the pillows. The three chief members of the mission were attended not only by their own police officers, but by two women who looked after their clothes and tidied their rooms. When the Soviet envoys were absent in London these women kept constant guard over their masters' rooms, only coming down one at a time for their meals." Molotov's room and bed were the objects of special search and care. "At night a revolver was laid out beside his dressing gown and dispatch case. . . . For myself," Churchill comments, "when I visited Moscow I put complete trust in Russian hospitality."[3]

A Soviet leader led a life of total tension at home and could not relax abroad.

Roosevelt invited Stalin, then Molotov, for one purpose: to discuss military operations and supplies. Stalin was circumspect. Addressing Roosevelt on April 20, 1942, he said he was sending Molotov to Washington "for an exchange of views on the organization of a second front in Europe in the near future." No mention of postwar frontiers.[4] Addressing Churchill two days later Stalin put frontiers first: Molotov was going to London "for personal talks with a view of settling the issues holding up the signing of the treaties" on boundaries.[5]

Churchill also treated the issue of frontiers with care. "I propose," he notified Roosevelt by telegram on April 24, "to agree to discussion of our drafts, and would hope to clear main difficulties out of the way. But I will suggest to him [Molotov] that he should then go on to Washington and see you before anything is finally signed."[6]

The Prime Minister hoped to clear away the difficulties and agree to the postwar settlement Stalin desired. In view of Roosevelt's negative attitude, however, he intended not to sign unless F.D.R. withdrew his veto. The problem would thus be laid in the President's lap on the assumption that, if lightning struck, the White House had a better lightning rod than No. 10, Downing Street.

No lightning struck.

The treaty negotiations were conducted by Eden and Permanent Under Secretary Sir Alexander Cadogan with Molotov and Maisky. "We insist-

3. Winston S. Churchill, *The Second World War. The Hinge of Fate*, p. 337.
4. *Correspondence*, Vol. II, p. 23.
5. *Ibid.*, Vol. I, pp. 41–42.
6. Churchill, p. 331.

ed," writes Maisky, "on the immediate recognition of the Soviet-Polish frontier as it stood before June 22, 1941." The Russians, furthermore, asked British sanction for Russia's absorption of the Baltic countries and "the conclusion by the Soviet Union of pacts of mutual assistance with Finland and Rumania." ("Mutual assistance" was standard Kremlinese for annexation. The fate of Estonia, Latvia, and Lithuania under "mutual assistance" remained fresh in memory.)

Secretary of State Cordell Hull was a white-haired southern gentleman whose mild countenance belied his bulldog devotion to a few simple principles: reduction of tariff barriers and no annexations. Hull, a former senator from Tennessee who retained considerable influence with southern senators, reinforced and sometimes forced Roosevelt's hand on the question of the Russian frontier issue. When Hull learned from Winant of the Molotov-Maisky territorial demands he drafted a stern telegram which, to his surprise, the President approved, indicating that if Britain signed the proposed treaty "we might not remain silent since silence might give tacit consent. On the contrary, we might have to issue a separate statement clearly stating that we did not subscribe to its principles and clauses."[7]

"The British position," Hull writes, "now began to veer toward our view." Eden, Maisky declares, offered "alternative proposals [which] completely avoided the questions of the frontiers of the U.S.S.R. The reaction of the Soviet side was sharply negative." But Soviet diplomats do not decide, nor do Soviet Foreign Ministers. The text of the British draft treaty together with the Molotov-Maisky hostile reactions were cabled to Moscow. "And suddenly from Moscow came an unexpected reply: the Soviet delegation was instructed to withdraw all its previous proposals and conduct the further negotiations on the basis of the British draft."[8]

Roosevelt, by being resolute, had won the day. In international politics it is often desirable to be absent. Stalin was a practical statesman. Franklin D. Roosevelt, the new source of billions of dollars in arms, food, and other commodities, the best hope of a second front, was the big figure in the western coalition. His opinion was law for the moment. He rejected wartime sanction of aggrandizement. Stalin genuflected. Churchill too. There was no Soviet separate peace with Germany.

Stalin's thought process in this matter is not difficult to demarcate. Why insist on getting something from somebody who does not have it to give? The Baltic States were held by the German army. If in time the Soviets drove out the Wehrmacht the Baltics would be Russia's without or with Anglo-American consent. Why stir a storm and disturb a rich ally

7. Cordell Hull, *The Memoirs of Cordell Hull,* Vol. II, p. 1172.
8. Ivan Maisky, *Memoirs of a Soviet Ambassador. The War 1939–43,* pp. 266–267.

when the only profit would be the abstract recognition of a right? Stalin let Roosevelt have his victory.

*   *   *

With the frontier problem adjourned, if not solved, it was unnecessary to delay the treaty signing until Molotov saw Roosevelt. The Anglo-Soviet treaty of alliance was signed in London on May 26, 1942, and ratified by both governments in June. The two parties would aid one another in the struggle against Nazi Germany and her European associates and maintain their alliance for twenty years. "In Articles V–VII," Maisky summarizes, "the parties undertook not to take part in any coalition against the other, and not to seek territorial aggrandizement for themselves or to interfere in the internal affairs of other states."⁹

The alliance between Britain and Russia was already in effect before the document was signed. Stalin thanked Churchill on March 14 "for the information on the steps you have taken to ensure deliveries to the U.S.S.R. and to intensify the air offensive against Germany." On being told by Maisky that the German army might use gas against Russia in the spring of 1942, Churchill assured Stalin on March 21 that "His Majesty's Government will treat any use of this weapon of poison gas against Russia exactly as if it was directed against ourselves." Eight days later Stalin urged Churchill to make a public statement warning Germany and Finland that British retaliation awaited them. Churchill did. On March 29, 1942, Stalin thanked Churchill for the promise "that the British Air Force will not hesitate to use the large store of gas bombs available in Britain for dropping on suitable targets in Germany."¹⁰

Delivery of supplies, bombing Germany, threats of reprisals. But the issue of a second front was now supreme. On this question Churchill's view remained unchanged and unchallenged in his Cabinet. Beaverbrook, a kinetic Canadian, might have been more adventurous had he been the King's First Minister. But Churchill, with all his ebullience, was a cautious man. He would not gamble with British manpower in a stab via northern France at the heart of Hitler's power. Memories of blood spilled in the first world war were too vivid. He preferred to nibble at the peripheries of the German-held continent, at Norway or Greece, and meanwhile fight on the fringes and on the highways of the British Empire, in North Africa, the Middle East, the Mediterranean. Stalin's hot claims to a second front stirred Churchill's dormant resentment of the pro-Nazi phase in the Kremlin: "They certainly have no right to reproach us. They brought their own fate upon themselves when, by their pact

9. *Ibid.*, p. 267.
10. *Correspondence,* Vol. I, pp. 41–43.

with Ribbentrop, they let Hitler loose on Poland and so started the war. They cut themselves off from an effective second front when they let the French Army be destroyed. . . . We were left alone for a whole year while every Communist in England, under orders from Moscow, did his best to hamper our war effort. If we had been invaded and destroyed in July or August, 1941, or starved out this year in the Battle of the Atlantic, they would have remained utterly indifferent."[11]

If this is not perfect history, it is good Churchill, and enough generals and civilians shared his sentiments to make them the law of the British Isles for two more years while Russia battled the bulk of the Nazi legions. Molotov moved on to Washington with Churchill's military *non possumus* arguments ringing in his ears; Britain lacked the force to cross the Channel in the face of German might on the other shore.

The armed Commissar arrived at the White House at 4 P.M. on May 29, 1942.

The United States, "foremost citadel of capitalism," had always evoked Stalin's admiration. He publicly praised its industrial efficiency, advanced technology, and progressive management methods. In five and a half months Hitler and Tokyo had linked Russia and America in a great struggle and made Stalin Roosevelt's colleague. This was food for Stalin's insatiable ego. It was good for Russia. U.S. Ambassador Laurence A. Steinhardt informed Deputy Foreign Commissar Andrei Yanuarevich Vyshinsky on November 2, 1941, that under the Lend-Lease Act adopted by Congress on March 11, 1941, and in accordance with a message from Roosevelt to Stalin, shipments of supplies would begin immediately "up to the value of $1 billion." No interest would be charged "on such indebtedness" and "payments shall begin only five years after the end of the war" and extend over a 10-year period.[12]

Stalin replied that this "is accepted by the Soviet Government with heartfelt gratitude as vital aid to the Soviet Union in its tremendous and onerous struggle against our common enemy—bloody Hitlerism."[13] On February 18, 1942, Stalin wired: "Your decision, Mr. President, to grant the Government of the U.S.S.R. another $1 billion, under the Lend-Lease Act on the same terms as the first $1 billion, is accepted by the Soviet Government with sincere gratitude."[14] F.D.R. had, in telling Stalin of the new loan, invited "counter-suggestions" about repayment which would be given "careful and sympathetic consideration."[15]

Two billion dollars graciously given should have created the right

11. Churchill, *The Second World War. The Grand Alliance.* pp. 472–473.
12. *Correspondence*, Vol. II, p. 14.
13. *Ibid.*, p. 15.
14. *Ibid.*, pp. 20–21.
15. *Ibid.*, pp. 19–20.

atmosphere for the Roosevelt-Molotov talks. At their first meeting the President told the Foreign Commissar that America would "remain on the defensive in the Pacific until the European front is cleared up." All this, cocktails shaken by the powerful arms of the President, and a room in the White House with every convenience: "I went for a moment to talk to him [Molotov] after the conference," Hopkins stated, "and he asked that one of the girls he brought over as secretaries be permitted to come [to the White House] and that has been arranged."[16] What else could one want?

Molotov wanted a second front. Hopkins told Sherwood that the President felt "unusually uncomfortable" and "his style was cramped" by the delays due to translations and the whispered exchanges between the American interpreter, Samuel H. Cross, Harvard professor of Slavic Languages and Literature, and Molotov's interpreter, Vladimir N. Pavlov, about "shadings of meanings. There was also the fact that in all of Roosevelt's manifold dealings with all kinds of people, he had never before encountered anyone like Molotov."

The Foreign Commissar had been toughened in the live-and-don't-let-live school of Bolshevik politics where no quarter is asked because no quarter is given. He was conscious during every minute of his Washington stay that he would soon stand before "The Boss" in the Kremlin and woe unto him if he omitted one argument or permitted himself one mite of softness. A blood-curdling whiplashing from Stalin's tongue, richly garnished with mother oaths, and perhaps a push of several rungs down the Soviet hierarchy would be the least punishment awaiting him. Being a Russian communist, moreover, it never occurred to him that there was a side to an issue except his. Neither F.D.R. nor Hull nor General George C. Marshall nor Hopkins recorded what he thought of Molotov's face. It was round and flat, which he could not help, and its expression (like Gromyko's in later years) was an unvaried blank with no smile to add a degree of human warmth. Roosevelt and Hopkins distinguished between Molotov and "Litvinov who, although qualifying as an old Bolshevik, had a Western kind of mind and an understanding of the ways of the world that Roosevelt knew." Litvinov had lived long in the West and married an Englishwoman.

Molotov acquitted himself well. At lunches, dinner, and other occasions between May 29 and June 1 inclusive, the Commissar, according to minutes kept by Professor Cross and Hopkins, spoke as follows on the central topic: "although the problem of the second front was both military and political, it was predominantly political. There was an essential difference between the situation in 1942 and what it might be in 1943. In

16. Robert E. Sherwood, *Roosevelt and Hopkins. An Intimate History,* pp. 559–560.

1942 Hitler was the master of all Europe save a few minor countries. He was the chief enemy of everyone. To be sure, as was devoutly to be hoped, the Russians might hold and fight on all through 1942. But it was only right to look at the darker side of the picture. On the basis of his continental dominance, Hitler might throw in such reinforcements in manpower and material that the Red Army might *not* be able to hold out against the Nazis. Such a development would produce a serious situation which we must face. The Soviet front would become secondary, the Red Army would be weakened, and Hitler's strength would be correspondingly greater since he would have at his disposal not only more troops, but also the foodstuffs and raw materials of the Ukraine and the oilwells of the Caucasus. In such circumstances the outlook would be much less favorable for all lands, and he would not pretend that such developments were all outside the range of possibility. The war would thus be tougher and longer. . . .

"Amplifying his remarks, Mr. Molotov observed that the forces on the Soviet front were large and, objectively speaking, the balance in the quantity of men, aviation, and mechanized equipment was slightly in Hitler's favor. Nevertheless, the Russians were reasonably certain they could hold out. This was the most optimistic outlook, and the Soviet morale was as yet unimpaired. But the main danger lay in the probability that Hitler would try to deal the Soviet Union a mighty crushing blow. If, then, Great Britain and the United States, as allies, were to create a new front and to draw off 40 German divisions from the Soviet front, the ratio of strength would be so altered that the Soviets could either beat Hitler this year or insure beyond question his ultimate defeat.

"Mr. Molotov therefore put this question frankly: could we undertake such offensive action as would draw off 40 German divisions which would be, to tell the truth, distinctly second-rate? If the answer should be in the affirmative, the war would be decided in 1942. If negative, the Soviets would fight on alone, doing their best, and no man could expect more from them than that. He had not, Mr. Molotov added, received any positive answer in London. Mr. Churchill had proposed that he should return through London on his homeward journey from Washington, and he had promised Mr. Molotov a more concrete answer on the second front. Mr. Molotov admitted he realized that the British would have to bear the brunt of the action if a second front were created, but he was also cognizant of the role the United States plays and what influence this country exerts in questions of major strategy. Without in any way minimizing the risks entailed by a second front action this summer, Mr. Molotov declared his government wanted to know in frank terms what position we take on the question of a second front, and whether we were prepared to establish one. He requested a straight answer.

"The difficulties, Mr. Molotov urged, would not be any less in 1943. The chances of success were actually better at present while the Russians still have a solid front. 'If you postpone your decision,' he said, 'you will have eventually to bear the brunt of the war, and if Hitler becomes the undisputed master of the continent, next year will unquestionably be tougher than this one.' "

Molotov halted.

The President asked General Marshall whether the developments were clear enough "so that we could say to Mr. Stalin that we are preparing a second front."

"Yes," replied Marshall.

"The President then authorized Mr. Molotov to inform Mr. Stalin that we expect the formation of a second front this year."

Here began the misunderstandings from the loose use of words. General Marshall answered "Yes" to the question are we preparing a second front? This does not mean we would launch a second front. Nor did Roosevelt's "we expect the formation of a second front this year."

Marshall added that "we were making every effort to build up a situation in which the creation of a second front would be possible. . . . Frankly speaking we had the troops, all adequately trained; we had the munitions, the aviation, and the armored divisions. The difficulties lay in transport." Many ships, he explained, were needed to bring supplies to Murmansk for the use of the Red Army. ". . . the delivery of aircraft to the British Isles . . . was limited by present deliveries to the Soviets.

"Strategically, the idea was, said General Marshall, to create as quickly as possible a situation on the continent under which the Germans would be forced into an all-out air engagement, but they will not engage on this scale without the pressure of the presence of our troops on the ground . . . while Mr. Molotov based his considerations on the number of divisions (40) which the Soviets would like to see diverted from their front, what we had to base our action on was the number of men we could ship across the Channel in order to provoke an all-out air battle for the destruction of the German air-force. The essential preliminary to a successful continental operation was to make the German aviation fight; we must therefore have an air-battle."

This further modified his yes.

The President asked Admiral Ernest J. King to give his views. The admiral, in reply, spoke exclusively about convoys bringing military equipment to Murmansk and Archangel. "German reconnaissance planes shadowed our convoys from Iceland to Murmansk and, when a convoy approached, they caused it to be attacked by both submarines and surface craft. The complex situation also rendered it necessary for large forces of the British Home Fleet to remain at sea to guard against attacks from heavy German ships which are stationed nearer to the convoy routes. Similarly, the United States Navy has had to reinforce the British fleet with such heavy ships so that the British should have enough such ships on hand in order to maintain their convoying forces on the requisite level. . . ."

It was time for lunch.

F.D.R. pronounced a toast to Stalin.

Molotov rose to drink to the President's health. He "wished to remind his hearers that the Soviet, by bitter experience, knew best what Hitler is. Hitler wanted more territory, and has become more insatiable day by day. The Red Army was doing its best, we must reckon fully with all possible dangers."

After lunch the President returned to his study where Ambassador Litvinov introduced the crew of Molotov's bomber and his secretaries. This achieved, Roosevelt handed Molotov a list of eight million tons of Lend-Lease material "which we should produce during the year from July 1, 1942, but stated that we could ship only 4,100,000 of this total."

Left alone with Marshall, King, and Hopkins later that day the President said he thought "the matter was a little vague and the dangerous situation on the Russian front required that he make a more specific answer to Molotov in regard to the second front."

F.D.R. cabled Churchill: "I am especially anxious that Molotov shall carry back some real results of his mission and give a favourable report to Stalin. I am inclined to believe the Russians are a bit down in the mouth at present."

This bit of long-distance psychiatry boomeranged.

Before anything was done for the second front, the President cut down the shipping schedule he had just given to Molotov. That had provided for 4,100,000 tons of supplies to Russia consisting of 1,800,000 tons of planes, tanks, guns, and 2,300,000 of general supplies. The revised plan retained the tonnage of arms but reduced the general supplies—food, clothing, trucks, machinery, raw materials, etc.—to 700,000 tons.

The last day of Molotov's stay, June 1, was spent in desultory discussions about postwar disarmament, the abandonment of the League of Nations' mandate system, the future of colonies, a separate peace with Finland, and unrelated subjects. On the second front, the President said, "Every week we were building up troop and plane concentrations in England with a view to getting at the Germans from there as quickly as possible.

"We were also shipping landing craft. But the time-element depended on available ships. We hoped and expected to open a second front in 1942, but we could progress more rapidly only with more ships." This meant a reduction of shipments to Russia. "The Soviets," F.D.R. said, "could not eat their cake and have it too.

"To this statement Mr. Molotov retorted with some emphasis that the second front would be stronger if the first still stood fast, and inquired with what seemed deliberate sarcasm what would happen if the Soviets cut down their requirements and then no second front eventuated. Then, becoming still more insistent," Molotov asked, "What is the President's answer with respect to the second front?"

After days of talk the answer remained unclear. The nearest the President came to a reply was, "We expect to establish a second front." With this and with a photograph of the President, Molotov departed for England.

Summing up blithely, Hopkins wrote Ambassador Winant in London: "Molotov's visit went extremely well. He and the President got along famously and I am sure that we at least bridged one more gap between ourselves and Russia."[17]

This was a public relations approach: you get along famously, you bridge gaps, and real relations remain the same or deteriorate.

VII CHURCHILL IN THE KREMLIN

It was obvious to the British and Americans, after Molotov's return to London from Washington, that there would be no second front in France in 1942. Before the Foreign Commissar flew back to Moscow Churchill handed him a memorandum which said, "We are making preparations for a landing on the Continent in August or September, 1942." Soviet historians and officials, experts in selectivity, quote this sentence only and charge the British government with "premeditated treachery" for breaking a promise. The Churchill memorandum, however, continued to explain that it was impossible to know in mid-June what conditions would be in September: "We can therefore give no promise in the matter."[1]

The only defensible accusation is that Churchill knew in June the western allies could not attack the continent in September. Out of a subconscious sense, perhaps, that he should have been more ingenuous, he took a dramatic step. He decided in August to give Stalin the bad news in person rather than use the telegraph or an intermediary.

17. *Ibid.*, pp. 556–577.
1. Winston S. Churchill, *The Second World War. The Hinge of Fate*, p. 342.

It was a strange errand. It was Churchill's first visit to Russia—Tsarist, Kerensky, or Soviet. As he flew up along the Volga, he wrote subsequently, "I pondered on my mission to this sullen, sinister Bolshevik State I had once tried so hard to strangle at its birth, and which, until Hitler appeared, I had regarded as the mortal foe of civilised freedom." The revulsion, he felt, was mutual. "We had always hated their wicked regime, and, till the German flail beat upon them, they would have watched us being swept out of existence with indifference and gleefully divided with Hitler our Empire in the East."[2]

Nazi imperialism had buried the mutual animosity under a half inch of frozen ground. If Churchill harbored the slightest illusions about Moscow's attitude toward him, Roosevelt, full of illusions regarding his own status in the Kremlin, tried to dispel them. "I know," he wrote the Prime Minister in a letter dated March 18, 1942, "you will not mind my being brutally frank when I tell you that I think I can handle Stalin better than either your Foreign Office or my State Department. Stalin hates the guts of all your top people. He thinks he likes me better, and I hope he will continue to do so."[3]

Stalin's rich fund of hate sufficed for the guts of all temporary associates, Roosevelt included.

Churchill had much to tell Stalin, who could hardly have listened with sympathy.

Despite the Japanese attack on Pearl Harbor, the U.S. government and the Churchill Cabinet agreed that Germany should be the first target, for if the two western powers defeated Japan, the effect on Germany would not be decisive, whereas a knockout blow at Germany would doom Japan. This approach pleased Moscow. But the Japanese armed forces, insistent on attention, diverted Anglo-American strength from the struggle against Germany. Churchill's evaluation of the Japanese seizure of Singapore as "the greatest disaster in our history" was heavy with emotion, yet the loss of the great base did, within a few months, bring a Japanese army to the eastern gate of India while Rommel pressed toward Suez. A Japanese-Gereman conjunction in India—and India seething—would ruin the British Empire, deny England the oil of the Middle East and the use of the Suez Canal, cut the Anglo-American supply route to Russia via Iran, and prolong the war by years. Even Mahatma Gandhi, who in June, 1942, launched his "Quit India" movement, took cognizance of the grave British military position and, in answer to my question when I was his hut guest, said the British army could stay. The British army was reinforced in the entire India-to-Tunis region.

Against this background the British and Americans weighed their ca-

2. *Ibid.*, p. 475.
3. *Ibid.*, p. 201.

pacity for a stab at Nazi-held France, and recoiled. The German rail and road communications between east and west, between the Soviet front and France, were so good that Hitler could shift enough manpower and weapons from Russia to crush quickly an invader of the continent. The second front in Europe would thereby be delayed indefinitely.

Other considerations affected the decision to postpone the second front in Europe, but these were not mentioned in the Churchill-Stalin parley. The first was Churchill's attachment to India, the richest jewel in the British imperial crown. Equally important, if not more so, was Soviet military prowess. The longer the Russians held back the Germans the less urgent the European second front seemed to the western allies. Yet even if these two factors had been absent, it emerges, in hindsight, that the U.S.A. and the U.K. lacked the manpower, landing craft, and air-power to land on and stay on the continent in 1942.

It was to deliver this disturbing message that Churchill traveled via Cairo and Tehran to Moscow, where he arrived on August 12, 1942. Strenuous flight notwithstanding, the talks began the same evening.

Churchill opened with a rosy prospect: a million American troops will have reached the United Kingdom by the spring of 1943. To these 27 divisions Britain would add 21 for "a very great operation in 1943." How-ever, the Prime Minister thought it possible that Hitler would then have a stronger army in the West than he now had.

"At this point," Churchill writes, "Stalin's face crumpled into a frown, but he did not interrupt."

Churchill explained that "I have good reasons against an attack on the French coast in 1942." Landing craft to move only six divisions were now available. In 1943 the western allies would have eight to ten times as many. "Stalin," Churchill observed, "who had begun to look glum, seemed unconvinced by my argument, and asked if it was impossible to attack any part of the French coast."

Churchill unrolled the maps he had brought along. Planes could cover ships crossing to and from France, but that was all. Stalin "did not seem to understand, and asked some questions about the range of fighter planes." Could they not, he inquired, come and go all the time? "I ex-plained that they could indeed come and go" across the Channel, but then "they would have no time to fight." If they got to France and fought a dogfight they would have no gasoline to return home. "An air umbrella to be of any use has to be kept open."

Stalin thereupon changed the angle of attack and contended that not one German division in France was of any value. Churchill begged to differ: there were 25 Nazi divisions in France, 9 of first-class quality.

Stalin shook his head to say no.

Churchill told Stalin it served no purpose to debate this question any further, his mission included General Sir Archibald Wavell, who spoke Russian, and the Chief of the Imperial General Staff; they could discuss the matter with their Soviet colleagues.

Stalin's "glumness . . . increased." In his opinion the western allies, to sum up, were unable to create a second front with a sizable force and unwilling to try with six divisions. Churchill concurred; they could land the six divisions but such an operation would be "more harmful than helpful" and "injure the big operation planned for next year. . . . If by throwing in 150,000 to 200,000 men we could render him aid by drawing away from the Russian front appreciable German forces, we would not shrink from this course on the grounds of loss. But if they drew no men away and spoiled the prospects for 1943 it would be a great error."

Stalin "had become restless." His view of war was "different. A man who was not prepared to take risks could not win a war. Why were we afraid of the Germans? He could not understand. His experience showed that troops must be blooded in battle. If you did not blood your troops you had no idea what their value was."

Churchill drew on his experience. Had Stalin ever asked himself why Hitler did not invade England in 1940 when the British army counted only 20,000 trained men, 200 guns, and 50 tanks? "It is not so easy to cross the Channel."

"This is no analogy," Stalin replied. Hitler would have encountered a hostile nation whereas the western armies could expect a liberator's welcome from the French.

On the other hand, Churchill argued, the French who greeted the Anglo-Americans would be punished after the invaders had been forced to withdraw, and these were the very people needed in the 1943 operation.

"There was an oppressive silence," Churchill records. Finally Stalin said he did not agree but had no right to insist.

Churchill thought it desirable, as the session grew old, to mention one subject, the "bombing of Germany, which gave general satisfaction. M. Stalin emphasized ,the importance of striking at the morale of the German population. He said he attached the greatest importance to bombing, and that he knew our raids were having a tremendous effect in Germany."

This lighter "interlude . . . relieved the tension" between the two statesmen and created the appropriate atmosphere, Churchill felt, for the introduction of a second, positive, message he had come to deliver: the news of "Torch," code name for the planned campaign that would carry an Anglo-American army to Morocco and Algeria.

To Churchill's astonishment and joy Stalin immediately grasped the import of the proposed expedition and itemized its main benefits: "it would hit Rommel in the back," "overawe Spain," encourage Frenchmen to resist Germans, and "expose Italy to the whole brunt of the war." Churchill dilated on further gains: the enemy, he said as the company gathered around a large globe, would be cleared out of the Mediterranean, and an Anglo-American air force could be sent to the southern flank of the Russian armies in the Caucasus.

The meeting had lasted almost four hours. The British Prime Minister thought the ice had been broken and "a human contact established." He so telegraphed the War Cabinet and Roosevelt and "slept soundly and long."

* * *

Half an hour's drive from the Kremlin, in a Moscow suburb, stands State Villa Number Seven, where Churchill and several of his fellow travelers were housed during their August, 1942, sojourn. Churchill describes it: "State Villa Number Seven was a fine, large, brand-new country house standing in its own extensive lawns and gardens in a fir wood of about twenty acres. There were agreeable walks . . . several fountains, and a large glass tank filled with many kinds of goldfish, which were all so tame that they would eat out of your hand . . . around the whole was a stockade, perhaps fifteen feet high, guarded on both sides by police and soldiers in considerable numbers. About a hundred yards from the house was an air-raid shelter. . . . It was of the latest and most luxurious type. Lifts at either end took you down eighty or ninety feet into the ground. Here were eight or ten large rooms inside a concrete box of massive thickness. The rooms were divided from each other by heavy sliding doors. The furniture was stylish 'Utility,' sumptuous and brightly coloured."

Number Seven was the dacha of either Stalin or another first-rank Soviet leader.

The next morning, in Dacha Number Seven just outside Moscow, Churchill remembered, as he did every year, that this was August 13, the day in 1704 when Marlborough, his direct ancestor, won the battle of Blenheim. Having slept amidst Russian ostentatious splendor, the scion of a victor proposed a resumption of talks at 10 P.M. Stalin preferred 11 P.M. At that hour Churchill and Major Arthur H. Birse, his interpreter, together with W. Averell Harriman, representing President Roosevelt, joined Stalin, Molotov, and Vladimir N. Pavlov, their interpreter. "Then," writes Churchill, "began a most unpleasant discussion."

The unpleasantness consisted of a two-hour verbal wrestling match in which Stalin and Molotov repeated all the insulting remarks of the day before: the westerners were afraid of fighting Germans; they had broken their promise to land in France in 1942, and they—Americans as well as

British—sent Russia the supplies they themselves did not need.

Churchill did not understand this performance. In a report from Moscow to the War Cabinet he speculated on the reason for it. "I think," he groped, "the most probable is that his Council of Ministers did not take the news I brought as well as he did. They may have more power than we suppose, and less knowledge."

Churchill's Kremlinology limped because he carried the psychology of Whitehall with him; Stalin's Council of Commissars became the democratic Cabinet sitting at No. 10, Downing Street. Stalin's Council were zeros, he was the one. What actually took place was an approved Soviet negotiation gambit: by repetition it tries the adversary's patience in the hope that he will retreat from an entrenched position. Stalin explained the method to U.S. Secretary of State George C. Marshall in 1947 during a long unproductive Four-Power Foreign Ministers' Conference. "Don't take these matters so seriously," Stalin said. "After diplomats exhaust themselves in dispute they are ready to compromise."[4] And compromise of course meant the opponent's compromise.

Churchill did not compromise. He could not. There could be no second front on the continent in 1942. Having used the gambit and failed, Stalin, all joviality, "abruptly invited us to dinner at eight o'clock the next night."

It was a gay Kremlin dinner attended by some forty people, "including several military commanders, members of the Politburo, and other high officials." Stalin and Churchill chatted through Interpreter Pavlov. Stalin talked lightheartedly about British military intention in Russia in 1919–1920 and who was responsible, Lloyd George or Churchill. He inclined to blame Lloyd George. But Churchill said, "I was very active in the intervention, and I would not wish you to think otherwise."

Stalin smiled amiably.

"Have you forgiven me?" Churchill asked.

"All that is past and the past belongs to God," Stalin replied.

Judgments of the past by Soviet historians and politicians are shaped by relations in the present. History is rewritten with every shift in Kremlin foreign policy.

The evening's festivities included numerous toasts during the many-course meal, several speeches in English and Russian (Wavell spoke in Russian), and friendly banter between guests and hosts. Churchill left at 1:30 A.M., which is rather early for such a Kremlin affair. The German army stood 50 miles from Moscow.

The British party was leaving at dawn on August 16. At six o'clock on the evening of the 15th the Prime Minister went to bid the communist

4. Repeated to me by U.S. Ambassador General Walter Bedell Smith, who was present at the interview.

commissar in chief farewell. Most of the exchange centered on the Russian front with Stalin expressing confidence that the Germans would be held. "Our hour's conversation drew to a close, and I got up to say goodbye. Stalin seemed suddenly embarrassed, and said in a more cordial tone than he had yet used with me, 'You are leaving at daybreak. Why not go to my house and have some drinks?' "

Churchill was not one to decline a drink, especially when accompanied by a rare invitation to visit a Soviet home, and Stalin's at that. They walked to the Kremlin apartment and Stalin showed him through it: a dining room, workroom, bedroom, and large bathroom, all moderate in size, simple, dignified, Churchill reported. "Presently," he continues, "there appeared, first a very aged housekeeper and later a handsome red-haired girl [16-year-old Svetlana] who kissed her father dutifully. He looked at me with a twinkle in his eye as if, so I thought, to convey, 'You see, even we Bolsheviks have family life.' Stalin's daughter started laying the table, and in a short time the housekeeper appeared with a few dishes. Meanwhile Stalin had been uncorking various bottles, which began to make an imposing array. Then he said, 'Why should we not invite Molotov? He is worrying about the communiqué. We could settle it here. There is one thing about Molotov—he can drink.' "

Business combined with pleasure. And a peek into the Soviet past: "Tell me," Churchill asked, "have the stresses of this war been as bad to you personally as carrying through the policy of the Collective Farms?"

"Oh, no," Stalin replied, "the Collective Farm policy was a terrible struggle."

"I thought you would have found it bad," Churchill agreed, "because you were dealing with . . . millions of small men."

"Ten millions," Stalin elaborated, holding up his hands. "It was fearful. Four years it lasted [1933 to 1937, according to Stalin]." The peasant talked it over with his wife and friends and, the dictator added, "After he has talked it over with them he always answers that he does not want the Collective Farm and he would rather do without tractors."

They sat at the table from 8:30 P.M. to 2:30 A.M., normal for a Georgian-Kremlin repast. "I had half an hour to drive to the villa," Churchill writes, "and as long to the airport. I had a splitting headache, which for me was very unusual."

Summing up in a cable to the War Cabinet and Roosevelt, Churchill asserted, "On the whole I am definitely encouraged by my visit to Moscow. I am sure that the disappointing news I brought [no second front in 1942] could not have been imparted except by me personally without leading to really serious drifting apart. . . . Now they know the worst, and having made their protests are entirely friendly; this in spite of the fact that this is their most anxious and agonising time."

Often in the history of Soviet foreign relations the Soviet government made vehement protests, exerted maximum pressures, uttered ominous threats, and, if resisted, relaxed into passivity or cordiality. The flow of screaming editorials ceased, the denunciations halted. This has sometimes conduced to optimism, as in Roosevelt after Molotov's stay in the White House and in Churchill after his 1942 talks in the Kremlin. Optimism is apparently a necessary ingredient of the politician. It acts like a life jacket and gives him the feeling he will not drown and onlookers the impression he is not drowning. The leader seeks to succeed, for the public dislikes failures. During the second world war such optimism—in itself a desirable quality for all human beings—was deceptive. For Stalin's war aims remained unchanged. Nowhere in Churchill's narrative of his 1942 visit to Moscow[5] are Russia's territorial aspirations noted. Neither Stalin nor Molotov mentioned them. But they were there. Their fulfillment would wait upon the outcome of the agonizing battle that raged while the statesmen talked and supped.

VIII THE AGONIZING BATTLE

The total military collapse of the Soviet Union was never absent from the calculations of Britain and America during 1942. In part this was due to the Red Army's poor performance in the 1939–40 winter war against Finland and to its many defeats after June 22, 1941. The astounding victory at Moscow in December, 1941, lifted many hearts and hopes in the West and won plaudits for Russian arms. But some of the credit was ascribed to General Brutal Winter and German unpreparedness to cope with him. When fighting resumed early in 1942 spirits sank again both in Russia and in the West, for the reinforced Wehrmacht registered heavy gains while the Soviet officer corps demonstrated its inadequacies.

Molotov, lunching in the White House on Saturday, May 30, 1942, did not conceal this. In the presence of Ambassador Litvinov, Secretary Hull, Harry L. Hopkins, General George C. Marshall, Admiral Ernest J. King, James Forrestal, and others the Foreign Commissar, answering President Roosevelt's question on the current military situation, dealt with the fighting in the Crimea. The Wehrmacht, spilling out of the Ukraine on

5. Churchill, pp. 475–502.

September 25, 1941, poured through the narrow Perekop neck which connects the Crimean peninsula to the mainland, and on November 16 captured Kerch, a thumb or peninsula sticking out of the bigger Crimean peninsula in the direction of the Caucasus. From Kerch it is a hop and skip to the grain of the Kuban region in the North Caucasus, and from there it is a jump to the oil of the North Caucasus and the Caucasus proper. Unwilling to yield the springboard, the Russians on December 29 landed some 40,000 troops on Kerch and advanced to Feodosiya, a city at the eastern end of the Crimea.

This was the same kind of operation as "Sledgehammer," a code name for the proposed Anglo-American assault on the French Cotentin Peninsula where the Atlantic port of Cherbourg is situated. Stalin had been eager to see Sledgehammer carried out. Churchill told him in Moscow that it would be "hazardous and futile" and end in "disaster." If at first the allies succeeded they would be penned in "this confined bomb and shell trap . . . under ceaseless bombardment and assault . . . It would bleed all other operations."

In his reply to F.D.R., Molotov said, "Marshal Timoshenko had begun his Kharkov offensive as an offset to the German drive on the Kerch peninsula."

Throughout January and February, 1942, the Red Army push which had relieved Moscow in December gradually ground to a winter halt. The Germans too were quiescent, licking their wounds and repairing their equipment. On January 18, 1942, Field Marshal Erich von Manstein struck the Russians at Feodosiya and forced them back into the Kerch thumb. On May 8 he hit the thumb. To deflect him Timoshenko prematurely opened a major offensive in the Kharkov region. Kerch was "bleeding" another operation.

" . . . the German drive on the Kerch peninsula," Molotov's White House account continued, "resulted unfavorably for the Russians. The Soviets had originally possessed superiority of forces in the Eastern Crimea, but had used this superiority ineffectively because of the inefficiency of the local commander, General [D. T.] Kozlov, who had proved weak and had not, as a matter of fact, taken part in previous operations against the invading forces. A concentration of aviation and of armored units, supported by Rumanian troops, had enabled the Germans to achieve a relatively easy success. This was regrettable but there was no use disguising the facts. The German drive in the Crimea necessitated speeding up by several days the opening of Marshal Timoshenko's Kharkov offensive. As far as personalities went, the Soviets had found that inexperienced officers and men were the least effective. For example, Marshal Timoshenko was the more dependable because he had had field experience since the beginning of the invasion, while Kozlov was an instance of the opposite state of affairs."[1]

The 1937 purge of the military—an estimated 15,000 to 30,000 officers shot on Stalin's orders—was taking its toll in 1942.

The official Soviet history of the war against Nazi Germany clothes Molotov's generalizations in technical detail and adds the sequel: Kozlov and most of his fellow officers were demoted. Colonel General Lev Z. Mekhlis, a member of the editorial board of *Pravda* in the 1930's, head of the Political Administration of the Red Army since the 1937 purge and Deputy Commissar of Defense, was expelled from both those high posts because as Kozlov's commissar and superior he exhibited a "personal lack of discipline." The same charge was made against Kozlov: "In the critical days of the operation Lieutenant General D. T. Kozlov, commander of the front, and First Rank Army Commissar L. Z. Mekhlis wasted time in fruitless sessions of the War Council lasting many hours instead of giving concrete leadership to the troops."[2]

The debacle at Kerch enabled Manstein to concentrate heavy forces against the great Soviet Black Sea naval base at Sevastopol, which fell on July 3.

The premature Kharkov offensive under the experienced Timoshenko ended in a calamity of far vaster proportions than the Kerch misadventure. Timoshenko moved his armies into battle on May 12 with a view to encircling the German forces on the southwestern front and retaking the key city of Kharkov. For two days the Russians made moderate progress. The evening of May 14, according to the official Soviet *History,* would have been the right time to throw the tank divisions into the fray. But "the command of the Southwestern front, misled by the unfounded information of the reconnaissance section of the Staff," delayed the introduction of its armor, giving the enemy the opportunity to bring up reserves, mostly tanks. Timoshenko lost the initiative to Field Marshal Ewald von Kleist's Panzers, infantry, and aviation. Kleist unleashed a counteroffensive on May 18. On its first day he broke through the defense of the Soviet Ninth Army whose staff headquarters were smashed by German planes. Now Timoshenko's entire force, which had set out to surround the Germans, was in danger of being surrounded. Nikita S. Khrushchev, Timoshenko's chief commissar, telephoned Stalin asking permission to shift from the offensive to the defensive. "But the High Command," reads the official *History*'s account, "insisted on the fulfillment of the original

---

1. Robert E. Sherwood, *Roosevelt and Hopkins. An Intimate History,* pp. 566–567.

2. *Istoria Velikoi Otechestvennoi Voiny Sovietskovo Soyuza 1941–1945. Tom Vtoroi* (The History of the Great Fatherland War of the Soviet Union 1941–1945, Vol. II), pp. 404–406. Hereafter this six-volume history will be designated by the anagram of its Russian initials: IVOVSS.

orders." Using superior aviation and withering artillery and tank fire, Kleist opened a broad breach in the Russian line. The Red Army, still obeying Moscow instructions, continued to advance into the tightening Nazi noose. Finally the High Command confirmed Timoshenko's plan to change to the defensive. But it was "too late," says the *History*. Two Soviet armies under Lieutenant General F. Y. Kostenko "fought a heroic battle against the superior forces of the enemy who enjoyed complete control of the air [while the Russians suffered from] a tremendous short-age of ammunition, fuel, and food." Kostenko was killed. Three other army commanders were killed. Timoshenko and Khrushchev were flown out of the giant trap. The Germans claimed 240,000 prisoners. Hundreds of tanks were captured. "Thus," the *History*'s sad tale concludes, "the offensive operation in the region of Kharkov, initiated successfully by Soviet troops, ended with the grave defeat of almost three armies of the Southwestern and Southern front." The 1961 *History* puts the blame on the Moscow High Command, pseudonym for Joseph Stalin.[3]

German soldiers wrote home that the war would soon be over, they would soon be back in the Fatherland. The Soviet catastrophes at Kerch and Kharkov seemed to justify their optimism. "The Russian is finished," Hitler exclaimed on July 15, 1942.

Colonel General Franz Halder, Wehrmacht Chief of General Staff, agreed: "I must say, it is beginning to look uncommonly like it."

Halder's assent smacks of veiled dissent which he did not dare express. Colonel General Alfred Jodl, sharing a secret thought with Lieutenant General Walter Warlimont, his deputy on the eastern front, said, "A dictator, as a matter of psychological necessity, must never be reminded of his own errors—in order to keep up his self-confidence, the ultimate source of his dictatorial force."[4] Jodl had distilled this wisdom from long experience at the elbow of Hitler. Nor should a dictator be contradicted. If Hitler decided in July, 1942, that Russia was finished she was finished and the conduct of Halder and other generals would be influenced by this view, as was Hitler's. Like Stalin, Hitler dominated the military decision center. In fact, during most of 1942 he stayed at staff headquarters in Vinnitsa in the western Ukraine not too far from the front. No important step could be taken against his wishes and few were made without him. This may have been Hitler's major contribution to Russia's ultimate victory. For his concept of military strategy encompassed no defeats or retreats; that proved Germany's undoing at Stalingrad as it had at Mos-cow and in the siege of Leningrad. Much of Europe had fallen before his legions. He could not imagine that the abominable Russian would alter the rhythm of German conquests.

3. IVOVSS, Vol. II, pp. 411–416.
4. Alan Clark, *Barbarossa. The Russian-German Conflict, 1941–1945*, p. 234.

Nazi philosophy also served Bolshevik Russia. The Nazis regarded Germans as the superior race; Russians, Poles, and Jews were subhumans to be gassed or "shot while trying to escape" or fried alive in their surrounded villages or transported to Germany for slave labor. Before the Hitlerite invasion the Russians and Ukrainians had not been distinguished by love of the communist system, and entire national minorities in the North Caucasus and Crimea seethed with unrest generated by collectivization, purges, religious persecution, restraints on personal freedom, and Russification. Many of these would have preferred the newly arrived brown devil they did not know to the Red devil they had learned over the decades to hate. Millions among them defected to the German side. But Nazi racism in action gave others, especially Great Russians, a foretaste of the future if Germany won the war. Burned villages and Gestapo and SS firing squads poured fuel on the pallid flame of Soviet patriotism which the Kremlin had been fostering. Stalin was so much Hitler's brother in brutality that he had had to neglect the education of the Soviet population on Nazi concentration camps, torture, anti-Semitism, and repression. Hitler now did the job for him.

Other factors began to operate in Russia's favor. As the Wehrmacht advanced, its lines of supply and communication lengthened over scorched earth. The Red Army was receiving more weapons from factories whose ponderous equipment had been lifted bodily onto endless freight trains and transported out of enemy reach eastward to be set up again by true heroes of labor. Soviet soldiers, baptized in blood, enraged by Nazi atrocities, gaining confidence in themselves and, slowly, in their green officers, fought better. Russia's enormous manpower resources, which the Kremlin expended with uninhibited prodigality, her vast spaces and cruel climate would defeat the Nazi state—but only after a thousand more days and millions of fatalities and casualties. On June 22, 1942, the first anniversary of war's outbreak, the Soviet Information Bureau announced that German killed, wounded, and captured in the fighting with the Red Army numbered 10 million, Soviet killed, wounded, and captured numbered 4.5 million. The late Alexander Werth, a Russian-born British-and-French-educated British journalist, and long an avowed Russian nationalist and Soviet sympathizer (the 1968 invasion of Czechoslovakia was his "Kronstadt"), called the figure for Russian losses "an underestimate."[5] The statistic for Germans was clearly arrived at by deciding what multiple would make the high Russian casualties publicly palatable. Two and two tenths was the arbitrary answer.

The Soviet Union won its war against Germany and contributed largely to victory in the second world war because Stalin was ready to pay

5. *Russia at War 1941–1945,* pp. 401–402.

the human price. The battle of Stalingrad exemplifies this.

The Wehrmacht renewed its Russian offensive in the summer of 1942 as soon as the tardy sun had dried the land. Rostov fell on July 28. In explanation of this crippling blow, Werth, on the scene during much of the war, writes, "certain Red Army units panicked and fled . . . officers and generals had lost their heads under the fierceness of the German onslaught . . . no orders had been given to abandon the city . . . there was here a clear case of disobedience. Many were shot and demoted: generals, officers and ordinary soldiers."[6] On July 30 Stalin issued his "not a step back" order. The Wehrmacht continued its advance. It captured the minor Maikop oil field on August 11 and the Mineralny Vody railhead and the famous nearby spas at the approaches of the Caucasus on August 21. Units of the German army moved down the Black Sea coast toward Taupse. Confident of their power and impatient to win and go home, the Germans divided their forces: one group of armies lunged at the strategic, oil-rich Caucasus isthmus, the gateway too to Iran through which Anglo-American munitions and food were reaching the Soviets; the second pointed its spearhead at Stalingrad, where it could cut off the communist retreat to the east, sever the Volga lifeline, and then perhaps join with other forces in encircling Moscow. These were motives enough. Yet an element of personal prestige was also involved: Stalingrad was the city of Stalin where he had fought during the Bolshevik Civil War; its name was changed from Tsaritsin to honor him. For Hitler the capture of Stalingrad would have been a symbolic triumph because of its name. Neither dictator would yield. Both adopted the slogan "not a step back." And the heaps of dead grew higher and higher.

The German attack on Stalingrad began August 23 with a raid of 600 bombers. Less than a fortnight later the Wehrmacht entered the city. The Russians stayed and fought for every yard, every foot of street, every house. By the end of October the Nazis controlled most of the city. They also controlled the air. Pockets of resistance remained inside Stalingrad, and from the east bank of the Volga Red artillery fired across the river at the Wehrmacht in the town. When, therefore, the Russians opened their counteroffensive on November 19 the enemy was exhausted, his spirit low. The Red Army surrounded Stalingrad. Soviet soldiers penetrated into the city in small groups to harass the occupiers. The Luftwaffe maintained contact and replenished the fast-diminishing supplies of munitions and food by parachute drops. It was clear, however, that the Germans could not hold out indefinitely unless a breach was made in the Red iron ring that had been forged around the city. The question remained who would make the breach. Was Field Marshal Friedrich Paulus to smash the ring and abandon the smoking city of jagged walls

6. *Ibid.*, p. 407.

and water-filled craters? Or should a German army outside Stalingrad crash through the encirclement and reinforce Paulus inside?

Paulus, entrapped and desperate, asked headquarters for permission on November 23 to ram through the ring and fight in the open field. But being shut in and under constant bombardment, he did not know the strength of the encircling Russian forces. Marshal Georgi K. Zhukov, commanding the Russian forces, had planted 2,000 guns around Stalingrad to hold Paulus in. Field Marshal Erich von Manstein, sent by Hitler to save Paulus' Sixth Army of almost a quarter of a million men, reconnoitered and decided that flight for Paulus would be too expensive in terms of troops and equipment. He accordingly planned to relieve Paulus by dispersing Zhukov's perimeter of fire and penetrating into Stalingrad.

Manstein collected armor and infantry from far and near, but when his attack commenced on December 12 he found he had less strength than Paulus within the city. It was therefore necessary for Paulus to try to break out simultaneously with Manstein's effort to break in. This conflicted with the Nazi code of war: Germans must not flee before Russians. Hitler had forbidden the surrender of Stalingrad.

Manstein continued to press Paulus to force an exit for the Sixth Army. Paulus demurred. The regrouping would take six days, it would cause casualties and, he radioed on December 20, "the general debility of the troops and the reduced mobility of units following the slaughtering of horses for food made it most unlikely that such a difficult and risky undertaking—particularly when carried out under conditions of extreme cold—could possibly succeed."[7] These seem to have been thin excuses. The basic explanation of Paulus' timidity was fear of disobeying Hitler. This is borne out by his response to a Russian offer on January 8 of an honorable surrender: "sufficient rations . . . care for the wounded . . . officers to keep their weapons . . . repatriation after the war to Germany or any other country." Paulus, in daily contact with Hitler over the shortwave radio, said no.

Nor could Manstein crack the ring from without. The Russians outnumbered the Germans 2 to 1 in the entire Volga-Don battlefield and 5 to 1 in some of its sectors. Inside Stalingrad German corpses littered the streets and filled former living rooms, offices, and cellars; thousands of wounded lay moaning and dying with no medical care; starvation had set in; ammunition was rationed while the Red Army intensified its sniping from behind ruins and shelling from beyond the Volga. The Wehrmacht soldiers were prostrate from fatigue, noise, dust, filth, undernourishment, and hopelessness.

Russian assaults grew hotter. The Nazi forces retreated step by step into contracting pockets. Paulus and a portion of his units were captured

7. Quoted by Alan Clark, p. 272.

on January 30. The remainder surrendered on February 1. Hitler was beside himself with anger. He complained that they should "have closed ranks, formed a hedgehog, and shot themselves with their last bullet."[8] So, with variations, he died.

Hitler's fury was more than justified. The Soviet victory at Stalingrad was the beginning of his end. It changed the course of the war and the course of world history. Stalin sensed this.

*　　*　　*

The German thrust to Stalingrad was part of a grandiose German conception to win the war and the world. As disclosed by Colonel General Jodl, Chief of the German Armed Forces Operations Staff, Hitler planned to break through at Stalingrad and in Egypt and to join these two mighty salients in the Middle East.[9] Marshal Rommel's divisions, advancing from Suez, would link up with the victorious Wehrmacht descending from Stalingrad through Turkey, forced into war on the Nazi side. Another branch of the Wehrmacht, traversing the Volga region by land and water, capturing the Caucasus oil fields and cutting through Iran to the Persian Gulf, could move into western India while the Japanese stood on India's eastern doorstep. A junction of the German and Japanese armies at the expense of Britain and Russia was conceived as a guarantee of the success of Hitler's world-encircling dreams. But Field Marshal Sir Bernard Montgomery's victory over Rommel at El Alamein in October, 1942, and the Red Army's victory at Stalingrad broke the grandiose scheme to shards. This was the dawn of victory in the second world war.

IX THE EXAGGERATED REPORT OF
THE DEATH OF THE COMINTERN

After the Russian victory at Stalingrad in January, 1943, Stalin could have been fairly certain that he would achieve his minimum war aims: the restoration to the U.S.S.R. of the frontiers accorded it by his arrangements with Hitler in 1939–1940. In the back of his brain, as subsequent

8. *Ibid.,* p. 288.
9. War Department, *Biennial Report of the Chief of Staff of the United States Army to the Secretary of War, July 1, 1943 to June 30, 1945,* p. 9.

events proved, he was planning to get more. The boundaries of 1941 were merely an appetizer before a gourmand's meal.

To smooth his road to empire Stalin dissolved the Comintern, or Third International, the union of world communist parties founded on March 4, 1919.

Stalin always disliked foreign communists. In fact he disliked communists. Nothing in his private life or political career indicates that he was a radical or rebel or revolutionary. He was a conservative. He killed more communists than anybody else in history, far more than Chiang Kai-shek. Foreign communists were particularly irksome to him. Their sycophancy won his scorn. They came to Moscow cap in hand asking for money and the privilege to serve Russia. They slavishly followed every twist in Soviet domestic policy. When Stalin persecuted the so-called leftists in the Soviet Communist Party the Comintern affiliates followed suit. When, having crushed Trotsky, he assailed Rykov, Bukharin, and Tomsky, the Comintern parties discovered and hounded "rightists" in their ranks. Attacks on "proletarian culture" in the Soviet Union for purely Russian reasons were followed by similar attacks in the Chilean and Greek communist parties.

The Kremlin dealt brutally with entire communist parties. The Polish Communist Party, for instance, was disbanded in the summer of 1938. Simultaneously the Soviet secret police executed all Polish communist leaders except those like Gomulka who, mercifully, had been jailed by the reactionary government of Poland. No reason for the executions was ever divulged. Presumably the victims, and the rank-and-file communists in the Polish underground, were too Polish to please Russian patriots.

"An internationalist," Stalin said in 1937, "is one who is unreservedly, unwaveringly, unconditionally ready to defend the U.S.S.R., for the U.S.S.R. is the base of the world revolutionary movement and it is impossible to defend, to advance that revolutionary movement apart from and against the U.S.S.R."[1]

By this topsy-turvy logic, a Soviet nationalist was an internationalist and a foreign communist became a Soviet nationalist. Foreign communists were expected to obey two precepts: (1) My country, right or wrong, wrong; (2) Russia, right or wrong, my country. This flowed from their perverted communism. For if they made objective judgments of the Soviet Union, if they conceded that it was less than paradise, that it was despotic, antiegalitarian, caste–ridden, and backward, how could they offer it to their native lands as an alternative of perfection to the present? They forfeited their critical judgments and became idolators. Nonpagans quit the movement.

1. Louis Fischer, *Russia's Road from Peace to War. 1917–1941*, p. 177.

Conformist weaklings do not make revolutions. The foreigners of the Comintern never made and maintained a revolution. After 1923 the Comintern no longer tried. Nor were the non-Russian communist parties an effective fifth wheel of Soviet foreign policy. In 1943 Stalin foresaw that his army and secret police, not Comintern comrades, would give Russia an empire.

Imperialism is not congruous with internationalism or revolution. The Comintern, in theory an instrument of internationalist revolution, no longer made sense. Stalin closed its doors.

The leaders of the Comintern had misled world communists with foolish prophecies of revolutions about to burst into bud. Underestimating the stability of capitalism and the menace of fascism, they directed their fire at the social democrats and other reformist socialists whom they maligned as "social fascists." They thereby divided the working class, helped lift Hitler into power, and weakened resistance to reaction everywhere.

The Comintern had done its work. The Comintern could go. Rarely had so much crusading zeal wedded to crass purpose produced such barren seed. What the individual communist parties could accomplish on behalf of Russia they would do without a central organization in Moscow because the Soviet Union was still their only model, their only new Jerusalem; the Kremlin could easily communicate its wishes to them. Later, when Maoist China and Castro Cuba became rival centers of dogma, gold, and guns, when Moscow's image, moreover, had been tarnished by blatant imperialist depredations, some communist parties ventured to criticize, but many did not dare cut the umbilical cord. *Pravda* of January 28, 1969, for example, reported from Helsinki that the plenary session of the Central Committee of the Finnish Communist Party opposed "the extension of [Finland's] economic collaboration with the northern countries"—Norway, Sweden, and Denmark. The Finns were seeking a Scandinavian counterweight to Russia. They did not wish to put all their commercial eggs in the Soviet basket and thereby subject themselves to Kremlin pressures. But, said *Pravda*, "the Finnish Communist Party rejects everything that could complicate the trade and general economic collaboration with the Soviet Union and other socialist countries which are so important to the life of Finland." That was Moscow speaking through its ventriloquist dummy.

Stalin's liquidation of the Comintern was thus a masterstroke of political strategy. He rid himself of an organization he had always loathed and often purged. He smoke-screened his imminent imperialist ventures. He lost nothing. The foreign communist parties, insensitive to maltreatment, would continue to pray to Moscow. Mother Russia would pay.

A special convention of the United States Communist Party had voted on November 16, 1940, to end its affiliation with the Comintern. Jewish and other anti-Nazis in the party abhorred Moscow's bond with Hitler. Earl Browder, secretary general of the party, a Kansan, realized that the tie with the Muscovite body was a kiss of polio in anticommunist America. The party's strength among workers and intellectuals had grown in consequence of its expensive espousal of Loyalist Spain, its militant trade unionism, and the muffling of silly talk about overthrowing American capitalism. Browder sought members, votes, influence, and power; he was a politician in the American tradition. None of these reasons, however, induced the party to sever relations with the Comintern. It shrank from cutting the lifeline. But in October, 1940, the U.S. Congress passed the Voorhis Act which required the party to register with the federal authorities as an "agent of a foreign government" and, as such, to give Washington a list of members—thus offering them up for prosecution.

Nevertheless, the Comintern leadership used the example of the American party's disaffiliation to explain the burial of the parent body. Changes in the international situation and in the working-class movement, the May 15, 1941, resolution stated, "demanded greater flexibility and independence of its sections in meeting the problems confronting them." The communist parties, the Comintern resolution continues, had grown and matured. During the war "some sections had raised the question of the dissolution of the Communist International as a directing center of the international working class movement." (It was merely the directing center of foreign communist parties.) Therefore the Presidium of the Executive Committee of the Comintern, without awaiting the end of the war when a world congress could determine its fate, administered the ax. Stalin was in a hurry.

The coroner's declaration closed with an appeal of "all friends of the Communist International" to concentrate their energies "on the whole-hearted support of and active participation in the war of liberation of the peoples and the states of the anti-Hitler coalition for the speediest defeat of the deadly enemy of the working class and toilers—German Fascism and its associates and vassals." No appeal to prepare for revolution. Moscow had long since abandoned the idea of revolution. The Messianism of the Comintern yielded to the militarism of Russia. Lenin had written a book entitled *Imperialism, the Last Stage of Capitalism*. Stalin wrote a chapter of history entitled "Imperialism, the Latest Stage of Sovietism."

The symbol of the Comintern was a burly workingman with bulging muscles wielding a massive sledgehammer against a globe wreathed in chains. Karl Radek, the cynical Puck who was one of the Comintern's leaders, used to say, "A file would be more effective." Stalin scrapped the hammer and chose the bayonet—which does not break chains.

The Comintern's suicide note is dated May 15, 1941, but for an undisclosed reason it was published in the Soviet and foreign press on May 23, 1941. The next day the decision to inter the Comintern was widely hailed in Britain and America for what it said. The *Times* of London declared that it "refutes the insinuation that the spread of communism in Europe is the Russian peace aim and the natural sequel of a Russian victory. . . . It is not too much to say that the future of the world turns on the establishment of confidence between Russia, Britain, and the United States. In dissolving the Communist International, Russia has made a notable contribution to that common purpose."

The *New York Times* of May 24 was far more skeptical than its London contemporary. Its editorial considered the Comintern's demise "one of the most momentous developments of this war" but immediately diluted that appraisal by calling the text of the Moscow declaration "equivocal" because it "left many loopholes open for continuing, and even strengthening, Communist activities in all countries." The effect of the decree would depend on whether "the Communist parties in their countries became really patriotic, which means their dissolution. . . . It will depend on whether the French Communists abandon their efforts to put themselves in the saddle and join in a real unification of the French nation."

Naïve hope.

The *New York Times* also made the ultimate value of the Comintern's death contingent on "whether Moscow drops the 'Union of Polish Patriots' led by the wife of an assistant Commissar for Foreign Affairs" and on the cessation of Soviet meddling in Yugoslav affairs. Here the editorial touched the nub of the matter. The death of the Comintern meant no flagging of communist activity, it merely veiled the intensification of Stalin's efforts to seize eastern Europe and as much else as possible. He told Dimitrov in 1941, shortly after the annexation of the Baltic countries, that he intended to liquidate the Comintern.[2] The gleam of empire in Stalin's eye dispelled the dream of world revolution. The first step toward Russian expansion inspired the first decision to liquidate the Comintern. It was created by and for Russia, and its founding fathers expected and got submission from their children.

Russian predominance outside matched Russian predominance inside the Soviet Union which, only 50 percent or less Russian, is, in theory, an international in itself. Russian supremacy was an old story. The war intensified it. "Coincidentally with the publication of the declaration [of the Comintern's death]," the *New York Times* reported from Moscow on May 23, "the Army newspaper Red Star prints an editorial entitled 'The Great Tradition of the Russian People' devoted to Russian patriotism which Red Star says every Russian takes with his mother's milk. The

2. Dimitrov told this in 1944 to Milovan Djilas, then a leader of the Yugoslav Communist Party. Djilas repeated it to me.

article calls on all non-Russians in the Red Army to take inspiration from it.

"When the Soviet Union was busy building itself up, Red Star writes, not much time was spent looking back at the past, and sometimes now, in education for the Army, there has been too much modesty about the Russians' great culture. The many nationalities on the front know how much they owe to the Russian people for their liberation in the past, it is asserted, and they, too, can be proud of the words of [Tsarist Field Marshal] Suvorov, who called on his armies to remember before battle that 'we are Russians.' "

So Armenians, Georgians, Tartars, Tadjiks, Buryats, Ukrainians, and Latvians were to remember that they were Russians. This was Russification at its worst. It flew in the face of the avowed Bolshevik-Leninist policy of respect for the rights of ethnic minorities. But where individuals are not respected neither are groups.

Red Star was proclaiming the primacy of Russians. Theoretical internationalism ceded to Russian supremacy at home. Stalin advocated this as early as 1922. Paper internationalism officially ceded to Russian nationalism abroad in 1941.

Neither Churchill nor Roosevelt understood the imperialistic implications of the Comintern's demise. Roosevelt regarded it as facilitating smoother relations with Moscow. The Kremlin's advocacy of world revolution had antagonized many business, trade union, and church circles in the United States and was hence a barrier to the friendly postwar collaboration between the two superpowers envisaged by F.D.R. He wanted it out of the way. Roosevelt's great design was nobly conceived. It ignored the nature of nations and the character of Stalin, whose only interest was his power over Russia and what she might acquire. The rest of the world was the enemy.

X MURDER IN THE FOREST

Dr. Paul Joseph Goebbels, that remarkably vile Nazi Minister of Public Enlightenment and Propaganda, continued throughout the war to darken the minds of Germans. But he aspired to greater things. He hoped to shape what Germans call "The Big Politics." Chance met him more than halfway. Was Moscow the beneficiary?

On April 13, 1943, the entire Goebbels press—all the newspapers of Germany and Nazi-occupied Europe—and all his radio stations published a communiqué: 12 kilometers west of Smolensk the German authorities had made a "most horrific discovery. A great pit was found, 28 metres long and 16 metres wide, filled with 12 layers of bodies of Polish officers, numbering about 3000. They were clad in full military uniform, and while many of them had their hands tied, all of them had wounds in the back of their necks caused by pistol shots. The identification of the bodies did not cause great difficulties because of the mummifying property of the soil and because the Bolsheviks had left on the bodies the identity documents of the victims. It has already been ascertained that among the murdered is a General [M.] Smorawinski from Lublin. These officers had been previously in Orel, from whence they had been brought in cattle wagons to Smolensk in February and March, 1940. . . . The discovery of and search for further graves is taking place. Under layers dug up already, new layers are found. The total figure of the murdered officers is estimated at 10,000 which would more or less correspond to the entire number of Polish officers taken as prisoners of war by the Bolsheviks."[1]

Two days later the Soviet Information Bureau replied: Goebbels' charges were "vile fabrications," "monstrous inventions," and "unscrupulous and base lies" launched "to cover up crimes which, as has now become evident, were perpetrated" by the Nazis themselves. "These arrant German-Fascist murderers, whose hands are stained with the blood of hundreds of thousands of innocent victims, who methodically exterminate the populations of countries they have occupied without sparing children, women, or old people, who exterminated many hundreds of thousands of Polish citizens in Poland itself, will deceive no one by their base lies and slanders."[2]

That thousands of Polish commissioned and noncommissioned officers were murdered and buried in the Katyn (pronounced kateen) Forest west of Smolensk is not questioned. What has been disputed is who did it. Germane to that issue is when it was done. The Soviet communiqué of April 15, 1943, gave the date as 1941, "after the withdrawal of the Soviet troops from the Smolensk area." The Goebbels announcement put the grim event in 1940 when the Soviets were there.

One other aspect is beyond controversy: Nazis as well as Bolsheviks were capable of committing the crime. The Hitlerite record is thick with the blood of millions of innocents. And if Stalin could have had 15,000 to 30,000 of his own Red Army officers executed he would not shrink from

1. General Sikorski Historical Institute, *Documents on Polish-Soviet Relations, 1939–1945.* Vol. I: *1939–1943,* pp. 523–524.
2. *Ibid.,* pp. 524–525.

killing thousands of Polish officers. However, psychological capacity for murder is no proof of crime.

The Soviet government did not deny that the murdered Poles had been its prisoners. When Germany invaded Poland on September 1, 1939, many Polish civilians and later many Polish military withdrew to the east. Some, like Foreign Minister Joseph Beck, reached Rumania. A larger number entered eastern Poland, assigned by the Soviet-Nazi pact to the U.S.S.R., where the Red Army apprehended them. The Polish officers were interned in camps in the Soviet Union. The Soviet communiqué of April 15 speaks of "the former Polish prisoners of war who in 1941 were engaged in construction work in areas west of Smolensk . . . and fell into the hands of the German-Fascist hangmen."

Two questions arise: (1) Why did the Polish officers become prisoners of war? The Soviet Union was not at war with Poland. (2) Why were officers "engaged in construction work" and why, when the Wehrmacht approached Smolensk, were these healthy men, if they were there, not allowed to run away? How is it that not one escaped?

The Polish authorities had been looking for the officers long before the Goebbels communiqué. The investigations and inquiries began informally even before the signing of the Soviet-Polish treaty of July 30, 1941, which provided for the renewal of relations, mutual aid in the war, and the formation of a Polish army on Soviet territory. On July 4, 1941, General Wladyslaw Sikorski, Polish Prime Minister and Commander in Chief, met Foreign Secretary Eden at the latter's request in the British Foreign Office. Sikorski said, "The figures given by Ambassador Maisky concerning Polish nationals are false and tendentious. According to the calculations of the Moscow *Pravda* there are about 190,000 soldiers in [Soviet] concentration camps, including 10,000 Polish officers, besides many thousand Poles of military age deported into the depths of Russia."

The next day Sikorski discussed the same question with Maisky: "Monsieur Maisky inquired what exactly General Sikorski had in mind in regard to Polish prisoners of war in the Soviet Union.

"General Sikorski replied that these men, who, according to official Soviet statistics, recently published, numbered 191,000 men and some 9,000 officers, the majority of whom are in military concentration camps east of the river Volga, should be formed into an independent, sovereign Polish Army in the Soviet Union. If the Soviet Government did not desire the presence of such an army, it might perhaps be possible to transport it elsewhere to continue the fight against Germany.

"Monsieur Maisky suggested that this Polish Army would be under the orders of the Soviet General staff."[3]

3. *Ibid.*, pp. 114–119. The Sikorski-Maisky interview was witnessed by Sir Alex-

On July 11, 1941, Polish Foreign Minister August Zaleski conferred with Maisky in the British Foreign Office in the presence of Eden. "As regards the Polish prisoners of war . . ." Maisky said, "the Soviet Government stated that there were only 20,000. The remainder were released as the Soviet Government had not considered it possible to keep these as prisoners of war, and were now dispersed throughout Russia."[4]

These words, uttered by Maisky on July 11, were based on information that would have come to him the day before at the latest, probably several days earlier. But according to the official Soviet *History* of the war the Germans had not yet taken Smolensk on July 11. As late as July 12 and 16 the Red Army was still fighting fiercely and launching counterattacks west of Smolensk.[5] Neither Moscow nor Maisky explained why, if so many Poles were released and dispersed throughout Russia, 20,000 should have been retained in captivity, why 9,000 to 10,000 of them were officers, and why they would have remained on the Smolensk battlefield where, as the Soviet communiqué of April 15, 1943, alleged, they were "engaged in construction work" and fell into German hands.

A Soviet decree dated August 12, 1941, liberated all Polish citizens "deprived of their freedom as prisoners of war or on other grounds." General Wladyslaw Anders, released after twenty months in Soviet prisons, was designated commander in chief of the Polish army to be created on Soviet soil.[6]

Polish Ambassador in Moscow Professor Stanislaw Kot said to Deputy Commissar of Foreign Affairs Andrei J. Vyshinsky on October 7, 1941, during a lengthy conversation, "I wish to quote here some figures now. Altogether 9,500 officers were imprisoned in Poland and deported inside the USSR, while there are only 2,000 officers in our army. What happened to 7,500 officers? . . . We tried to find them everywhere, we thought that they had been delivered to the Germans, we made enquiries in German prisoner-of-war camps, in occupied Poland, everywhere they might be. I would have understood the missing of some dozens of people, or, let us say, several hundred, but not several thousand."

Vyshinsky expressed puzzlement.[7]

Ambassador Kot raised the same question with Vyshinsky on October 14 and got no satisfaction. General Sikorski on October 15 took the matter up in London with Soviet Ambassador Bogomolov who was accredited to the Polish, Czechoslovak, and other governments-in-exile there. Meanwhile the Soviet government had agreed to the formation of only two

ander Cadogan, British Permanent Under Secretary for Foreign Affairs, who initialed these minutes.

4. *Ibid.*, p. 128.
5. IVOVSS, Vol. 2, p. 60.
6. Sikorski Institute, Vol. I., p. 151.
7. *Ibid.*, pp. 173–174.

Polish divisions. The Polish authorities claimed they could organize many more.

Chairman Stalin received Ambassador Kot in Moscow on November 14, 1941. Foreign Commissar Molotov was in attendance. During the preliminary exchange of pleasantries Kot referred to the Poles and Russians as "neighbors." Stalin said, "Not only neighbors, but also of the same blood" ("Yedinokroviye" in Russian). Next Kot asked whether Stalin wished a frank discussion of requests and grievances. Stalin said he did. "But let bygones be bygones," he urged. Kot then stated that 150,000 Poles were available for military service in the Soviet Union but permission had been granted for only 30,000 soldiers. Stalin pleaded shortages of arms and food and promised to investigate. Kot came to the missing Polish officers.

Kot: "We have names and lists: for instance, General Stanislaw Haller has not been found, and the officers from Starobielsk, Kozielsk, and Ostakhov [prisoner-of-war camps] who were moved in April and May, 1940, are missing."

Stalin: "We have released all the Poles. . . ."

Kot: ". . . I beg you, Mr. President, to issue an order to effect the release of the officers whom we need for the organization of our army. We have official reports stating the dates on which they were removed from the camps."

Stalin: "Are there any detailed lists?"

Kot: "Every name was entered into the lists held by the Russian commanding officers of the camps who used to make a roll-call every day. Moreover, the NKVD interrogated each officer separately. None of the officers who served with the Staff of the army which General Anders commanded in Poland has been returned."

Stalin dialed the NKVD.

Stalin: "Stalin speaking. Have all the Poles been released from prisons? The Ambassador of Poland is here and he tells me that not all have been released." He put down the receiver but had no news for Kot. A minute later the telephone rang. Stalin answered, listened, put down the receiver, but said nothing.[8]

In the course of the two hour and ten minute conversation with Kot, Stalin made a statement of general importance. "For my part," he said, "it is essential for me to contribute personally to the restoration of the Polish State, whatever might be its internal constitution." Ambassador Kot was overjoyed and wondered whether he might publish this declaration or would the Chairman. Stalin: "I will do so at the first opportunity." Stalin was a good host. He liked to please his guests. The moment they

8. *Ibid.*, pp. 205–213.

left, his mood changed. He never published the declaration.

The mystery of the missing Polish officers remained. Even Stalin had not thrown any light on it. For the Poles, however, the 10,000 officers, a few hundred more or less, were the cadres of their future army and hence of a future reconstituted Poland.

At the height of the battle of Moscow General Sikorski, newly arrived from London, was received by Stalin in the presence of Molotov, Kot, and General Anders. Date: December 3, 1941. Two minutes after the opening of the meeting Prime Minister Sikorski invoked the subject of the vanished officers. "I confirm in your presence, Mr. President," he said, "that your declaration about the amnesty is not being fulfilled. Many of our people, a great number of very prominent men, are still kept in labour camps and in prisons."

Stalin: "This is impossible, as the amnesty has referred to all and all the Poles have been released."

General Anders: "This is not in accordance with the real facts. . . ."

Sikorski: ". . . I have ordered that checks be made whether they are in Poland, with whom we have steady contact. It has been proven that not one of them is there, likewise as in our prisoner of war camps in Poland. Not one of them has returned."

Stalin: "That is impossible, they have escaped."

Anders: "Where then could they escape?"

Stalin: "Well, to Manchuria."

Anders: "It is impossible that all could escape, the more impossible considering the fact that since they have been deported from prisoner of war camps to labour camps and prisons their correspondence with their families has stopped completely. . . ."

Sikorski: "If anyone would succeed to get beyond the boundaries of Russia he would report to me."

Neither Stalin nor Molotov said anything more on the matter; the conferees passed to other aspects of the Polish military situation. Anders requested better facilities for training the two approved Polish divisions and more punctual delivery of food, fodder, and equipment for them. Stalin exclaimed that if the Poles did not wish to fight "they may go elsewhere." Anders persisted: men were living in tents in freezing temperatures. Stalin admitted he was "crude," he wanted to know, yes or no, did the Poles wish to fight. Sikorski and Anders assured him they could, given the facilities, mobilize and train 150,000 Poles for combat in Russia, but conditions had to improve. Stalin said, "When you go to Iran then perhaps you have to fight in Turkey against the Germans. Tomorrow Japan will enter the war, then against Japan. So as the English order. Perhaps in Singapore."

Anders contradicted: "From here it is closer to Poland."

Stalin: "It seems to me the English need your army."

"No," Sikorski affirmed, "it was I, seeing what difficulties we have to face here, that requested the English and Americans to move our soldiers to better conditions." Anders dilated on the problems. If a better training region were available, in the warmer republics of Central Asia, for instance, he could count on 150,000 men or more "but among them there is also a great number of Jews who do not want to serve in the army."

Stalin: "Jews are poor warriors."

Sikorski agreed. Anders too. "Two hundred Jews," he reported, "deserted from Buzuluk upon hearing" a rumor that Kuibyshev, the substitute capital, had been bombed.

Stalin: "Yes, Jews are bad warriors."

Sikorski: "I must evacuate 25,000 people from here for the air force, navy, and Panzer units" to be trained in England. They could return to join the Polish army in Russia.

Stalin praised the British airmen stationed on Soviet territory.

Sikorski: "Our airmen have excellent vision and quick orientation."

Stalin: "The best and most valiant airmen are Slavs. They act very quickly because it is a young race which as yet has not been worn out."

Sikorski: "The present war will make the Anglo-Saxons younger. The British are not the French, who are already finished."

Stalin: "I don't agree with this opinion. . . . The Germans are strong, but the Slavs will crush them."

The racist discussion was resumed the next evening at the customary festive dinner for visiting dignitaries. General Anders said to Stalin across the table: "Many Ukrainians were and are Germanophils, the present war proves it, and that is why we, and later on you, had much trouble with them, even with those among them who pretended to be Communist. . . ."

Stalin: "Yes, but they were your Ukrainians, not ours. Jointly with you we shall destroy them in future. We shall finish with them once and for all."[9]

Despite agreement between Stalin and the Polish generals on genetics and on the evacuation of 25,000 Poles to foreign countries, not even the dictator-master of the NKVD offered a clue to the fate of the thousands of lost Polish officers. Stalin's only contribution to the unremitting Polish quest was the unsupported assertion that the men whose corpses were subsequently examined by Germans and Russians in mass graves near Smolensk in Russia's far west had escaped across the vast expanse of

9. *Ibid.,* pp. 231–243.

Russia and Siberia to Manchuria in the Far East without writing a single letter to their relatives or announcing their presence to the Polish authorities or anybody else.

Jovial banquets and cordial interviews between foreign leaders and Soviet statesmen promise nothing. Stalin, Sikorski, and Anders saw eye to eye on a number of abstract ideas and concrete problems, and Stalin manifested good will toward the Poles. But the Polish visit marked the beginning of a precipitous deterioration in Soviet-Polish relations. The Red Army's victory over the Wehrmacht at Moscow was ominous for Poland; Stalin's plans for territorial expansion took on a cast of reality. He would therefore not have welcomed the wish expressed by his Polish guests to fight in Russia and be the first to re-enter their homeland. Moreover, a foreign body, especially a foreign army, fits ill into the Soviet system with its xenophobic overtones. The Poles did not help matters by asking for their soldiers and civilian refugees civilized living conditions unattainable for most Soviet citizens in normal times, not to speak of wartime. Stalin was glad to see Polish divisions in the U.S.S.R. depart via Iran for the Palestine and other Middle East fronts. A Polish officer who accompanied General Anders to Stalin and heard the dictator's statements exclaimed, "Our dream of creating here an army as powerful as possible and for the return to the liberated homeland through battle collapsed today."

Sensing danger, Sikorski pressed Churchill in London and Roosevelt in Washington not to allow Russia to annex Polish and other East European lands. The Polish Prime Minister wrote Eden on April 16, 1942, on the menace of Russia's looming new imperialism. Within the Soviet Union the NKVD arrested and in several notable instances executed Polish nationals of known anti-Nazi convictions. The case of Victor Alter and Henrich Ehrlich, leading Polish-Jewish socialists who fled into Russia when the Wehrmacht occupied Poland, is notorious; the Soviet secret police shot them as pro-Nazi spies. In the second half of 1942 employees of the Polish embassy in Kuibyshev were repeatedly arrested. General Anders, encountering Churchill in Cairo on August 22, 1942, on the Prime Minister's return from seeing Stalin, said, "There is no justice or honour in Russia, and there is not a single man in that country whose word can be trusted."[10]

Given these acts and attitudes Soviet-Polish relations grew worse in the early months of 1943. During March, 1943, the Kremlin unveiled the "Union of Polish Patriots," potential parent of a future communist government of Poland, presided over by Wanda Wassilewska, a Polish novelist and wife of Alexander Korneichuk, Assistant Commissar for Foreign Affairs in Moscow. It was shortly thereafter, on April 13, 1943, that Goeb-

10. *Ibid.*, p. 422.

bels exploded his bombshell about the discovery in the Katyn Forest near Smolensk of a huge pit crammed with the cadavers of thousands of Polish officers in uniform and hundreds of civilians.

The Polish reaction was expectedly emotional. Recent irritations in Russia had given freer rein to historic antagonisms. The thought that the Soviets might have killed the remnant of the nation's military caste removed restraints and precluded recourse to political hypocrisy. The first move of the Polish government-in-exile in London was the publication on April 16 of a statement by General Marian Kukiel, its Minister of Defense: Three Soviet prisoner-of-war camps had been set up for Poles late in 1939; one at Kozielsk east of Smolensk held approximately 5,000 men, including 4,500 officers; another at Starobielsk, southeast of Kharkov, accommodated 3,920 officers, medical officers, and civilians; the third, at Ostakhov, some 10 miles from Kalinin, housed some 6,570 men, including 380 officers. Between April 5 and the middle of May, 1940, the camps were dismantled. The occupants of the Kozielsk camp were sent in the direction of Smolensk. The statement then mentions the numerous Polish inquiries about the officers which failed to elicit information from the Soviets. The Polish government "has therefore approached this institution [the International Red Cross] with a view to their sending a delegation to the place where the massacre of the Polish prisoners of war is said to have taken place."[11]

This unleashed the whirlwind. Though the Polish government on April 17 condemned Nazi Germany's cruelty against Poles and others and rejected the right of "all who are themselves guilty of such crimes" to make "political capital" out of this one, the furies were loose. The relations between Stalin and Churchill and Roosevelt had been evolving in superficial calm. On April 7, 1943, Stalin congratulated Churchill on British success against Rommel in Tunisia and said, "I welcome the stepped up bombing of Essen, Berlin, Kiel and other industrial centres of Germany." When Churchill asked Stalin's permission to broadcast this message to the Royal Air Force Stalin assented. "I am glad," he added, "you intend to go on bombing German towns on an ever-increasing scale."[12] But the Polish government's invitation to the International Red Cross in Switzerland to exhume the Katyn corpses shrouded the Allied sky in gray clouds. "The fact that the anti-Soviet campaign has been started simultaneously in the German and Polish press and followed identical lines," Stalin wired Churchill on April 21, "is indubitable evidence of contact and collusion between Hitler—the Allies' enemy—and the Sikorski government in this hostile campaign." The Polish government in London "having descended to collusion with the Hitler government" had, "in practice," severed its relations of alliance with the

11. *Ibid.,* pp. 525–527.
12. *Correspondence,* Vol. I, pp. 115–119.

U.S.S.R. and adopted a hostile attitude to the Soviet Union. "For these reasons the Soviet Government has decided to interrupt relations with that Government."[13]

Simultaneous actions become "indubitable" proof of contact and collusion. Moscow, wishing to sever relations, pretends that the other party has already done so. Blame must never attach to the Soviets.

Churchill attempted to argue. "Far from being pro-German or in league with them," he told Stalin, "Sikorski is in danger of being overthrown by the Poles who consider that he has not stood up sufficiently for his people against the Soviets. If he should go we should only get somebody worse." The Prime Minister therefore hoped the Kremlin would not "interrupt" its relations with the Polish government; the public announcement of a break would "do the greatest possible harm in the United States, where the Poles are numerous and influential." Stalin replied immediately that "the matter of interrupting relations with the Polish Government has already been settled. . . . All my colleagues insisted on this." The news would be published.[14]

Roosevelt too sought to dissuade Stalin. "I cannot believe that Sikorski has in any way whatsoever collaborated with the Hitlerite gangsters," the President telegraphed. To be sure, Sikorski had erred in turning to the International Red Cross, but Churchill would "find a way of prevailing upon the Polish Government in London in the future to act with more common sense."

"Incidentally," F.D.R. remarked as if casually, "I have several million Poles in the United States . . . all of them are bitter against the Hitlerites. [The President had adopted Stalin's favored name for the Nazis.] However, the over-all situation would not be helped by the knowledge of a complete diplomatic break between the Soviet and Polish Governments." Stalin replied: it was too late; relations had already been interrupted.[15]

A note of April 25, 1943, by Foreign Commissar Molotov revealed what animated the Soviet mind. He attributed the action of the Polish government on Katyn to its desire to wrest from the Soviet Union "territorial concessions at the expense of the Soviet Ukraine, Soviet Byelorussia and Soviet Lithuania."[16] The Soviet Ukraine, by virtue of the Soviet-Nazi agreements of 1939, had absorbed large pieces of Poland. Likewise Soviet Byelorussia. Independent Lithuania, having received a free gift of Polish Vilna from Moscow, had been annexed by Russia. Stalin wanted no Poles to dispute his claim to these lands. Goebbels' announcement of the discovery at Katyn and the London Poles' reaction to it offered a happy

13. *Ibid.*, pp. 120–121.
14. *Ibid.*, pp. 121–123.
15. *Correspondence*, Vol. II, pp. 60–62.
16. *Documents on Polish-Russian Relations*, Vol. I, pp. 533–534.

opportunity to exclude the Polish government in London from the potentially victorious alliance.

"So far," Churchill telegraphed Stalin on April 30, "this business has been Goebbels' triumph. He is now busy suggesting that the USSR will set up a Polish Government on Russian soil and deal only with them." Churchill knew the score. "We should not, of course," he added, "be able to recognize such a Government and would continue our relations with Sikorski who is far the most helpful man you or we are likely to find."[17] Stalin knew better. He had already found pliable Polish puppets. He needed them; an independent postwar Poland, not bound hand and foot to Moscow, would be an intolerable neighbor disputing Russia's territorial aspirations.

Now everything fell into place. In March the Kremlin launched the Union of Polish Patriots, which waited in the wings ready to serve Russia. In April Moscow broke relations with the government of Poland in London. Stalin, shrewdly anticipating, had encouraged the nationalistic Anders army to leave for Iran. In its stead, on May 9, 1943, the Soviet government sanctioned the formation of the communist-led Tadeusz Kosciuszko Division for Poles remaining in Russia. These moves revealed Stalin's design: he intended to have Poland after the war. Churchill believed that General Sikorski, whom he frequently consulted on military matters, could mend the Polish rift with Moscow. On July 4, 1943, Sikorski was killed in a plane crash at Gibraltar. Accidents play their role in world affairs. But a British Court of Inquiry and later a Polish Commission of Inquiry found no clue to an accident. Some therefore cried "Sabotage." There were those who suspected Stalin, others, incredibly, Churchill, still others the extreme reactionary Poles in England. Nobody adduced any proof.

The Soviet-Polish conflict was more than a bilateral affair. The fate of Poland was central to the future of Europe. In the spring of 1943, in the middle of the war, when the first rays of victory appeared above the horizon, the boards on which stood the Anglo-American-Russian alliance had commenced to creak. But the West, engrossed in battles and fretting lest Russia defect from the triangle, was not listening.

* * *

Under pressure from Churchill and Roosevelt, Sikorski withdrew his request to the International Red Cross to investigate. Only the German Red Cross, not the German government, had invited the Swiss society to Katyn. The Soviet government did not want the International Red Cross

17. *Ibid.,* p. 539.

to come to Smolensk. Without invitations from all governments concerned, the International Red Cross refused to go to the scene of the ghastly murders. Germany in April, 1943, accordingly organized an International Commission consisting of 11 medical scientists from Nazi-occupied and Nazi-allied countries and a Swiss expert. From German-held Poland at the same time came a 12-man Polish Red Cross team. The Soviets, having driven the Wehrmacht out of the Smolensk region in September, 1943, also investigated the mass graves.

The Special Soviet Commission's report, dated Smolensk, January 24, 1944,[18] is signed by its Chairman, Academician Nikolai I. Burdenko; Alexei Tolstoy, a novelist with the title of Academician; Metropolitan Nikolai of the Orthodox Church in Moscow; Lieutenant General Gundorov, Chairman of the All-Slav Committee; Kolesnikov, Chairman of the Executive Committee of the Union of Red Cross and Red Crescent Societies; People's Commissar of Education of the Russian Federation Academician Vladimir P. Potemkin, former ambassador to France and Greece; Colonel General Smirnov, Chief of the Central Medical Administration of the Red Army; and Melnikov, Chairman of the Smolensk Regional Executive Committee. The commission invited five Soviet medicolegal experts "to take part in its work."

The commission begins its analysis by answering why the Polish prisoners of war, who were "building and repairing roads" near Smolensk when the German army approached, were not moved out of harm's way: no railway cars were available. Moreover, the railway line "was already under fire." And it was impossible to get in touch with Moscow for permission to allow the Poles "to set out on foot." To anybody who knows Soviet bureaucracy this sounds plausible; it is just the kind of explanation that would occur to a Russian official. But it leaves a riddle unsolved: what did Stalin hear from the NKVD when he telephoned in the presence of Ambassador Kot for information about the Polish prisoners? He did not tell Kot that the officers had been captured by the Germans. And when Sikorski inquired Stalin said the men had escaped to Manchuria. The first time the Soviets said the prisoners had fallen into German hands was on April 15, 1943, two days after Goebbels' announcement.

Next the Soviet Commission recounts testimony it took from local Soviet inhabitants who saw Polish prisoners in the region, who heard shots at night during the German occupation, and who witnessed German searches for escaped Polish prisoners. One woman schoolteacher said she had harbored a Polish prisoner. Mikhailova, another Soviet woman, described an episode. "From all that took place," her story ended,

18. Published in English in London in the *Soviet War Weekly* of February 3, 1944. Reprinted in full in Zdsislaw Stahl, *The Crime of Katyn, Facts and Documents*, pp. 139–171.

"I concluded that these two Poles had been shot." There is further deduc-
tive and earwitness testimony. No witness saw the shootings.

The minor and major Moscow trials of the 1930's showed that Soviet
citizens, even political figures of high intellectual caliber, will repeat in
open court false tales concocted for them in the secret chambers of the
secret police. Scores of Soviet military and civilian leaders, who had
confessed to heinous political crimes and were executed or sentenced to
long periods in concentration camps during Stalin's reign of lawlessness,
were officially declared innocent after the despot's death. A few survivors
published their memoirs in Russia. The testimony of Soviet witnesses
taken in camera and reproduced in the report of the Soviet Commission
on Katyn must therefore be discarded.

Several witnesses before the Soviet Commission affirmed that "Just
about the beginning of March, 1943" some 500 Red Army prisoners of war
were conveyed to the Katyn graves and assigned the grisly task of disin-
terring the bodies and emptying the pockets of their clothing. "Then the
Germans made the [Russian] prisoners put into the pockets of the Polish
officers some papers which they took from cases or suitcases (I don't
remember exactly) which they had brought along." Subsequently the
Red Army soldiers were shot. One escaped but was captured and "taken
away."

No proof, and all possible witnesses liquidated. The Soviet allegation
would therefore have to be taken on trust.

"The medico-legal examination of the bodies carried out between
January 16 and 23, 1944," reads the Soviet Commission's report, "testifies
that there are absolutely no bodies in a condition of decay or disintegra-
tion. . . . Properties of the soil in the place of discovery were of certain
significance in the preservation of the tissues and organs of the bodies."
This complicated the task of fixing the date of the executions. Nevertheless, the Soviet experts, says the report, assert "that this shooting dates
back two years ago, i.e., between September and December, 1941."

However, the Soviet report contains a strange discrepancy. An appendix gives the dates of the only nine documents found on the Polish bodies:
a letter from Warsaw dated September 12, 1940, rubber-stamped Moscow,
September 28, 1940, and inscribed in Russian "Ascertain and forward for
delivery, November 15, 1940"; a postcard stamped Tarnopol Nov. 12, 1940;
a receipt stamped March 14, 1941; another receipt marked March 25,
1941; a small paper ikon with the image of Christ bearing the date of
April 4, 1941; a receipt for a sum in rubles dated April 6, 1941; another
receipt dated May 5, 1941; a receipt dated May 15, 1941; and an unmailed
postcard in Polish addressed to Irene Kuszinska in Warsaw dated June
20, 1941. After enumerating these finds, there follows a remarkable comment: The Commission "regards the fact of the discovery by the commis-

sion of medico-legal experts, in the clothes of the bodies, of valuables and documents dated 1941, as proof that the German-Fascist authorities who undertook a search of the bodies in the spring-summer season of 1943 did not do it thoroughly. . . ." In other words, they overlooked the nine documents. An intelligent Soviet censor would have deleted this criticism of German efficiency. For the documents need not have disturbed the Germans; they pertain to the time before the Wehrmacht arrived at Katyn. The Germans were not less than thorough. They had no reason to remove the documents. And since the documents relate to the Soviet period and none are dated after it the Poles must have died during the Soviet period before the Germans arrived at Katyn. This emerges from the Soviet Commission's report.

Alexander Werth, then still a Soviet sympathizer, joined other foreign correspondents for the trip from Moscow to Katyn on January 15, 1944, when the Soviet Commission arrived there for its investigation. He cites the testimony of Soviet witnesses and comments, "All this was very thin." The foreign press was admitted to only one session of the inquiry. "The whole procedure," he wrote, "had a distinctly prefabricated appearance. Altogether, the Russian starting-point in this whole inquiry was that the very suggestion that the Russians might have murdered the Poles had to be ruled out right away; the whole idea was insulting and outrageous."[19]

* * *

Moscow was so certain of the rewards of victory and so impregnated with the idea of the indivisible tie between politics and jurisprudence that it wished to include the Katyn murders in the indictment of the major war criminals at the Nuremberg trials.

The cross-examination of witnesses at Nuremberg on the Katyn murders took place on July 1 and most of July 2, 1946.[20] By agreement the Soviet prosecutor called three witnesses, the German attorney three. None of the evidence is impressive or conclusive. One of the witnesses called by the Soviet prosecutor was Marko Antonov Markov, a Bulgarian national and professor at the University of Sofia who participated in the International Commission sponsored by the Nazis. At the Nuremberg trial he withdrew the signed statement he had made as a member of the Commission, contending that he acted under duress because his country was under German occupation. When he appeared in Nuremberg it was under Russian occupation.

19. *Russia at War 1941–1945*, pp. 661–667.
20. International Military Tribunal. *Trial of the Major War Criminals before the International Military Tribunal, Nuremberg, 14 November 1945–1 October 1946.* Vol. XVII: Proceedings 25 June 1946–8 July 1946, pp. 274–371.

The most interesting Soviet witness was Professor Victor I. Prosorovski, chief medical expert of the Ministry of Public Health of the Soviet Union and chairman of the Soviet Medico-Judicial Commission of experts to exhume and examine the Polish corpses. He revealed at Nuremberg that, although his appointment to the commission came at the beginning of January, 1944, Soviet persons had exhumed and examined 925 corpses in September and October, 1943. The tribunal did not ask him why he and other high-level experts and the prominent members of the Special Commission like Alexei Tolstoy, Metropolitan Nikolai, and Education Minister Potemkin, included to lend credibility to the findings, did not reach Katyn until January, 1944, when the corpses had undergone autopsies three and four months earlier. Nor is it comprehensible why it was necessary to examine 925 or more bodies. They were all killed in the same way, by a bullet fired into the nape of the neck which exited through the forehead or remained lodged in the cranium. This is the Soviet method of execution, but the Nazis had also resorted to it. The bullets, fired at point-blank range, were of German manufacture, but lethal weapons and ammunition are notoriously no respecters of national boundaries, and in view of the close relations until 1933 and after August 23, 1939, between the Soviet and German military it would not have been difficult for the NKVD to obtain German-made means of murder. The Poles, at the time of their death, as stated by all investigators and by Nuremberg witnesses, wore winter clothing, some wore fur coats and many long heavy greatcoats. This is not helpful in fixing the month of the crime. The victims might have been asked to line up wearing their winter coats, for the coats were useful in the executions: in a large number of cases the tails of the coats were thrown over the heads of the officers and tied tightly around the neck with a rope which also fastened the hands of the victims behind their backs. If they pulled on the rope to get free they would choke themselves. The ropes were of Russian manufacture; the Germans, however, could have obtained them after they took Smolensk on July 16, 1941. Some officers did apparently struggle, for they were pierced by bayonets, and the bayonets, judging by the perforations, were not the knife kind known in western countries and Germany but fluted and shaped like tapered daggers—the regular Soviet bayonet.

Professor Prosorovski told the tribunal that "most of the pockets were turned out or cut; but some remained intact. In those pockets, and also under the linings of the overcoats and of the trousers we discovered, for instance, notes, pamphlets, papers, closed and open letters and postcards, cigarette paper, cigarette holders, pipes, and so forth, and even valuables were found, such as ingots of gold and gold coins."

The witness was asked about the dates of the papers. Professor Prosorovski gave a number of dates, the latest being June 20, 1941, when the Soviets ruled the Smolensk district. According to the Nazi-sponsored commission the numerous diaries of the Polish officers ended in April or May, 1940, and the last entries often described the trips in those months of the men from their camp in Kozielsk to a railway station near Katyn. No letters from relatives and friends found in the dead men's pockets were dated later than April or May, 1940.

Absent from all Soviet accounts is any reference to the thousands of Polish officers who disappeared without trace from the Soviet prisoner-of-war camps at Starobielsk and Ostakhov. All Soviet commissions, testimony, and reports have dealt only with the unfortunates of Kozielsk who were carried to Katyn at a disputed date. If the date was 1940 or any time before July 16, 1941, the Russians committed the multiple crime, if after the capture of Smolensk on July 16, 1941, the Germans.

Decades after the black event of Katyn it would seem that there is one circumstantial fact and one political consideration which bear on a judgment of who perpetrated the act. The German and Russian investigators agree that no papers or documents found in the Katyn graves are dated later than June 20, 1941 (the Germans put the date at April-May, 1940, the Russians at June 20, 1941), before the Germans had entered the area. This points to the Russians as the criminals.

After the Nuremberg International Military Tribunal, which included Soviet jurists, heard the flimsy evidence on the Katyn murders it decided not to include that atrocity in the final indictment against the Nazi war criminals.

XI CRACKS IN THE TRIANGLE

In public life as in private life the knowledge of what one wants helps in achieving it. During the second world war Churchill and Stalin appear to have had a fairly clear idea of their national war aims. Churchill made no secret of his wish to preserve the British Empire. He aimed to eliminate Germany as a menace to England's security at the lowest possible cost in British lives. Stalin's first purpose was to oust the Nazi invader. Even before the outlook of crushing defeat yielded to the prospect of brilliant victory the Soviet leadership began to think of territorial expansion. This lust for land can be interpreted as arising out of a desire for national security or as an urge to spread the rule of communism. Objectively it was imperialism.

American goals in the second world war are more elusive. The search therefore sometimes becomes slightly frantic and irrational. A central U.S. intention, it has been alleged, was to break up the British Empire and inherit the pieces. This thesis stems from the traditional concept of imperialism as the key to capitalist wealth. It rests on Lenin's fallacious proposition that imperialism represented the fullest flowering of capitalism, that the next phase was the loss of empire, the end of capitalism, and the triumph of socialism. "Imperialism is the eve of the socialist revolution," Lenin wrote on July 6, 1920, in a foreword for the German and French translations of his book, *Imperialism, the Highest Stage of Capitalism.*

Lenin's views on imperialism have been repudiated by history. Japan lost her possessions on the Asiatic mainland after the second world war and has made unprecedented economic progress despite or perhaps because of that loss. West German capitalism is robust without colonies. Holland, poorly endowed, was deprived of Indonesia, a treasure house of natural resources, yet enjoys a much higher standard of living than during her imperial heyday. France is no worse off from losing Algeria or Britain after losing India. The capitalist powers would be paying dearly if today they were sitting on the hot lids of seething colonies.

"The era of imperialism is ended," U.S. Under Secretary of State Sumner Welles, often F.D.R.'s spokesman, said at Arlington Cemetery on May 30, 1942. "The new democracy, by definition, abhors imperialism," Vice-President Henry Wallace declared on November 8, 1942. Wendell Willkie, Roosevelt's Republican opponent, repeatedly spoke against imperialism when he came home from his "One World" trip.

These Americans, a cynic might say, desired the destruction of other people's empires. The fact is that the United States has not converted the fragments of the British, French, Dutch, Belgian, and Italian empires into American political or economic colonies, and the disastrous involvement in South Vietnam in the 1960's could scarcely have been in Roosevelt's mind in 1942 and 1943. In modern times the price in blood, money, and diversion from domestic problems of winning and keeping an empire can never be repaid.

There is no evidence that Franklin D. Roosevelt or the people who had his ear dreamed of territorial or materialistic aggrandizement. The United States had no need of colonies or spheres of influence. Its burgeoning economy and rising military power would be the guarantee of a bright future at home and abroad if peace reigned.

The United States, like the Soviet Union, went to war because it was attacked. Unlike Russia, however, America was openly aiding Britain before the attack. This can be attributed to common heritage and kindred political institutions, but in far larger measure to that hostility toward the domination of Europe by one power which brought the U.S.A. into the first world war. In both world wars the prospect of a German victory triggered American intervention just as the fear of Soviet domination of Europe subsequently persuaded the U.S. to return in strength to the continent.

Once in the war the Roosevelt administration fought the war to win the war. F.D.R. differed from Stalin and Churchill in having no specific war aims. His country needed nothing. Provided no great power won the war so decisively as to shut out American enterprise the dollar would easily find new fields to conquer. Empires are for conservatives mired in a nineteenth-century mentality. The best capitalist profits are earned at home and in other highly developed nations; colonies or former colonies cost money.

To the extent, therefore, that the White House Chief and his advisers contemplated the postwar future they saw it in terms of a secure peace and hence not of a Pax Americana but of a Pax Soviet-Americana; the two superpowers would guard the globe. This suited Stalin. It spelled a recognition, eagerly desired by a historically inferiority-complex ridden Russia, of the Soviet's paramount role in world affairs. But in implementing this high purpose Roosevelt defeated it.

Paradoxically, the immediate goal of Roosevelt's diplomacy had little in common with postbellum collaboration, it aimed first to prevent Russia's military collapse and a Russo-German separate peace. The Soviet-Nazi pact of August 23, 1939, haunted western policy makers. In desperate straits and in different circumstances the Kremlin might do it again.

Under Secretary Sumner Welles said to me on May 18, 1943: "The British feel the chief emphasis should be placed on defeating Hitler [rather than Japan] for three reasons: because the Red Army might not be strong enough to withstand continued Nazi onslaughts, because there might be a Nazi-Soviet separate peace, and because the British are eager to maintain their position rather than assure their domination of the Mediterranean." The United States shared Britain's concern over the first two possibilities and, not having experienced the crippling loss of life and limb suffered by England in the first world war, was willing to open a second front in France in 1942 or 1943. Unable to override Churchill's veto, America accepted the invasion of North Africa as a substitute for a second front in France. This made it all the more necessary to reassure Stalin that the West stood staunchly behind him. Hence Roosevelt's "unconditional surrender" declaration.

In his annual State of the Union address to Congress on January 7, 1943,

Roosevelt spoke in generalities about a peace after victory that would enlarge "the security of man here and throughout the world" and guarantee "Freedom from Fear." Four days later he took off from Miami for Casablanca. The Roosevelt-Churchill conference in the Moroccan town discussed military problems and, together with their chiefs of staff, drew up a list of priorities: security of communications across the Atlantic by the introduction of more escort vessels for merchant ships; second, assistance to Russia; then the invasion of Sicily; an attack across the English Channel to the Channel Islands and Cherbourg; finally, offensive action in the Pacific.[1]

There followed the customary briefing of the press at which Roosevelt uttered his famous "Unconditional Surrender." Subsequently the President explained that "Winston and I had had no time to prepare for [the press conference] and the thought popped into my mind that they had called [General Ulysses S.] Grant 'Old Unconditional Surrender' and the next thing I knew, I had said it."[2]

Franklin D. Roosevelt loved giving himself a casual and extemporaneous air. But Harry Hopkins, who was present, wrote in his description of the news conference that the President spoke from notes, and he quotes those notes: ". . . peace can come to the world only by a total elimination of German and Japanese war power. This involves the simple formula of placing the objective of this war in terms of an unconditional surrender by Germany, Italy, and Japan. Unconditional surrender by them means a reasonable assurance of world peace."[3]

Elliott Roosevelt, who was with his father in Casablanca, has a diary entry in his book *As He Saw It* for Saturday, January 23, reading: "At lunch that afternoon, there were just Harry [Hopkins], the P.M., Father, and I. And it was at that lunch table that the phrase 'unconditional surrender' was born." Hopkins liked it immediately and Churchill, after some moments, exclaimed, "Perfect! And I can just see how Goebbels and the rest of 'em 'll squeal!" The son then quotes Father as saying, "Of course, it's just the thing for the Russians. They couldn't want anything better. Uncle Joe might have made it up himself."

So the two controversial words did not "pop into" Roosevelt's mind. They were not directed at Germany, Italy, and Japan. With imperfect information about conditions and morale in those countries it would have been folly to tell liberals, radicals, and disaffected generals and diplomats that not even the overthrow of their totalitarian masters and militarists could shorten the war and give them decent conditions of

1. Robert F. Sherwood, *Roosevelt and Hopkins, An Intimate History*, pp. 690–691.
2. *Ibid.*, p. 696.
3. *Ibid.*, pp. 696–697.

peace; the three aggressor states would have to submit unconditionally to the mercies of the victors. Faced with this prospect of the unknown and the likelihood of loss of territory and the imposition of reparations the people might rally around the dictators and fight after all hope of victory had vanished. Statesmen do make egregious errors, and it is conceivable that "unconditional surrender" was one, but Roosevelt can be absolved of the intention of deliberately prolonging hostilities. The two words were addressed to Stalin. The western powers, the President was saying, will never make a separate peace, they will go on until they force the enemy to surrender unconditionally; you need not fear Anglo-American defection from the triple coalition, and we expect the same of you.

But as Roosevelt reached Washington from Casablanca, Field Marshal von Paulus and his hungry, sleepless, frozen army, counting approximately 100,000 casualties, surrendered at Stalingrad. Stalin was not the man to sign a separate peace with Hitler when he felt hopeful of victory and its spoils. In the month after the Russians' return to the rubbled Volga city, Moscow organized the Union of Polish Patriots. The break with the Polish government in London was a further indication of Stalin's imperial design. It came into sharper focus in the light of the treatment accorded Paulus and his followers which bore no resemblance to the spirit of unconditional surrender. The Bolshevik reputation for terror gave the Germans no reason to await the fury of the battle, no title to expect a fate sweeter than death in Russian captivity. And in fact large numbers of the 70,000 German prisoners taken at Stalingrad died from exhaustion and wounds en route to prisoner-of-war camps. But what was the astonishment of Paulus and his generals when a special train carried several hundred officers with speed and in comfort to the environs of Moscow. Paulus became the guest of the government in a well-appointed suburban dacha with servants. Likewise a number of his staff and commanders. Some 2,000 officers of lesser rank were accommodated in locations where they could engage in sports, borrow books from libraries, and receive health rehabilitation care. All officer-prisoners were exempt from labor.

This was courtship rather than kindness.

The script for the courtship was written by Stalin. On November 6, 1942, at the traditional eve-of-the-anniversary meeting, he laid down two conditions for Germany after defeat. "We have no such aim as to destroy Germany," he said, "for it is impossible to destroy Germany, just as it is impossible to destroy Russia. But the Hitlerite State can and must be destroyed." Moreover, "It is not our aim to destroy all organized military force in Germany, for every literate person will understand that this is not only impossible in regard to Germany, as it is in regard to Russia, but it is also inexpedient from the point of view of the victor."

These were statesmanlike terms for the conditional surrender of Germany designed to appeal to German patriots and, above all, to the German military. The hope was to shorten the war by fostering defeatism within the Wehrmacht.

The first targets of the courtship were those in hand: the prisoners from Stalingrad. The train that carried Paulus and his colleagues out of the ruined city is slightly reminiscent of the train Ludendorff gave Lenin and his comrades to travel through Germany to sow dissension in Russia. There was some similarity between the situations. Not only did the Germans suffer from the physical shock of battle in the hellhole of hunger, frost, and fear of death, they resented having been kept in the Stalingrad inferno on orders from Hitler, who failed in his efforts to relieve them. What was probably worse, their eyes were opened for the first time since September 1, 1939, and instead of certain triumph they saw the specter of dismal defeat. Into this fertile mental field marched German communist intellectuals armed with Stalin's conditional surrender directive. Here was a possibility of saving oneself and saving one's country.

Friedrich Wolf, the playwright, Johannes R. Becher, the poet, and Alfred Kurella, an official, led the phalanx of propagandists who addressed mass meetings of prisoners in the communist phraseology acquired at party cells and schools before they fled from Hitler to Moscow: class struggle; historical materialism; world revolution; dictatorship of the proletariat. Anti-Nazi resolutions passed unanimously. But most of the captive auditors had been impregnated at home with the horror and terror of communism. Though they raised their hands their hearts did not respond to Marxist clichés. The "National Committee for a Free Germany," inaugurated at the end of June, 1943, was heavily weighted with veteran German communist émigrés long resident in the Soviet Union: Walter Ulbricht, Wilhelm Pieck, Erich Weinert, Johannes Becher, Hans Mahle, two private soldiers, and, for reality, Lieutenant Bernt von Kuegelgen and Captain Dr. Ernst Haldermann. These were not names to charm generals from Stalingrad, much less top Wehrmacht officers still fighting on the fronts of Europe and Africa.

The Kremlin now introduced the drug of nationalism. In July Dmitry Z. Manuilsky, until its dissolution in May the power behind Georgi Dimitrov in the Comintern, told a Moscow assembly of chosen prisoners that it was Stalin's wish to see a strong committee. The émigré communists present proposed the black-red-gold flag of the Weimar Republic of Germany as the committee's emblem. Manuilsky rejected it in favor of the black-white-red banner of the Kaiser monarchy.[4] This revealed a policy. In the 1920's and early 1930's a constant struggle, often taking the form

4. Bodo Scheurig, *Freies Deutschland, Das Nationalkomitee und der Bund Deutscher Offiziere in der Sowjetunion 1943–1945*, p. 42.

of mass pitched battles, had raged in Germany between reactionary groups, Stahlhelm war veterans, and embryo Nazis carrying the black-white-red colors of the past and socialists and democrats bearing the black-red-gold symbol of the republic. Moscow knew whom it was courting. It preferred the black-white-red. Manuilsky was consistent; he ordered the émigré communists to abandon communist clichés and exalt German nationalism. Under his instructions the committee leaders drew up an appeal early in August, 1943, taking note of Russian military victories on a broad front during the current summer "and what then will the winter bring?" It alluded to the fall of Mussolini and the impending collapse of Germany's other allies. "Hitler is played out as a statesman and military leader." The continuation of the war therefore means "suicide for the German nation and the Wehrmacht. . . . Put an end to the war," it urged.

The appeal was signed by Erich Weinert, a German communist poet and former member of the International Brigade in Spain, now chairman of the National Committee for a Free Germany, and by two vice-chairmen: Major Karl Hetz and Count Heinrich von Einsiedel, a great-grandson of Prince Otto von Bismarck, who had sponsored a German pro-Russian policy. The collaboration of Einsiedel was a propaganda coup, but the young Luftwaffe lieutenant meant little to the prisoner-generals and their staff officers. The preponderance of communists on the committee repelled the commanders.

Never easily daunted in choosing alternative routes to its goals, the Kremlin moved quickly to organize a second body: the Union of German Officers in the Soviet Union. Its September, 1943, proclamation to the "German generals and officers, the nation and the Wehrmacht" signed by its president, General of Artillery Walther von Seydlitz, four other generals, and several hundred colonels, majors, captains, and lieutenants, called for the "immediate resignation of Hitler and his government" in order to save Germany from "chaos and collapse."[5]

Soon the National Committee and the Union were collaborating and issuing statements together. Paulus, however, remained aloof. He did not put his name to an appeal until December 8, 1944, when fifty generals, all captured by the Red Army, signed their names and ranks below his. It attacked Hitler, said "The war is lost," and declared "There is no miracle that can still help" the German people.

Hitler was not listening. The German people were powerless, the men of July 20, 1944, clumsy, inhibited, unaccustomed to the role of conspirators. Yet they did lift themselves above mindless discipline and belatedly learned to distinguish between government and nation.

5. *Ibid.*, pp. 232–233.

All Stalin's efforts to shorten the war by subverting the German army came to naught. There is no demonstrable evidence that the Union of German Officers changed anything except their living conditions in Russian captivity. Nevertheless, the fact that Moscow made the effort throws light on Soviet foreign policy then and subsequently. The Kremlin recruited members of the reactionary class of Prussian Junkers and militarists. Germans were not repulsive, not even Germans known for their evil deeds against Russians. Neither Stalin nor his agents gave any indication that the Soviets intended to partition Germany, disarm her, or convert her to communism. "Communism fits Germany as a saddle fits a cow," Stalin said to Mikolajczyk in August, 1943.

Although Stalin on November 6, 1942, had enunciated a wise policy of conditional surrender for Germany, Roosevelt did not hesitate to announce his policy of unconditional surrender in which Churchill reluctantly acquiesced. Conscious that he was deviating from western views, Stalin persisted in courting German generals; he hoped to gain an advantageous position in postwar Germany to the detriment of the U.S.A. and Great Britain.

Simultaneously, Roosevelt courted Stalin on the assumption that Russia would be a superpower after hostilities ceased while Britain's strength would wane. For many reasons Roosevelt wished to meet Stalin. One reason never mentioned was sheer curiosity. Moreover, the rupture of Soviet-Polish relations after the discovery in the Katyn Forest had caused some friction between Washington and Moscow. The delay in opening a second front in France troubled Stalin. Roosevelt, as he wrote Stalin on May 5, 1943, believed Russia's military successes might "cause a crack-up in Germany next winter. In such a case we must be prepared for the many next steps. We are none of us prepared." (Stalin had prepared by attempting to recruit German officer-prisoners.) "Therefore," Roosevelt continued, "it is my belief that you and I ought to meet this summer."

The question was when and where. Africa would be too hot in summer "and Khartoum is British territory." The President did not like the idea of meeting in Iceland "because for you and me it involves rather difficult flights and, in addition, would make it, quite frankly, difficult not to invite Prime Minister Churchill at the same time." The President accordingly suggested a tryst "either on your side or my side of the Bering Straits."[6]

Despite the shared Anglo-Saxon heritage, the tie of language and culture, the personal tie between Churchill and Roosevelt, the gulf between dictatorship and democracy, the conflict between communism and capitalism, Roosevelt wished to exclude Great Britain and limit the discus-

6. *Correspondence,* Vol. II, pp. 63–64.

sion of the future to representatives of the two superpowers. The proposal was dropped because Stalin would not travel so far from Moscow. But it exposed another crack in the Anglo-Soviet-American coalition and not on class or ideological lines. That triangle was born cracked and it grew cracks as it aged.

A steady stream of secret messages flowed from Roosevelt to Stalin, from Churchill to Stalin, and from Stalin to Roosevelt and Churchill. Marshal Stalin congratulated Roosevelt on the victory "which has resulted in the liberation of Bizerta and Tunis from Hitler tyranny," and Roosevelt thanked Stalin for the message. The President and Prime Minister congratulated Stalin on Russian victories and he telegraphed his thanks. Churchill went to Washington in May, 1943, and Stalin was informed. But when Roosevelt on June 4 wired Stalin the results of those Washington talks the Marshal could not contain his anger. First the western allies had promised to prepare for a second front in France in 1942, he telegraphed Roosevelt on June 11. Later they deferred it to 1943. "Now, in May, 1943, you and Mr. Churchill have decided to postpone the Anglo-American invasion of Western Europe until the spring of 1944. . . . Your decision creates exceptional difficulties for the Soviet Union . . . and leaves the Soviet Army, which is fighting not only for its country, but also for its Allies, to do the job alone, almost single-handedly, against an enemy that is still very strong and formidable. . . .

". . . the Soviet Government . . . cannot align itself with this decision, which, moreover, was adopted without its participation and without any attempt at a joint discussion."[7]

This was more than a crack, it was a crevice with a creaking bridge of telegrams across it. The western Allies felt that their military default created a political debt. The stage was set for a summit conference.

XII SWEET AND SOUR IN MOSCOW

If Stalin had expected Germany to collapse in 1943 he would not have pressed Britain and America so hard to build a second front in northern France, he would have preferred to see Germany occupied by the Red Army only. But he knew that the Nazi armed forces in Russia were still powerful, that Soviet victories, however impressive, were being bought

7. *Ibid.*, pp. 70–71.

at the expense of millions of Soviet casualties, and he did not wish to reach the end of the war with the U.S.S.R. exhausted and the U.S. and Britain fresh and potent.

Roosevelt, thinking or wistfully hoping that Germany might collapse in the 1943–44 winter, suggested meeting Stalin in Alaska or Siberia. It would have been better if their armies met in the middle of Germany. The President and Army Chief of Staff General George C. Marshall, as well as others in authority in Washington, therefore argued the wisdom of a second front in western Europe in 1943. This would have had the added advantage, as Secretary of War Henry L. Stimson explained, of putting a large American army in Britain to defend the islands in case Russia collapsed or capitulated and Hitler attacked England. But the United States was unprepared and Churchill unwilling. Lord Louis Mountbatten, British Chief of Combined Operations, a Royal Navy man, told Harry Hopkins at Casablanca "that crossing the Channel was a hell of an enterprise. The Germans [in France] have armed to the teeth."

What might Roosevelt have said to Stalin in Alaska? Explain why the second front in Europe had been put off? That would not bind Russia's wounds or assuage Stalin's wrath. The President's purpose could only have been to cement the bond between the two superpowers and plan postwar collaboration, especially economic aid for Soviet reconstruction.

The shape of the peace interested Stalin enormously, but tomorrow was a relentless master. The war consumed ravenously and destroyed pitilessly. Stalin made ever-growing demands on the West. Roosevelt offered bombers and crews for the defense of the Caucasus. Stalin asked for "aircraft, especially fighters, but without crews, whom you now need badly." The President promised hundreds of planes, some to be ferried from Alaska to Siberia. In view of a possible Japanese attack on the Soviet Far East, Roosevelt proposed sending Air Corps General Follett Bradley with a small staff to study the situation. Stalin replied: "I was rather surprised at your proposal that General Bradley should inspect Russian military objectives in the Far East and elsewhere in the U.S.S.R. It should be perfectly obvious that only Russians can inspect Russian military objectives, just as U.S. military objectives can be inspected by none but Americans. There should be no unclarity in this matter." In the same telegram Stalin wondered why F.D.R. wanted to send General Marshall to Russia: "I must say I am not quite clear about his mission."[1] There was no mission.

To exalt the West's contribution, Roosevelt, in a May 20, 1943, telegram to Stalin listed German and Italian losses in the fighting in North Africa from December 8, 1940, to May 12, 1943: personnel, 625,000; planes, 7,596

1. *Correspondence,* Vol. II, p. 50.

destroyed, 1,748 probably destroyed; tanks, not less than 2,100 disabled; ships sunk, 625 totaling approximately 2,200,000 tons.[2]

Stalin did not respond. But several days later he telegraphed that he was waiting for the second front in Europe. Roosevelt, on June 16, 1943, informed Stalin he had given instructions for 78 B-25 bombers and 600 P-40 N fighters to be dispatched to Russia during the remainder of 1943. Stalin on June 24 wired Roosevelt and Churchill at great length complaining about the absence of a second front in western Europe.[3]

The second front was a deeply felt Soviet need; it was also Stalin's alibi: but for the delinquent West, Russia would suffer less. The anguish over the millions of dead, crippled, and blind that would otherwise have assailed the Kremlin was turned against the Americans and British. Stalin's genius for blackmail matched his talent for brutality. The more he complained about the absence of a second front the greater the western inclination to placate him. The second-front campaign gave Roosevelt and Churchill a guilty conscience and softened them up for political concessions.

Stalin had risen to the pinnacle of power by first dividing his enemies. The invitation to the Bering Straits—to elude Churchill—must have aroused all his wild combative instincts. That Roosevelt did not understand this is astonishing. That none of his advisers was given the opportunity to warn him is tragic. The President had a deserved reputation for understanding the psychology of the American people. He misread Stalin's.

The descent to the Tehran summit had commenced.

Political differences did exist between Britain and America, and they affected military strategy. The U.S. was interested in the quick defeat of Germany so it could knock out Japan with Russian help. But the smashing of Germany would create a power vacuum in eastern and central Europe accessible to Russia. To cope with this contingency and keep open the road to empire the British wanted victory over the Axis army in North Africa, thereby reinforcing their grip on Egypt and preventing a junction between Germany and Japan somewhere in India. This achieved, the plan was to leap across the Mediterranean, break Italy off from the Axis, and press into the Balkans. The proximity of an Anglo-American force and the fear of an expanding Russia would presumably pull Turkey into the war on the side of the Anglo-Soviet-American coalition with a view to blocking Russia's domination of the Balkan Peninsula.

During his wartime travels Churchill stopped in Turkey and tried to persuade the Turkish leaders to come off their neutral perch. But before

2. *Ibid.*, p. 65.
3. *Ibid.*, pp. 74–76.

Mussolini fell and before a British army invaded eastern Europe this was too much of a gamble for the Turks, who had suffered heavily in the Balkan wars and the first world war and had lost an empire and the taste for another.

All these subtle schemes would be frustrated by a cross-Channel invasion of France requiring every ounce of British military force. The United States, on the other hand, had no feel for Balkan politics, regarded North Africa as a sideshow, and believed in doing big things in a big way first, and the big thing was to strike at Nazi Europe by fording the English Channel.

Stimson and Marshall had bowed to the Presidential-Prime Ministerial decision to fight in North Africa, but their hearts were in northern France. Roosevelt accordingly let Stimson go to London for an eye-to-eye debate on strategy. It was mid-July, 1943; the western Allies had landed in Sicily on July 10. "I told [Churchill]," Stimson reported to F.D.R. several weeks later, "that the American people did not hate the Italians but took them rather as a joke as fighters; that only by an intellectual effort had they been convinced that Germany was their most dangerous enemy and should be disposed of before Japan; that the enemy whom the American people really hated, if they hated anyone, was Japan which had dealt them a foul blow. . . . I asserted that . . . if we allow ourselves to become so entangled with matters of the Balkans, Greece, and the Middle East that we could not fulfill our purpose of Roundhammer [the cross-Channel effort, subsequently dubbed Overlord] in 1944, that situation would be a serious blow to the prestige of the President's war policy and therefore to the interests of the United States."

Stimson did not give a detailed report on Churchill's answer but wrote: "Towards the end he confined his position to favoring a march on Rome with its prestige and the possibility of knocking Italy out of the war. Eden on the other hand continued to contend for carrying the war into the Balkans and Greece."[4]

There were thus two wars, a war within a war, the war of the United States, Great Britain, the Soviet Union, and their small allies against Germany, Italy, and Japan and their allies, a war of fire, hunger, and death, and another war, a preview of the postwar, a war for land, power, and influence. For the Soviets it began on August 23, 1939; for England, centuries ago, when the island stretched out its arms across the seas; for America it was soon to begin.

International politics moved along battle lines. The Germans launched a heavy offensive in central Russia on July 5, 1943. The Red Army quickly turned this into its own counteroffensive, and on August 5 captured Orel

4. Henry L. Stimson and McGeorge Bundy, *On Active Service in Peace and War,* pp. 429–430.

and Byelgorod. On August 23 Kharkov was liberated from the Nazis. In celebration Moscow shook from 20 salvos fired by 224 guns. On August 30 Taganrog was retaken. By September 8 the Donets coal basin was cleansed of Wehrmacht invaders. Again 20 salvos by 224 guns in the Soviet capital. The successful Soviet offensive continued throughout September. With every victory Moscow trembled from its own joyous artillery.

Hitler withdrew from Russia one of Guderian's best Panzer divisions to guard Greece against invasion. Guderian seethed with helpless anger. The Royal Air Force continued to bomb German cities and industrial sites. Yet German arms output grew in 1943, and at Peenemuende on the Baltic preparations were being made to produce pilotless, long-range, jet-propelled rockets for the destruction of London and other great British urban complexes. "In the summer of 1943 there was still only one American field division in the United Kingdom, with about 150,000 ground, base and air personnel. But in the spring of 1944 it was expected that at least a million American troops would be based there, including fifteen fighting divisions."[5] Until they arrived Britain concentrated on Italy and the Balkans.

Mussolini had taken Italy into the world war when he thought the fall of France meant the war was over. He miscalculated. Since his country was in no condition to fight (and now with the landing in Sicily it would have to fight), the Grand Council of the Fascist Party voted against him on July 24, 1943, and the next day King Victor Emmanuel dismissed him and appointed Marshal Pietro Badoglio to head a new nonfascist government. Mussolini was arrested as he left the King. To deceive Germany Badoglio stated that Italy remained in the war, but on August 15 he opened secret negotiations with the West; September 8 Italy signed the terms of surrender. Hitler was in the Ukraine wrestling with the problem of the Red Army's successes.

The western assault on the Balkans depended on the capture of Rome and at least the lower half of the Italian peninsula. But the Anglo-Americans, short of landing craft and deficient in daring, came ashore at Salerno, south of Naples. Hitler, defiant, rescued Mussolini from captivity by a spectacular commando raid, sent reinforcements into northern Italy, and put Rommel in charge of resistance to Allied progress up the boot. Rommel held for months. Rome was not taken until June, 1944. By that time the western powers were ready and eager to move into the continent. For the Russians were coming. On September 25 they captured Smolensk and moved on toward Poland. On November 6 they recaptured

5. Arthur Bryant, *The Turn of the Tide, A History of the War Years Based on the Diaries of Field-Marshal Lord Alanbrooke, Chief of the Imperial General Staff*, pp. 532–539.

Kiev, capital of the Ukraine. They, not the Anglo-Americans, were advancing toward the Balkans. This reduced the probability of Turkey going to war. The Turks had no heart to tangle with Russia, no stomach for casualties; no appetite for foreign territory, no faith in western military strategy; they remembered the futile first world war.

Turkey was a central item on the agenda when Secretary of State Cordell Hull, Foreign Secretary Anthony Eden, and Foreign Commissar Vyacheslav Molotov convened in Moscow on October 19. A split emerged. To Hull from Tennessee the Balkans were on the moon. Roosevelt, Stimson, Marshall, and all the American military saw that the entry of Turkey into the war might mean a diversion from the landing in northern France. Britain and Russia, however, wanted Turkey to join the fight. Britain's case is clear: she needed Turkish air and naval bases for the protection of Greece and the Middle East, and eventually for establishing a sphere of influence in southeastern Europe. Soviet motives are equally transparent. Turkey's adherence to the alliance would, to be sure, give her greater immunity to the kind of claims Russia made on her territory and sovereignty in 1939 and repeated after the war. On the other hand, Germany's strength remained immense; Hitler might, with brutal pressure, bring Turkey into his camp against Russia, giving the Luftwaffe an easy platform from which to bomb the Caucasus oil fields.

These considerations built a bridge carrying two-way political traffic: (1) British anti-Russian interests in the Balkans and the Middle East; (2) Russia's desire to acquire an ally and deny an ally to Hitler. Molotov and Eden accordingly signed a protocol in Moscow on November 2, 1943: "The two Foreign Secretaries agree that it should be suggested to Turkey on behalf of the United Kingdom and the Soviet Government ... that she enter the war before the end of 1943 ..."[6] But when Eden met the Turkish Foreign Minister in Cairo on November 4 he received Turkey's refusal. Fearing Germany today, the Turks preferred to preserve their neutrality. Fearing Russia tomorrow, they wished to conserve their strength.

Cordell Hull demonstratively dissociated himself from the Eden-Molotov effort to draw Turkey into the war. Not that he scorned Turkey's military prowess or was less eager for victory; he saw Britain and Russia maneuvering for dominion. Hull was another Woodrow Wilson, except that Wilson envisaged the League of Nations as a sparkling penthouse above a stinking slum tenement of annexations and empires (the Versailles treaty), whereas Hull thought his Four-Power Declaration, adopted by the Moscow Conference, would launch a United Nations organization capable of eliminating nationalistic rivalries and imperialistic contests. To a joint session of Congress on November 18, 1943, soon after

6. J. R. M. Butler (Ed.), *History of the Second World War. Grand Strategy.* Vol. V, John Ehrman, *August 1943–September 1944,* p. 101.

his return from Moscow, he said that when the Declaration was put into effect there would be no further need for "spheres of influence, for alliances, for balance of power or any other of the special arrangements through which, in the unhappy past, the nations strove to safeguard their security or to promote their interests."[7] Alas, poor Hull! The UN did none of these things.

Hull won a losing battle. He had to fight for his Declaration before he left Washington. "During the spring of 1943 I found there was a basic cleavage between him [Roosevelt] and me on the very nature of the postwar organization. The President favored a four-power establishment that would police the world with the forces of the United States, Britain, Russia, and China. All other nations, including France, were to be disarmed. . . . At that time," Hull writes in his memoirs, the President "did not want an over-all world organization." Churchill also opposed it; he believed in regional organizations. "Only vapid and academic discussions," Hull paraphrased the Prime Minister as saying, "would result from calling in countries remote from a dispute." Unfortunately, United Nations experience has justified this view if not the political philosophy that lay behind it.

Hull persuaded Roosevelt and Churchill to acquiesce in his Four-Power Declaration and carried it to Moscow. But such men do not change basic beliefs on major matters because someone presents a counterargument. They obviously wrote off Hull's beloved declaration as mere words. Eden gave it one two-line sentence in his nine-page account of the conference.[8]

Hull's draft declaration brought from Washington was eviscerated in Moscow. Eden and Molotov accepted his proposition regarding postwar consultation but not mandatory agreement and common action. Hull's original text would have required the victorious nations to consult and agree after the war before "employing their military forces within the territories of other states." The words "and agree" were deleted. Consultation costs nothing and its results can be ignored. Eden attempted to add a clause to Hull's text forbidding the great powers from concluding treaties with small countries during the war except by consent. Molotov objected. The objection held.[9]

The debate on the declaration showed that the U.S., the U.K., and the U.S.S.R. would keep in touch and talk, but would go their separate ways when it appeared profitable. Result: the Soviet Union alone occupied East European countries and the United States excluded the Soviet Union from the occupation of Japan. The postwar world, the outlines of which

7. *The Memoirs of Cordell Hull,* Vol. II, pp. 1647–1648.
8. *The Memoirs of Anthony Eden, Earl of Avon. The Reckoning,* pp. 476–485.
9. Details of the amendment of the declaration in Herbert Feis, *Churchill * Roosevelt * Stalin: The War They Waged and the Peace They Sought,* pp. 207–210.

were first sketched on August 23, 1939, began to take concrete form in 1943. The more the powers conferred the clearer grew the differences between them.

But it was easy to create the opposite impression. At the gala dinner on October 30 marking the conclusion of the Moscow Conference Hull sat at Stalin's right. Stalin "astonished and delighted me," Hull writes, "by saying clearly and unequivocally that, when the Allies succeeded in defeating Germany, the Soviet Union would then join in defeating Japan. Stalin had brought up this subject entirely on his own. . . . He finished by saying that I could inform President Roosevelt of this in the strictest confidence. I thanked him heartily."[10]

Stalin's promise showed him as a friend and good ally; Russia's participation would reduce American casualties in the war against Japan. Subsequently, at Yalta, he presented a bill in advance of action: the Soviets demanded payment in the form of territory and bases. This did not conform with Hull's idealistic vision nor did it conduce to peace in the Far East or Soviet-American amity or global tranquillity. The blood the nations were shedding so copiously was drawn by the dragons' teeth sowed by the punitive, annexationist peace after the first world war. Yet the statesmen could not forbear, in the midst of the second conflict, from treating the coming peace in terms of power and influence over other peoples, of territory annexed and territory occupied, and of rivalry among themselves for these illusory benefits. Hull had, with the President's approval, carried a second declaration to Moscow "dealing," as he stated in his memoirs, "with dependent peoples—the inhabitants of colonies and mandates—and proclaiming the necessity to lead them gradually to a condition of independence." A rather tepid affirmation of anti-imperialist intent. Eden refused to discuss it. Politely, "Molotov said he felt the question of dependent peoples should receive further study and that his Government attached great importance to it."[11] England hoped to retain an empire, Russia to acquire one.

At the conference Molotov preferred a Three-Power Declaration; China was not a great power. During a recess for tea when, as Hull noted, wine and "an infinite variety of delicacies" were served in the garden of the Spiridonovka villa where Litvinov had lived in rooms above the garage, Hull intimated that the exclusion of China "might call for all sorts of readjustments by my Government to keep the political and military situation in the Pacific properly stabilized." A hint that America might give to China the supplies going to Russia. Eden supported Hull for the sake of good relations with Washington although Churchill had ridiculed the idea of China as a great power. Molotov yielded. China's signing or not signing was not worth a quarrel.

10. Hull, p. 1309.
11. *Ibid.,* pp. 1304–1305.

Hull's uncomplicated mind regarded a Foreign Ministers' conference as a place to discuss foreign policy. To the Soviets, however, the war was the primary fact of foreign affairs. They therefore put the second front in northern France at the top of the agenda. Molotov asked whether the western allies would land in northern France on May 1, 1944, as planned. General Sir Hastings Lionel Ismay, for Britain, and General John R. Deane, head of the American Military Mission in Moscow, for the U.S., answered in the affirmative subject, however, to two conditions: that on the day of the landing the German reserves in France and the Low Countries did not exceed 12 first-class divisions, and that there be a substantial reduction in the number of fighter planes in and near the area of combat. Eden gave the same reply to Stalin in a personal interview. When Stalin asked whether this meant a postponement of the attack and for how long, "a month or two?" Eden quoted Churchill: there was "no use planning for defeat in the field in order to give temporary political satisfaction"—in order, in other words, to mollify Moscow.

The three Foreign Ministers also discussed Germany and made tentative plans for her postwar administration. They agreed that the Reich be deprived of East Prussia. For Molotov this was probably the richest fruit he picked at the conference; not only did he see East Prussia going to Russia or to Russian-dominated Poland, he rejoiced in the acceptance, in principle, of further territorial "adjustments." For Hull Stalin's promise to fight Japan was the bacon he brought home to the White House. Eden sounded out Molotov on the resumption of Moscow's relations with the Polish government-in-exile in London and received a curt rebuff. But he had saved the British Empire from Russo-American meddling. Each statesman carried away a trophy from the Moscow Conference. This is how all international conferences should end: with a small sweet to kill the sour taste.

XIII THE BIG THREE

Franklin Delano Roosevelt was born to social status and wealth. He worked hard in political office but never had to work for a living. His assets—a handsome figure, a fine face, a smile that charmed, a mellifluous voice—came into the world with him and he cultivated them without effort. He attended the best schools, Groton and Harvard, and distinguished himself at neither. At the age of 23 he married Anna Eleanor

Roosevelt, a relative of President Theodore Roosevelt who gave away the bride at the wedding ceremony. She was in many respects greater than he and became a tower of strength to him. With all these advantages he did not shine as an elected member of the New York State Senate or as Assistant Secretary of the Navy. In 1920 the Democratic Party, expecting the defeat it got, nominated F.D.R. for vice-president. In August of the next year he was stricken with polio. Thereafter he never walked, and stood only when propped up. He had to be carried into bed, out of bed, to his desk, to meals, away from meals, into a train, into and out of an airplane. Swimming, his only exercise, helped him develop powerful arm and chest muscles and kept him in excellent health. Considering the length of American election campaigns and the amount of travel, political maneuvering, speechmaking, and baby kissing a campaign entails, it is indeed miraculous that this crippled person was twice elected governor of New York and, unprecedented in U.S. history, four times to the Presidency of the United States.

A man climbing the slope changes when he achieves the summit. It was only when Franklin Roosevelt became President that he emerged as a more than ordinary personality. In domestic affairs he fathered so many reforms that enemies accused him of introducing "creeping socialism" although they could not have known what socialism was because neither Marx nor Engels nor Lenin nor any of their followers had ever defined or described it. What Roosevelt did was to use the power and resources of the federal government to save capitalism from creeping decay. He injected into private capitalism a limited therapeutic measure of state capitalism, and it is by this mixture of free enterprise and state regulation and aid that all advanced capitalist systems now function. Roosevelt was a reformist, never a radical or revolutionary, unless revolution means rapid evolution in crisis. He did not rebuild. He patched the ripped sail and leaking hull when not to do so would have brought disaster.

In foreign affairs Roosevelt groped for a policy with a finger on the pulse of the public as his guide. The majority of the country's politicians and probably the majority of its citizens were isolationist and noninterventionist because, with few ignoble exceptions which modify the generalization, abstention from foreign entanglements was in the American tradition and proved beneficial to America's well-being. Thus hobbled the President did nothing to rescue the Spanish Republic from Franco or Austria from Hitler or Czechoslovakia from surgery at Munich. He made one attempt to preach the wisdom of preventive diplomacy; rebuffed, he relapsed into quiescence.

As the second world war loomed, Roosevelt conceived the idea of summoning Prime Minister Chamberlain, Premier Daladier, Hitler, Mussolini, Stalin to a save-the-peace conference. He believed that big men at the helm of big nations alter history. They often do, but Munich was a bad sample of their work. When two or three or more national leaders convene, the question is not whether they will make history, the real question is who will make history by prevailing and who by ceding. Statesmen in council or alone are not immune to the follies and blunders of ordinary mortals. The proposition that government leaders make history is subject to the amendment that most of modern history is a record of the mistakes of governments. But Roosevelt, having won so many towering successes despite his physical handicap, gained boundless confidence in himself and in his chances, at the Tehran Conference, of avoiding the pitfalls of postwar politics by charming Stalin into friendly collaboration. The intention was commendable.

Winston S. Churchill, seven years older than Roosevelt, was, like Roosevelt, born into a rich family. His grandfather was the Seventh Duke of Marlborough. All his life Churchill adored monarchs and not only wrote in high praise of King Alfonso XIII of Spain but had some charitable words for the ex-Kaiser, Wilhelm II, whom he regarded as "a very ordinary, vain, but on the whole well-meaning man."[1] His abiding hostility to Bolsheviks had several roots, one that they were regicides. Unlike David Lloyd George, he did not hate the church, army, and landlords; whether Liberal or Conservative Churchill held conservative views and glorified the army and navy. Lloyd George excelled Churchill in extemporaneous Parliamentary debate and in oratorical fire, but few could equal Churchill the political writer or the orator-author of his own exquisitely chiseled speeches. Even in a personal interview classic English sentences dropped from his lips as abundantly as the cigar ashes that fell to the waistcoat. He was the British lion and the English bulldog, the eager fighter with words and steel, the lover of royal pomp and global empire, the craver of action who wrote the history he made.

While England slept under Baldwin and Chamberlain, Churchill sought to awaken her to the menace of Hitler's mounting aggressiveness and Germany's rising power. The motive was not antifascism, for he hoped to bring Mussolini into the anti-German camp. He early advocated a triple alliance of Britain, France, and the Soviet Union to check Nazi expansion, and urged his country to rearm to meet new dangers. Because he disturbed Britain's peaceful dreams he was kept from the leadership until war came, when he was appointed First Lord of the Admiralty; the fall of Belgium and Holland lifted him into No. 10, Downing Street. His ambition now was to sustain Britain, bring America to Britain's side, and induce Russia to change sides.

1. Winston S. Churchill, *Great Contemporaries.*

Joseph V. Stalin enjoyed none of Churchill's or Roosevelt's advantages. Both his parents were born serfs; after the liberation of the serfs the father became a poor, small-town cobbler-drunkard; the mother did laundry for more prosperous families. Stalin received many paternal beatings and little education until his widowed mother enrolled him, at the age of fifteen, in the Tiflis Theological Seminary, a preparatory high school for the priesthood in the Greek Orthodox Church. There anti-Russian nationalism captured his mind and he, and not a few of his fellow students, blaming the Tsar for the poverty, backwardness, and forced Russification of their native Georgia, turned in protest to socialism. Of the two forms of socialism, Menshevism and Bolshevism, Stalin rejected the former which appealed for broad popular support and chose the small Leninist faction wedded to brigandage for funds and to conspiracy and violence for success through revolution. With the scantiest ability as speaker and writer but a supertalent for intrigue, ruthlessness, and organization, he had no place in the democratic Menshevik faction. In the Bolshevik group he mounted quickly up the hierarchical ladder, first in Georgia and then in Russia. Neither grace nor charm nor a pleasant presence was part of Stalin's personality equipment; he could, however, ingratiate himself. Principles were not his forte; he sniffed the wind and adjusted. When the Tsar fell he saw no possibility of a communist coup d'état. Lenin did, and passionately whipped all comrades, including Stalin, into obedience. Stalin was not an insignificant cog in the political machinery that launched the Bolshevik revolution, but he played nowhere near the stellar role performed by Leon Trotsky at the side of Lenin.

Stalin had, in effect, no father or, at best, a hated father. At the Tiflis Seminary he rejected God as father. Though he expressed surprise, after a first meeting, that the great Lenin, whom he wished to worship, was short in stature, he fastened on him as his father figure. Here began the feud between Stalin and Trotsky which shook the world more than the first ten days of the Bolshevik regime. Its purpose: to displace Trotsky as second to the master. The essence of Stalin's self-directed cult of personality was to locate himself next to Lenin in oil paintings, sculpture, distorted polemics, and the battle of quotations. "Stalin Is Lenin Today" millions were taught to chant after Lenin died. Stalin never forgave Trotsky for living and finally killed him, although the distant exile possessed only an envied tongue and pen. Trotsky quotes Stalin as saying, "The greatest delight is to mark one's enemy, prepare everything, avenge oneself thoroughly, and then go to sleep."[2]

Stalin was well served by his sense of inferiority, it fueled his ascent

2. *Trotsky's Diary in Exile 1935*, p. 64.

to the peak of the Soviet pyramid of power. Nature furnished him with the tools to work behind the scenes where deceit and unfounded denunciations toppled rivals and won followers through intimidation. The high walls of the Tsarist Kremlin are the true symbols of Stalinism; within them the Stalin system of government by murder, punishment without justice, and life without liberty evolved unseen and unhindered. In his first inaugural President Franklin D. Roosevelt declared "that the only thing we have to fear is fear itself—nameless, unreasoning, unjustified terror." The Soviet people did not fear fear itself, unjustified terror justified their fears. Their fears could not be exorcised by a psychological poultice of magic words. Stalin had turned Russia back to Tsarist tyranny and intensified it a hundredfold.

Soviet despotism is a twentieth-century phenomenon rooted in a nineteenth-century mentality. The Soviet population fears the Kremlin and the Kremlin fears its people, else it would grant them greater freedom. In war the people fight for their country, in peace a gulf opens between government and nation. This was so when Napoleon invaded and when Hitler attacked. It gives the Kremlin, with all its armed strength, a feeling of inner weakness, an instability that conduces to mediocrity. Stalin was not mediocre but he created a culture in which the best brains tend toward science and technology while politics receives the dregs and drudges who, in the Stalin pattern, seek foreign triumphs so they can keep afloat on a river of nationalism. Cell by cell the ideology of communism has been converted into the ideology of nationalism, and since it was communist ideology that formerly distinguished the Soviet Union from other countries whereas nationalism is something it now has in common with Pakistan, Portugal, and Brazil, one might say that the Soviets have no identifying ideology, they are identified by dictatorship, bureaucratic management, and other methods of administration. What they have is a mass of people (the exceptions are notable and increasingly numerous) who underwent so much oppression and privation that they are ready to live by "bread" alone and pay the government with obedience and obeisances for a period of tranquillity. Tsarism trained its subjects in such passive withdrawal. There was in Stalin's time, and there is today, a tension, a nervous throbbing in the Soviet Union which comes from the regime's feverish effort to reach the population by every means except democracy and surcease from exploitation. These elements in the Soviet condition propelled Stalin to yearn for empire, an extension of the nation, a fillip to nationalism. The opportunity appeared with the Soviet-Nazi pact in 1939 and again with the Red Army victories in 1943. Nor was the Bolshevik Kremlin capable of liberating itself, perhaps it did not wish to liberate itself, from the self-induced morbid nightmare in which world capitalism conspires to encircle Russia and overthrow the Soviet government. Lenin bequeathed this dread to Stalin, and Stalin, having the mind of a nineteenth-century imperialist, in this sense a kinsman of Churchill, believed that safety lay in the acquisition of more territory by the Soviet Union, already the largest country of the globe. Had he trusted Roosevelt and Churchill his fears might have abated. But he was a suspicious person, and the postponement of the second front in France fed his mistrust. Moreover, Stalin saw every situation as a struggle in which all succumbed and he won. In this spirit he went to Tehran where the Big Three met for the first time. Churchill was 69 years old, Stalin 64, Roosevelt 61.

XIV HIGH DIPLOMACY

A meeting of the Big Three would plan the defeat of Hitler Germany and, inescapably, outline the world's postwar peace. It would be high diplomacy. On May 5, 1943, President Roosevelt had invited Stalin to a conference somewhere in Alaska or Siberia and without Churchill. Stalin agreed to the time—"in July or August"—but not to the place. Churchill, not knowing about Roosevelt's invitation, proposed Khartoum. When Stalin turned that down, Churchill on June 13 suggested Scapa Flow, "our main naval harbour in the North of Scotland . . . the most convenient, the safest and, if desired, the most secret." On June 25 Churchill, having learned from Ambassador W. Averell Harriman that the President wished to meet "U.J." (Uncle Joe) "in Alaska *à deux*," saw the exclusion of Great Britain as a gift to enemy propaganda. It would be "serious and vexatious," bewildering and alarming, he told Roosevelt. The President denied it: "I did not suggest to UJ that we meet alone." He nevertheless dwelt, in the same message of June 28 to Churchill, on the advantages of such a two-man talk. F.D.R. added that "the Kremlin people do not like the idea of UJ flying across Finland, Sweden, Norway and the North Sea to Scapa, especially at this time of year when there is practically no darkness."

Stalin had never flown.

Meanwhile Roosevelt told Generalissimo Chiang Kai-shek he would like to meet him "sometime this fall." On July 21, however, T. V. Soong, Chinese Foreign Minister, wrote in Washington to Harry Hopkins saying the Generalissimo thought it would be "awkward" if the meeting were somewhere in Alaska and he touched Soviet territory going through Siberia without seeing Stalin, whom he apparently did not want to see.

Stalin informed Roosevelt by wire on August 8 that in view of the intense German-Soviet summer battle he had to put aside all other tasks and attend to "my chief duty, that of directing the front." He still considered it "highly advisable for responsible representatives of our two countries to meet . . . either in Astrakhan or in Archangel." If Roosevelt himself could not come he could send "a fully authorized man of confidence." He had "no objection to Mr. Churchill attending." Two days later Stalin told Churchill by telegram he agreed "that a meeting of the three heads of the Governments is highly desirable" but, in view of the situation at the front, he could not come to Scapa Flow "or any other distant point." On August 12 Churchill, in Quebec for a conference à deux with Roosevelt, acknowledged Stalin's message and said, "I am sending you a small stereoscopic machine with a large number of photographic slides of the damage done by our bombers to German cities."

From Quebec on August 18 Roosevelt and Churchill sent a dispatch to Stalin: "Neither Astrakhan nor Archangel are suitable, in our opinion." They suggested Fairbanks, Alaska. Stalin replied on August 24: "I cannot, in the opinion of my colleagues, leave the front without injury to our military operations to go to so distant a point as Fairbanks," although, he added, "Fairbanks would undoubtedly have been a suitable place for our meeting, as I indeed thought before."

On September 4 Roosevelt informed Stalin he still hoped for talks with "you and Churchill" and that since "under our Constitution," he could not absent himself from Washington "for more than twenty days" because "no one can sign for me when I am away," he was ready to go "as far as North Africa" between November 15 and December 15. Stalin replied on the 8th that he desired a meeting of the three "as early as possible" but in a country "where all three countries are represented, such as Iran."

Roosevelt explained to Stalin on September 11 that Congress was now in session, the Constitution required the President to act within ten days on legislation passed by Congress, and if flying weather was bad this might be impossible. Therefore he suggested meeting in Egypt, "a neutral state." The end of November would suit him.

Having himself suggested Iran, Stalin telegraphed Churchill and Roosevelt on September 12, "I have no objection" to Tehran, the capital of Iran, "which, I think, is a more suitable place than Egypt where the Soviet Union is not represented."

Presently Churchill had an inspiration. He drafted a telegram for Stalin which he first sent to Roosevelt for concurrence. In it he would tell

Stalin that Roosevelt faced "a very real constitutional difficulty" in going to Tehran and would he not agree to come from Moscow to Beirut or Cyprus? Or "One way of holding conference is for us each to have a ship and meet in one of the harbours of Egypt or Levant or possibly of Cyprus." Roosevelt responded: "I think your idea of enticing Uncle Joe to the Mediterranean with the offer of the use of a ship is excellent." But Churchill never sent the telegram to Stalin because he mistakenly assumed that Roosevelt had agreed to Tehran. However, on October 14 Churchill had another idea: to meet at Habbaniya, 50 miles west of Baghdad in Iraq, and he so wired Roosevelt. But the same day Roosevelt wired Stalin saying that, for constitutional reasons, Tehran "is too far." Would Stalin therefore not come to Cairo or Asmara, the former Italian capital of Eritrea, or "at some port in the Eastern Mediterranean, each one of us to have a ship?" That very day, on the other hand, Roosevelt agreed to Churchill's proposal of Habbaniya.

On October 19 Stalin telegraphed Roosevelt: "Unfortunately, not one of the places proposed by you for the meeting instead of Tehran is acceptable for me." His colleagues, Stalin said, feel that "my personal contact with the [Supreme] Command" was necessary every day. From Tehran he could be in constant telegraph and telephone communication with Moscow.

On October 21 Roosevelt pleaded with Stalin. He was "deeply disappointed," he said, "in your message received today." Stalin's "daily guidance" of the Supreme Command was "of high importance." But "there are other vital matters." He could not change the U.S. Constitution, which required him to act on legislation within ten days. "The trouble with Tehran is the simple fact that the approaches to the city often make flying an impossibility for several days at a time." The President therefore proposed Basra on the Persian Gulf as the place of the Big Three meeting. It could be guarded "by our respective national troops." Stalin could "easily have a special telephone, under your own control, laid from Basra to Tehran, where you will reach your own line into Russia." Then Roosevelt hinted at something which Stalin should have kept in mind because he knew Roosevelt's condition: "I am not in any way considering the fact," the President continued, "that from United States territory I would have to travel six thousand miles and you would only have to travel six hundred miles from Russian territory." And Roosevelt added, "It would be regarded as a tragedy by future generations if you and I and Mr. Churchill failed today because of a few hundred miles. . . . Please do not fail me in this crisis." F.D.R. offered Ankara, Baghdad, and Asmara as alternatives to Tehran and once more emphasized that it was the Constitution, not his personal comfort, that was decisive. To Churchill the same day Roosevelt wired, "The possibility of Tehran is out." Church-ill noted twenty-four hours later that Ankara was not suitable because "there are the Taurus Mountains to cross."

On the 25th Roosevelt informed Churchill "No word from UJ yet." If Stalin was "adamant, what would you think of you and me meeting . . . in North Africa." Uncle Joe could deputize Molotov. Secretary of State Hull spoke to Stalin in Moscow on October 25 recommending Basra.

Ambassador Harriman talked with Molotov in Moscow and asked him "bluntly" whether communications was the "only inhibition to Basra as against Tehran. He assured me that it was." Harriman also asked Molo-tov, he wired the President, "to accept your decision that Tehran was impossible."

Stalin, Molotov, Hull, and Harriman discussed the meeting place on October 26. Stalin said he would "have to consider . . . Basra . . . and consult his associates." Molotov declared that "both civil and military authorities in the Soviet Union were loath to have the Marshal absent himself at all." Stalin said the conference could be postponed to the spring, "when military operations would have been suspended during the thaw, at which time Fairbanks might be an appropriate place." On receiving this information Roosevelt instructed Hull to tell Stalin that "I suggest he fly as far as Basra even for one day." The rest of the time Molotov might substitute for him.

Churchill to Roosevelt on October 29: "It is very awkward waiting about for an answer from Uncle Joe." Roosevelt to Churchill October 29: "If he declines Basra I propose we go there with small staffs and meet Molotov and a small Russian staff and plead with UJ to come there if only for one day. I think it vital that we see him."

Hull pressed Molotov on October 29: why could not Stalin fly down to Basra for one day and have Molotov stay the rest of the time? "Molotov instantly dissented from this suggestion by saying he himself was in no sense a military man and would not fit into that sort of a situation."

Churchill to Roosevelt on October 30: "I am quite game to go to Basra, but I gather Joe will not come beyond Tehran." That evening Hull sat at Stalin's side at the usual Moscow end-of-conference banquet and in-formed Roosevelt by wire the next day that Stalin would go no farther than Tehran; the President and the Marshal could not meet "unless you . . . decide to fly to Tehran for a day."

Churchill to Roosevelt on November 2: "Uncle Joe will not come beyond Tehran." Therefore why meet at Basra? "I suggest that, when we are in Cairo, we try to wheedle him to Habbaniya, or if the weather is really good, make a six hours' hop ourselves to meet him in Tehran."

Roosevelt to Churchill on November 2: "I am wiring Hull to ask UJ if he could come to Basra for even one day. That would be infinitely better than no meeting with him at all."

Stalin to Roosevelt on November 5: ". . . Of course, the decision of whether you are able to travel to Tehran remains entirely with yourself. On my part, I have to say that I do not see any other more suitable place for a meeting, than the aforementioned city. . . . My colleagues in the Government consider, in general, that my travelling beyond the borders of the U.S.S.R. at the present time is impossible due to the great complexity of the situation at the front."

Roosevelt to Stalin on November 8: ". . . You will be glad to know that I have worked out a method so that if I get word that a bill requiring my veto has been passed by the Congress and forwarded to me, I will fly to Tunis to meet it and then return to Conference. Therefore, I have decided to go to Tehran and this makes me especially happy."[1]

* * *

If Stalin could not indeed leave Russia for a few days it means that no marshal or group of marshals, no generals or the General Staff were permitted to take, or were capable of taking, a major decision without him about the conduct of a battle in progress or about preparations for battle. The concentration of so much power in Stalin's hands deprived everybody else, on this supposition, of the skill, will, and courage to exercise power even temporarily. This suggests that one-man totalitarianism of the Stalinist type paralyzes minds, atrophies agility, and prepares a nation for its political and cultural decline no matter how impressive the dictator's achievements appear to be on the surface. Soviet history indicates that this assumption is in part justified. Stalin did not want anyone to make decisions without his being consulted at least by telephone; some leaders might begin to think they could manage the country alone.

It is equally probable that Stalin, obsessively afraid of assassination (hence the rigorous, almost ridiculous, protection of his homes and dachas and the precautions taken when he moved about Moscow or to its outskirts), did not wish to expose himself to an attempt on his life in a foreign country and, what is even more plausible, that he wondered whether the military, some of whom resented the 1937 purge of Red Army leaders, the shooting of generals during the second world war, and the despot's bungling before and after the beginning of that war, might not depose him in his absence from Moscow. The cult of personality,

1. All quotations from U.S. Department of State, *Foreign Relations [F.R.] of the United States. Diplomatic Papers. The Conferences at Cairo and Tehran 1943,* and from *Correspondence,* Vols. I and II.

exalting Stalin's genius, may have convinced him that he was indispensable, and it perhaps convinced others, but he could easily have imagined
that some were immune to idolatry and irked by his monopoly of decision
making and fulsomeness of the praise heaped upon him for their success
on the battlefield. Stalin's tyranny exterminated millions of human beings but it did not kill all human reactions. Stalin, a shrewd psychologist,
understood the passions and weaknesses of his marshals and generals.
Not a few of them were powerful, strong-willed soldiers whose ambitions
only he could hold in check, for they knew from what had happened in
1937 how utterly unrestrained he could be.

Stalin's psyche was multifaceted. One motive alone does not explain
his actions. He might well have reasoned that if Roosevelt and Churchill
were so eager to meet him they would come to him if he held out long
enough, and then his own subjects and all humanity would see that the
globe's greatest paid him honor. His Oriental mind would have attached
considerable significance to this. In 1945 he had Roosevelt and Churchill
travel all the way to Yalta in the Crimea, and later that year the leaders
of Britain and the U.S. came to Potsdam, then under Soviet occupation,
as Tehran was in effect in November, 1943; the Shah of Iran had been
induced to allow the Big Three powers to station troops along the entire
route from Basra, where their supplies for Russia were unloaded,
through Tehran, largely occupied by Russian soldiers, to the Caspian
Sea. Successful insistence on Tehran meant personal safety for Stalin
and prestige because the mighty of the world conferred on his doorstep.
Besides, he had won the contest of wills with the President and the Prime
Minister. This, he expected, would set the right atmosphere for the talks
at Tehran. The wealthy, aristocratic representatives of capitalism were
on their knees before him. What joy!

XV THE TEHRAN CONFERENCE

At 9:16 A.M. on November 12, 1943, President Roosevelt was transferred
from the yacht *Potomac* to the battleship *Iowa*. Under naval and air
escort, the *Iowa* carried the President and his large military and civilian
staffs to Oran, Algeria, which they reached on November 20. The same
day Roosevelt flew to Tunis, where he was quartered in the "White
House" at Carthage. Late the next evening F.D.R. took off from the Tunis

airport, flew 1,851 miles, and landed at Cairo at 9:35 A.M. Monday, November 22.

In Cairo the President received Churchill, Generalissimo and Madame Chiang Kai-shek, King Peter of Yugoslavia, and King George II of Greece. King Farouk of Egypt had been injured in an automobile accident and could not call. Roosevelt entertained the Prime Minister and a big group at a Thanksgiving dinner—turkeys brought from Washington—and saw the sights at the Sphinx and pyramids. Following a dizzying round of consultations with Americans, British, Soviet, Chinese, Egyptian, and other officials on the war in the Pacific, the Mediterranean, Russia, and Europe, he departed from Cairo early on the morning of November 27, crossed the Suez Canal, circled over Jerusalem, sighted the Euphrates and Tigris rivers, and, after six and a half hours in the air, disembarked at Tehran.

Churchill says simply, "So we [the President and he] sailed off into the air from Cairo at the crack of dawn on November 27, in perfect weather for the long-sought meeting place, and arrived safely by different routes at different times."

Marshal Stalin traveled by luxury train from Moscow to Baku and from there flew for about an hour to Tehran. Over the mountains the pressure hurt his ears; he vowed never to fly again. It was his first and last flight.

On arrival Roosevelt learned that Stalin had preceded him into Tehran. He invited the Marshal to dinner; the Marshal declined saying he had had a strenuous day. The next morning, Sunday, November 28, Roosevelt, who was staying at the U.S. Legation, received a message from Stalin: it was well known that Tehran was full of Axis sympathizers and he was concerned lest an unhappy accident occur to one of the heads of government while moving through town to visit one another. Would not the President, therefore, come and stay at the Soviet Embassy compound? The compound had high walls and a large Red Army guard. A house in the compound, Stalin stated, was being prepared for Roosevelt. Harriman urged the President to accept. Churchill, when consulted, said he felt relieved; the British Legation could offer the President only one bedroom and a sitting room. Roosevelt accepted and lived in the Soviet compound during the length of the Tehran Conference.[1] Churchill amplified this official American account. "Molotov," he wrote, "produced a story that the Soviet Secret Intelligence had unearthed a plot to kill one or more of the 'Big Three,' as we were regarded. . . . 'If anything like that were to happen,' he said, 'it could produce a most unfortunate impression.' This could not be denied. I strongly supported Molotov in his appeals to the President to move forthwith inside the Soviet Embassy."[2]

1. *F.R., The Conferences at Cairo and Tehran 1943*, pp. 463, 476, 867.
2. Winston S. Churchill, *The Second World War. Closing the Ring,* p. 343.

No doubt there were Nazi agents in Tehran. No doubt Stalin would not wish Roosevelt to be assassinated in Tehran. No doubt Roosevelt would have security but no secrecy in the Soviet compound. No doubt Stalin believed he had raised his prestige by having Roosevelt as his guest; he had once called himself "an Asiatic."

At his news conference in Washington on December 17, 1943, F.D.R. mentioned a plot to kill him, Stalin, and Churchill in Tehran. Roosevelt could not well have ignored such information coming to him from Stalin. Nor would Roosevelt have wished to reject Stalin's invitation to stay in the Soviet Embassy compound. For, while the purpose of the Tehran Conference was to concert wartime and postwar plans, Roosevelt's primary objective was to establish a human contact and working arrangement with Stalin. The U.S. had strong ties with Britain, whose dependence on America grew as the war sapped her strength and as it became clear that Hitler could not be defeated without American weapons and men. Roosevelt could not have been so certain of good future relations with the Soviet Union. Churchill thought Russia would of necessity rely on American aid in her postwar reconstruction. The President was not sure about what would happen after victory or during the war. Even after Stalingrad and after the Red Army's recapture of Smolensk, the gateway to Poland, Washington could not rid itself of the fear that Russia in her exhaustion might make a compact with Germany and quit the war. Secretary of State Cordell Hull said to me in his office on January 19, 1944, that he went to Moscow the previous autumn for the Foreign Ministers' Conference because "I wanted to get to the bottom of the many stories of a separate peace between Russia and Germany that we heard in Washington, London, and Chungking. We were in the dark on that."[3] Finally, Roosevelt was eager to win the Soviets for the stupendous task of beating Japan.

Roosevelt came to Tehran to court Stalin.

Stalin brought Roosevelt all the way to Tehran to squeeze every benefit from that courtship.

As Stalin's guest Roosevelt would be nearer the Marshal. As Roosevelt's host Stalin had separated the President from the Prime Minister. Strangely enough, this suited F.D.R.'s political strategy. He subsequently explained it to Mrs. Frances Perkins, a long-time friend and for many years his Secretary of Labor, who reproduced his words in her book, *The Roosevelt I Knew.* "He told me," she wrote, "he didn't believe there had been a plot and didn't think so at the time, but it was clear Stalin wanted him to come to the Russian Embassy." The conference met in that embassy. "For the first three days," Roosevelt told Mrs. Perkins, "I made

3. Louis Fischer, *The Great Challenge,* p. 246.

absolutely no progress. I couldn't get any personal connection with Stalin, although I had done everything he asked me to do. . . . I had come there [Tehran] to accommodate Stalin. I felt pretty discouraged because I thought I was making no personal headway. What we were doing could have been done by the foreign ministers.

"I thought it over all night and made up my mind I had to do something desperate. I couldn't stay in Tehran forever. I had to cut through the icy surface so that later I could talk by telephone or letter in a personal way. I had scarcely seen Churchill alone during the conference. I had a feeling that the Russians did not feel right about seeing us conferring together in a language which we understand and they didn't.

"On my way to the conference room that morning we caught up with Winston and I had just a moment to say to him, 'Winston, I hope you won't feel sore for what I am going to do.'

"Winston just shifted his cigar and grunted. I must say he behaved very decently afterward.

"I began almost as soon as we got into the conference room. I talked privately with Stalin. I didn't say anything I hadn't said before, but it appeared quite chummy and confidential. . . . Still no smile.

"Then I said, lifting my hand up to cover a whisper (which of course had to be interpreted), 'Winston is cranky this morning, he got up on the wrong side of the bed.'

"A vague smile passed over Stalin's eyes, and I decided I was on the right track. As soon as I sat down at the conference table, I began to tease Churchill about his Britishness, about John Bull, about his cigars, about his habits. It began to register with Stalin. Winston got red and scowled, and the more he did so, the more Stalin smiled. Finally Stalin broke out into a deep, hearty guffaw, and for the first time in three days I saw light. I kept it up until Stalin was laughing with me, and it was then that I called him 'Uncle Joe.' He would have thought me fresh the day before, but that day he laughed and came over and shook my hand.

"From that time on our relations were personal. . . . The ice was broken and we talked like men and brothers."[4]

If all this snuggling up to Stalin seems frivolous, Churchill did not think so; he took it seriously and found it distasteful: "The fact that the President was in private contact with Marshal Stalin and dwelling at the Soviet Embassy, and that he had avoided ever seeing me alone since we left Cairo, in spite of our hitherto intimate relations and the way in which our vital affairs are interwoven, led me to seek a direct personal interview with Stalin. I felt the Russian leader was not deriving a true impression of the British attitude." The audience was granted. "I began,"

4. Frances Perkins, pp. 83–85.

Churchill records, "by reminding the Marshal that I was half American [his mother was an American] and had a great affection for the American people." Stalin understood how to evaluate such an introduction: I love them but . . . "What I am going to say," Churchill continues, "was not to be understood as disparaging to the Americans and I would be perfectly loyal towards them. . . ."[5]

Stalin found this delightful. In the abstract, Roosevelt was the mediator between Churchill and Stalin. In practice, Roosevelt's extravagant exertion to open Stalin's closed mind had made the Marshal the arbiter of the Tehran Conference; even Churchill wooed him.

Unprecedented triumphs inclined Roosevelt to the belief that nobody could resist his charm. He dreamt of a postwar peace policed by four powers, the U.S., the U.S.S.R., the U.K., and China, chiefly the first two. Most important, he wanted Russia's aid in the war against Japan. At the first plenary session of the conference, held in the Soviet Embassy on Sunday, November 28, at 4 P.M., the President, presiding, began by discussing the situation in the Pacific theater. He described the war there as one of successful "attrition." "We were sinking more Japanese tonnage," the minutes read, "than the Japanese were able to replace." The Allies had also captured island steppingstones to the Japanese archipelago. China was being buttressed with arms.

When the President completed this statement, Stalin spoke. "The Soviet Government," he declared, "welcomed the successes of the Anglo-American forces against the Japanese . . . up to the present to their regret they had not been able to join the effort of the Soviet Union to that of the United States and England against the Japanese because the Soviet armies were too deeply engaged in the West. He added that the Soviet forces in Siberia were sufficient for defensive purposes but would have to be increased three-fold before they would be adequate for offensive operations. Once Germany was finally defeated, it would then be possible to send the necessary reinforcements to Siberia and then we shall be able by our common front to beat Japan."[6]

This promise, volunteered so early in the proceedings, would, in the President's mind, have justified his strenuous efforts to bring Stalin to the conference and his own fatiguing trip to it. Stalin had made a similar declaration to Hull in Moscow. But this time it was for the record in the presence of the heads of government and of their civilian and military staffs. The assurance, when implemented, would, it was expected, avert mountains of Anglo–American casualties and shorten the war. Stalin committed his country before the West put any pressure on him to enter the Pacific conflict. He asked no compensation. Yet his pledge to fight

5. Churchill, pp. 375–377.
6. F.R., *The Conferences at Cairo and Tehran 1943*, pp. 487–489.

Japan after Germany's defeat confirmed the West in its wish to win in Europe first—thus relieving Russia.

Charity was not a noticeable component of Stalin's character. Dexterity was. By giving the Americans what they wanted he won their hearts and support. General Deane, chief of the U.S. military mission in Moscow and a member of the delegation at Tehran, writes: "The Americans at the Conference . . . were all considerably and favorably impressed by him [Stalin], probably because he advocated the American point of view in our differences with the British. Regardless of this, one could not help but recognize qualities of greatness in the man."[7] He was greatly penetrating, greatly purposeful, greatly cunning. Tehran became a showcase of his talents.

The conference convened without an agenda. Its military discussions were evidence of the centrifugal tendencies in the Triple Alliance. All its private and plenary meetings witnessed the birth pangs of an unhealthy peace.

Roosevelt had promised Chiang Kai-shek at Cairo that Anglo-American forces operating from the Andaman Islands in the Bay of Bengal would soon invade Burma (Operation Buccaneer) with a view of opening a road into southern China. Before the first plenary session the President, Harry Hopkins, who served, in effect, as Secretary of State, and the U.S. Joint Chiefs of Staff met at 11:30 A.M. on November 28. General George C. Marshall said he "believed that the Prime Minister [Churchill] would use every wile to cut out BUCCANEER." Hopkins "observed that the Prime Minister considers that as between Rhodes and BUCCANEER, the former is more important." The President said, "we are obligated to the Chinese to carry out the amphibious operation BUCCANEER."[8]

Churchill's preference for Rhodes was part of larger strategy. He told the Tehran Conference that the trans-Channel invasion of northern France would take place as planned during May, June, and July, 1944, with a million Americans and Britons. May, 1944, however, was still six months away. The western Allies must not spend this period in idleness. Seven of their divisions in Italy were being transported to England for the assault on northern France. Their remaining strength in the peninsula would, nevertheless, suffice to move up the Italian leg, capture Rome, establish themselves on the airfields above Rome from which southern Germany could be bombed, and then reach farther north to the Pisa-Rimini line. This would open two possibilities: an invasion of southern France and a thrust northeast through Yugoslavia toward the Danube.[9]

7. John R. Deane, *The Strange Alliance,* p. 43.
8. *F.R.,* p. 479.
9. Churchill, pp. 350–352.

The President associated himself with the northeastern idea. It would not only help Tito, as Churchill proposed; with the assistance of Tito's Partisans they could drive into Rumania "and effect a junction with the Red Army advancing southward from the region of Odessa."

Hopkins scribbled a note to Admiral Ernest J. King: "Who's promoting that Adriatic business the President continually returns to?"

"As far as I know it's his own idea," King replied.[10]

If it was his own it was also Churchill's own. Britain had been giving help to Tito, the Prime Minister informed the conference, who "was holding a number of German divisions and doing much more for the Allied cause than the Chetniks under [General Draza] Mihailovic." That was not all. Looking east gave wings to Churchill's rich romantic imagination. Shortage of shipping prevented the transfer to England of further divisions now stationed in the Mediterranean area. With two or three of these and with the planes defending Egypt, Rhodes and all islands in the Aegean Sea could be captured. Turkey would then come into the war on the Allied side. That would open the Dardanelles, which still exercised their first-world-war fascination on the Prime Minister, and enable Britain and America to enter the Black Sea, knock Bulgaria out of the Nazi camp, and permit the West to supply Russia by the short route via the Mediterranean.

As much time was spent at the conference on Turkey as on any other subject. Churchill mustered all his eloquence and knowledge to paint the East Mediterranean expedition in radiant colors. (He feared a second Dunkirk or a repetition of first-world-war trench fighting unless German forces in the Balkans, the Aegean, and Italy were kept busy and thereby prevented from coming to the aid of the Wehrmacht divisions when Overlord began.) Stalin could not be shaken. Repeatedly he predicted Turkey's refusal to go to war. Churchill reminded Stalin of Britain's aid to Tito, leader of the communist Partisans who were holding numerous German divisions at bay. Stalin still insisted that all this was secondary to the cross-Channel invasion of France. Churchill said "Turkey would be mad" not to join the winning side. Stalin replied "that a number of people preferred to be mad, and all neutrals regarded those people who were waging war as fools to fight when they might be doing nothing."[11] (This, incidentally, supplies a key to Stalin's thoughts in 1939: he negotiated the Soviet-Nazi pact and secret protocol because he was not foolish enough to give up "doing nothing" and risk the Soviet regime in the fire and brimstone of war.) Churchill contended that Turkey at war and the West slicing into Yugoslavia, into Rumania—which had already made peace feelers to the Allies—and into Hungary "might start a landslide

10. Robert E. Sherwood, *Roosevelt and Hopkins,* p. 780.
11. Churchill, pp. 354–358.

among the [German] satellite states."[12] A delay of Overlord of a month or two, he held, was a small price to pay for these gains.

Stalin had seen too many postponements of the second front to relish mention of another. Turkey would not fight, he reiterated. Moreover, he opposed the dispersal of forces. Soviet experience in the war had demonstrated the wisdom of using maximum concentrations of arms and men in big operations. He therefore advocated an invasion of southern France "some two months before OVERLORD" to divide German strength and facilitate the major attack on northern France. He even expressed a preference for postponing the capture of Rome in order to invade the French Riviera. The Soviets had seen the enormous advantage, he said, of hitting the enemy "from two sides at once. . . . He added that he thought such a two-way operation in France would be very successful."[13]

Churchill persisted. Britain had twenty divisions in the Eastern Mediterranean and air squadrons in Egypt. Why keep them idle? Was the Soviet government in favor of trying again to bring Turkey into the war? "I am all in favor of trying again," Churchill quotes Stalin as replying. "We ought to take them by the scruff of the neck if necessary."[14] Was this wishful hearing on Churchill's part? The minutes kept by the U.S. Joint Chiefs of Staff read: "Marshal Stalin said the Soviets do want Turkey to enter the war but he felt she could not be taken in by 'the scruff of the neck.' "[15] On the other hand, the Soviet minutes twice quote Stalin as saying, "Yes, we must try to compel Turkey to enter the war."[16]

However, General Sir Alan Brooke, spokesman for the British military, stated at Tehran that operations in the Mediterranean "would require the retarding of the date set for Overlord."[17] This is what Stalin did not want. To be sure, Stalin promised Churchill and Roosevelt that, if Turkey went to war, Russia would go to war with Bulgaria. Molotov had, in November, 1940, revealed Russia's designs on Bulgaria. But "even so," Stalin added, "he did not think Turkey would come in. He continued that there was no difference of opinion as to the importance of helping the Partisans, but that he must say that from the Russian point of view the question of Turkey, the Partisans and even the occupation of Rome were not really important operations. He said that Overlord was the most important and nothing should be done to distract attention from that operation."[18]

12. *F.R.*, p. 493.
13. *Ibid.*, p. 495.
14. Churchill, p. 355.
15. *F.R.*, p. 505.
16. S. P. Sanakoyev and B. L. Tsibulevsky (Eds.), *Tegeran, Yalta, Potsdam* (Tehran, Yalta, Potsdam), pp. 13 and 15.
17. *F.R.*, p. 516.
18. *Ibid.*, p. 537.

If Turkey became a belligerent she would be entitled to British and American support should Moscow renew its 1939 pressure on Turkish territorial integrity. If western forces pushed up from the head of the Adriatic into Yugoslavia and Rumania, Soviet postwar expansion might be blocked. It is difficult to divest oneself of the thought that these political considerations were in Stalin's mind, and in Churchill's, throughout the Tehran debate on military strategy in the Eastern Mediterranean. Only the Americans at the conference were pure-minded; they were fighting the war. Stalin and Churchill, quite properly, were also fighting for position in the postwar.

To play a leading role when peace came, to save Russia from economic ruin, to keep the Soviet regime intact, it was necessary to shorten the war. Hence Stalin's insistence on an early landing in northern and, as a diversion, in southern France and a thrust from there at the heart of Germany. No more delays. He won the day at Tehran. Churchill's schemes were vetoed. Overlord was given topmost priority.

Throughout the proceedings at Tehran Stalin behaved the courtly gentleman, never raising his voice above a whisper; he spoke to his interpreters, who translated. He was brief and blunt, neither shy nor soft. When Stalin was informed that the British and American Chiefs of Staff had decided to launch Overlord in May and simultaneously to land in southern France, he asked, "Who will command Overlord?"

Roosevelt replied that the general had not yet been chosen.

Stalin said until he had the name of the commander he could not believe in the reality of the trans-Channel operation.

Here Churchill made a last attempt to win approval for interim campaigns in the regions of Turkey and the Balkans. Stalin turned to the Prime Minister and warned that he was about to put an "indiscreet" question to him: "Did the British really believe in Overlord or were they expressing their approval of it merely as a means of reassuring the Russians?"

Churchill promised to hurl maximum strength at the Germans across the Channel.[19] Stalin in turn promised to open an offensive on the Russian front to coincide with Overlord; Hitler then could not shift overwhelming force to meet the western armies as they landed on the beaches.

The fate of the Hitler Reich had been decided. The destiny of Russia too.

* * *

19. Sherwood, pp. 787–788.

Although the Americans, Cordell Hull in particular, opposed wartime discussions and dispositions about postwar territorial changes, Tehran showed that those changes were implicit in military planning. Who would be mistress in eastern Europe was already on the agenda. A second issue of transcendent importance intruded itself on the conference: the future of Germany. War is notoriously incalculable. Suppose the Nazi regime suddenly collapsed?

The difference between what was said at Tehran on Germany's future and what has actually happened can be measured in millions of political miles. The lesson? Nobody was wise enough to deal with the future. Stalin, Churchill, and Roosevelt brought to the conference no blueprint of world peace into which to fit a defeated Germany. They consulted either their greeds or their fears—a guarantee that the treatment of Germany would be punitive. But in the modern technological age the punishment of a nation cannot be effective unless it is total; the country must be sown with salt.

The Big Three, moreover, assumed at Tehran that they would unite in implementing their decisions for Germany. This was as indispensable as it was improbable. One did not have to possess the vision of a prophet; history is cluttered with the debris of shattered wartime coalitions. And disunity among the victors relieves the vanquished. The alternative at Tehran was a world in which peace is a built-in imperative, in which the national goals that cause hot and cold wars are abandoned and abolished. To this end the victors would have had to contain their appetites and restrain their actions. They would, in other words, seem to be punishing themselves but in effect securing their welfare and happiness. That was not the Tehran mood. The Big Three had neither time nor inclination nor incentive to solve basic problems; they were fighting a war against deadly enemies; they were harassed and tired.

Plans for a defeated Germany were tied inextricably to plans for a liberated Poland, the country with tragic geography. Wedged between Russia and Germany, her fortunes reflect their power. When Russia and Germany are strong Poland is partitioned. When both are weak Poland can be free and foolish. When Russia is strong and Germany weak Poland becomes a vassal of her big eastern neighbor. The dawn of German defeat, discernible at Tehran, put Germany and, ominously, Poland on the conference agenda.

Differences among the heads of government, particularly between Churchill and Stalin, were never suppressed or disguised. Stalin, for instance, asserted that Germany was maintaining nine divisions against Yugoslavia, three to four divisions in Bulgaria and nine in Italy. Churchill: "Our figures differ from those figures."

Stalin: "Your figures are wrong."[20]

On another occasion Roosevelt said, "We are now very hungry. Therefore I would propose that we adjourn our session in order to attend the dinner Marshal Stalin is tendering us today. I propose that our Military Commission continue its meeting tomorrow morning."

Stalin: "There is no need of a meeting of the Military Commission. It's superfluous. The meeting of the Military Commission will not speed our work. Only we ourselves can speed our work."[21]

The divergence on strategy and the postwar political settlement was sharper. Disagreements alternated with agreements. On strategy Roosevelt usually accepted Stalin's point of view. In the beginning at Tehran the President, like Churchill, felt that the Germans in Italy "should be pushed on toward the Alps. He thought it would be a good idea to go around the ends into France and Austria."[22] But he yielded to Stalin's adamant advocacy of Overlord without Italian and eastern or central European diversions, whereas Churchill, whose word count at Tehran exceeded those of Roosevelt and Stalin combined, continued relentlessly to press for operations in the Balkans and the Aegean.

Opinions among the Big Three on the shape of the peace followed a similar pattern, sometimes coinciding, sometimes clashing. The subject arose at a small dinner given by the President on Sunday, November 28, the first day of the conference. Present: Roosevelt, Hopkins, Harriman, and Charles E. Bohlen, future Ambassador to Moscow, who interpreted and kept the U.S. minutes; Churchill, Foreign Secretary Eden, Sir Archibald Clark Kerr, British Ambassador to Moscow, and Major Birse, their translator; and Stalin and Molotov with Vladimir N. Pavlov, an interpreter.

During the meal Stalin referred to "the entire French ruling class" as "rotten to the core." It had delivered France to Hitler and was now "actively helping our enemies." Therefore France should lose all her colonies after the war.

The President agreed "in part." He believed that "anybody over forty years old" should be eliminated from "the future government of France" (that would have kept out Charles de Gaulle). New Caledonia in the Pacific and Dakar on the hump of Africa should be denied the French. F.D.R. declared "he was speaking for twenty-one American nations when he said that Dakar in unsure hands was a direct threat to the Americas." A rather fantastic statement. (Stalin also believed that Marshal Pétain, not de Gaulle, represented "the real physical France.")

The conversation turned to Germany. Roosevelt said that "it was very

20. Sanakoyev and Tsibulevsky (Eds.), *Tegeran, Yalta, Potsdam*, p. 33.
21. *Ibid.*, p. 38.
22. *F.R.*, p. 480.

important not to leave in the German mind the concept of the Reich and that the very word should be stricken from the language.

"Marshal Stalin replied that it was not enough to eliminate the word, but the very Reich itself must be rendered impotent ever again to plunge the world into war." The victorious Allies, he added, must retain in their hands "the strategic positions necessary to prevent any recrudescence of German militarism." In further discussion Stalin emphasized that measures for the control of Germany and her disarmament "were insufficient to prevent the rebirth of German militarism." In this connection Stalin "stated definitely that the Russians would help the Poles to obtain a frontier on the Oder." (The Oder River in places is 40 miles from Berlin.)

Without dissenting, the President sketched his idea of "perhaps an international state in the vicinity of the Kiel Canal to insure free navigation in both directions through the approaches" to the Baltic Sea. Apparently Pavlov erred in translating or Stalin fastened on the name "Baltic" and thought F.D.R. wanted to internationalize the three Baltic countries. Stalin asserted "categorically that the Baltic States had by an expression of the will of the people voted to join the Soviet Union and that this question was not therefore one for discussion."[23]

The Baltic peoples "voted" in the presence of a Russian army of occupation after thousands of their leaders and intellectuals had been deported to Siberia. Local communists and the Soviet secret police supervised the plebiscites in the absence of any foreign observers except Russian. But Stalin was the good Leninist. Lenin asserted in January, 1918, that "no Marxist who has not abandoned the basic ideas of Marxism and in general of socialism can deny that the interests of socialism stand higher than the right of nations to self-determination."[24] By calling their country socialist the Soviets seek to wash away the sins of imperialist oppression. Lenin had branded Tsarist Russia "a prison of nationalities." Stalin dragged the Estonian, Latvian, and Lithuanian independent peoples back into prison and considered it legitimate because the conquerors bore the name of communists. At the Tehran dinner he made it clear that Russia meant to hold them in perpetuity.

After the meal Roosevelt withdrew to go to bed. Churchill led Stalin to a sofa where they, joined by Eden, discussed peacetime restraints upon Germany. Stalin expressed his attitude in one sentence: "All very good, but insufficient."

Stalin told Churchill and Eden he "thought Germany had every possibility of recovering from this war and might start on a new one within a comparatively short time. He feared the revival of German nationalism."

23. *Ibid.,* pp. 509–511.
24. Cited in Fischer, *The Life of Lenin,* p. 193.

"How soon?" Churchill asked.

Stalin: "Within fifteen to twenty years."

Churchill wanted safety for fifty years. He would "forbid them all aviation, civil and military, and I would forbid the General Staff system."

Stalin: "Would you also forbid the existence of watchmakers' and furniture factories for making parts of shells? The Germans produced toy rifles which were used for teaching hundreds of thousands of men how to shoot."

[In the 1920's and 1930's Germany also produced airplanes, tanks, and poison gas on Soviet territory, and there taught her men, and Russians, how to use them.]

Churchill argued that German disarmament, foreign supervision of German factories and "territorial changes of a far-reaching character" would, if England, America, and Russia remained close friends, "make the world safe for at least fifty years."

Stalin: "There was control [over Germany] after the last war but it failed."

Churchill: "We were inexperienced then" and Russia was not a party at the Peace Conference. "It will be different this time." He felt that Prussia should be "isolated and reduced" and dealt with "more sternly than other parts of the Reich." Bavaria, Austria, and Hungary "might form a broad, peaceful, unaggressive confederation."

Stalin: "All very good, but insufficient."

Churchill: The Big Three powers would be strong by land, sea, and air. "We are the trustees of the peace of the world. If we fail, there will be perhaps a century of chaos. If we are strong, we can carry out our trusteeship . . . the three Powers should guide the future of the world. I do not want to enforce any system on other nations. I ask for freedom and the right of all nations to develop as they like. We three must remain friends in order to ensure happy homes in all countries."

Impatient with oratory, Stalin asked crisply, "What is to happen to Germany?"

Churchill: He was not against "the toilers in Germany, but against the leaders and against dangerous combinations."

Stalin made no such distinction. German workers fought fiercely against the Russian army. He personally, he said, had interrogated German prisoners of war and asked them why they had burst into Russian homes and killed Russian women, and their only explanation was that they obeyed orders. "He shot such prisoners."

Churchill suggested they talk about Poland. Stalin invited the Prime Minister's views but remained noncommittal. Did Churchill think, he inquired, that Russia was going to "swallow" Poland? "Eden said he did not know how much the Russians were going to eat. . . . Stalin said the

Russians did not want anything belonging to other people, although they might take a bite out of Germany. Eden said that what Poland had lost in the East she might gain in the West. Stalin replied that she might, but he did not know. I then," Churchill writes, "demonstrated with three matches my idea of Poland moving westward. This pleased Stalin and on this note our group parted for the moment."[25]

With his three matchsticks Churchill indicated how he would recarve Europe: Russia would move west by annexing the eastern half of Poland; Poland would move west by annexing eastern parts of Germany; Germany would move west by standing still and losing her eastern marches.

The dinner and the postprandial conversation showed that the Big Three were concerned with maps, not with minds. The nations that defeated Germany did not exert themselves to extirpate the psychology of militarism in Germany. A few years after the war, for political reasons, they were encouraging militarism in two Germanys. And while manifesting anxiety over German militarism, Churchill and Roosevelt at Tehran failed to consider the resurgence of Russian imperialism. Churchill, by implication, welcomed it with his three-matches exercise. Except for casually announcing a "bite" here and there, Stalin feigned indifference to the entire matter.

The next afternoon, just as all delegates had assembled for the November 29 plenary session, Churchill presented Stalin with a specially designed and wrought Sword of Honor from King George VI to commemorate the victory at Stalingrad. Stalin lifted the sword to his lips and kissed the blade. Then he handed it to Voroshilov, Russia's most dispensable marshal, who dropped it.

That evening Stalin was host at dinner. The Americans present were Roosevelt, Hopkins, Harriman, and Bohlen; the British, Churchill, Eden, Clark Kerr, and Major Birse. Stalin did not invite Molotov or Voroshilov. He was alone with Valentin M. Berezhkov, his interpreter. The dinner was marked by a duel between Churchill and Stalin relieved, to some extent, by presidential comedy. The Prime Minister asked Stalin what territorial interests the Soviet Union had.

Stalin: "There's no need to speak at the present time about any Soviet desires, but when the time comes we will speak." On the other hand, the dictator was generous to Great Britain. She had fought well in the war "and he, personally, favored an increase in the British Empire, particularly the area around Gibraltar." He also thought the U.S. and the U.K. should "install more suitable governments in Spain and Portugal, since he was convinced that Franco was no friend of Great Britain or the United States." He wanted the Big Three to "retain possession of the

25. Churchill, pp. 359–362, and *F.R.*, pp. 509–512.

important strategic points in the world so that if Germany moved a muscle she could be rapidly stopped."[26] Churchill asserted that his country intended to hold on to her colonies and to reclaim what had been seized by Japan—specifically Hong Kong and Singapore—but that she might, without compulsion, release some portions of the empire.

The drama came in connection with Germany. Hopkins reported that throughout the evening Stalin engaged in "unremitting . . . teasing" of Churchill. The Prime Minister himself states that "there was a good deal of gaiety and many toasts were proposed. Presently Elliott Roosevelt, who had flown out to join his father, appeared at the door, and somebody beckoned him to come in."

Churchill avers that he did not resent the teasing until Stalin "entered in a genial manner upon a serious and even deadly aspect of the punishment to be inflicted upon the Germans. The German General Staff, he said, must be liquidated."[27] He recommended that "At least 50,000 and perhaps 100,000 of the German Commanding Staff must be physically liquidated."[28]

At this Churchill announced solemnly that "the British Parliament and public will never tolerate mass executions. Even if in war passion they allowed them to begin, they would turn violently against those responsible after the first butchery had taken place. The Soviets must be under no delusion on this point."

Stalin: "Fifty thousand must be shot."

Churchill: "I would rather be taken out into the garden here and now and be shot myself than sully my own and my country's honour by such infamy."

Obviously Churchill no longer thought Stalin was teasing or being mischievous. If Stalin could execute 15,000 to 30,000 of his own army officers and liquidate some 15,000 Polish army officers, it must have occurred to Churchill that the dictator was not joking.

"At this point," Churchill adds, "the President intervened. He had a compromise to propose. Not fifty thousand to be shot, but only forty-nine thousand. By this he hoped, no doubt, to reduce the whole matter to ridicule. Eden also made signs and gestures intended to reassure me that it was all a joke. But now Elliott Roosevelt rose in his place at the end of the table and made a speech, saying how cordially he agreed with Marshal Stalin's plan and how sure he was that the United States Army would support it. At this intrusion," Churchill continues, "I got up and left the table, walking off into the next room, which was in semi-darkness. I had not been there a minute before hands were clapped on my shoulders from behind, and there was Stalin with Molotov at his side,

26. *F.R.*, pp. 554–555.
27. Churchill, p. 373.
28. *F.R.*, p. 554.

both grinning broadly, and eagerly declaring that they were only playing, and nothing of a serious nature had entered their heads. Stalin has a very captivating manner when he chooses to use it, and I never saw him do so to such an extent as at this moment. Although I was not then, and not now, fully convinced that all was chaff and there was no serious intent lurking behind, I consented to return, and the rest of the evening passed pleasantly."[29]

The next day, November 30, the storm at last night's dinner had subsided and the diplomatic sea was smooth when the Big Three and their translators—nobody else—met for lunch. Stalin, in a mellow mood, "admitted frankly that had Russia not had at her disposal such a vast territory the Germans would have probably won the victory."

Such a large land mass as Russia, Churchill observed, deserved access to warm water ports; the peace settlement should settle this matter "as between friends."

Stalin said this could be discussed at the proper time, but since the Prime Minister had raised the question, he asked about the Dardanelles; "it would be well to relax that regime."

The regime he referred to was the Turkish control of the Straits. Churchill said it might not be advisable to do anything at present since they intended, when they arrived in Cairo from Tehran, to bring Turkey into the war. Stalin was in no hurry but "merely interested in discussing it here in general." The Prime Minister thought there could be no objection to Stalin's question, "furthermore, we all hoped to see Russian fleets, both naval and merchant, on all the seas of the world."

Responding to the waves of generosity, Stalin asked what could be done for Russia in the Far East. Vladivostok was only partly ice free. Roosevelt suggested Dairen in Chinese Manchuria as a free port. The Tsar had controlled Dairen and Port Arthur.

At this juncture Churchill made perhaps the most astounding pronouncement heard at the Tehran Conference. "It was important," he said, "that the nations who would govern the world after the war, and who would be entrusted with the direction of the world after the war, should be satisfied and have no territorial or other ambitions. If that question could be settled in a manner agreeable to the great powers, he felt then that the world might indeed remain at peace. He said that hungry and ambitious nations are dangerous, and he would like to see the leading nations of the world in the position of rich, happy men.

"The President and Marshal Stalin agreed."[30]

So ended the luncheon.

29. Churchill, p. 374. In the semidarkness Churchill must have mistaken Berezhkov for Molotov, for, according to Bohlen's minutes of the dinner (*F.R.*, p. 552), Molotov was not present.

30. *F.R.*, pp. 564–568.

Churchill's statement was audacious and cynical, and in the tradition of nineteenth-century imperialism. It echoed, too, the frightening lamentations heard from Germany, Italy, and Japan in the 1930's: they had been deprived, they cried; they were hungry. Hungry nations are dangerous, Churchill said. Hungry nations become ambitious. Churchill did not want "the leading nations of the world"—Britain, Russia, and America —to be hungry, ambitious, and dangerous. He preferred them rich and happy. They would be "entrusted" with the direction of the world after the war and they would use that trust to become rich and happy. At whose expense would they satisfy their hunger? What proof that one feast is not the prelude to another? Are rich men happy? Are not some rich men unhappy until they are richer? Have the poor no right to happiness? And what arrogance to assume that the three big powers would "direct" the world! Even if they had remained united it would have been undesirable and immoral. In the modern world power, fortunately, is sometimes powerless. In time, and time runs fast in the second half of the twentieth century, the slaves, serfs, and satellites throw off the shackles.

Churchill spoke. "The President and Marshal Stalin agreed."

There is no hint here of containment. The three big powers were all to become rich and happy.

The three delegations met in plenary session soon after that luncheon. They heard the report of the Military Commission that Overlord, the descent on the beaches of northern France, was fixed for May, 1944. At the same time a large supporting operation would be undertaken on the French Riviera. This was the decision for which Stalin had striven. The second front at last. The Red Army, he pledged, would launch a large-scale offensive "simultaneously" so that Hitler could not "transfer German troops to the west."[31]

It was appropriate now to think of the final communiqué.

Churchill: "The communiqué should be brief and mysterious."

Stalin: "But no mysticism."

Churchill feared the enemy would learn of our preparations.

Stalin: "You can't hide a big operation in a bag."

Churchill: "Our staffs should consider disguising those preparations so as to confuse the enemy."

Stalin: "In such a situation we deceive the enemy by building dummy tanks, airplanes, and by establishing false airfields. Then, with the aid of tractors, we move these dummy tanks and airplanes about. Intelligence reports these movements to the enemy, and the Germans think this is just the place where an attack is being prepared. At the same time

31. *Ibid.*, pp. 576–577.

there is complete calm where an attack is really being prepared. All transportation is done at night. In a number of places we build up to five to eight thousand dummy tanks, up to two thousand dummy airplanes, and a large number of false airfields. Besides, we mislead the enemy with the aid of radio. In those areas where no attack is intended, exchanges go on between radio stations. The enemy listens in to these stations and gathers the impression that large units are gathered here. Day and night the enemy sometimes bombs these places which are in fact altogether empty."[32]

Churchill: "Truth deserves a bodyguard of lies."[33]

November 30 was Winston Churchill's birthday and he had the pleasure of inviting thirty-two American, British, and Russian guests (including Roosevelt's son Elliott and son-in-law John Boettiger and his own daughter Sarah and son Randolph—no Russian relatives) to a gala dinner at the British Legation. There were many toasts. Churchill, playing to Stalin's great weakness, drank to him as "Stalin the Great."[34] Stalin delivered the most notable toast, the penultimate one: he drank to "the machine" and its role in the war, and expressed his "great admiration" for the productive capacity of the United States which was producing 10,000 airplanes a month. "Without these machines from America, through Lend-Lease, we would lose the war," he said.

Roosevelt, brimming over with good will and undiluted optimism, had the last word: "So as we leave this historic gathering, we can see in the sky, for the first time, that traditional symbol of hope, the rainbow."[35]

The next day, December 1, the day the Tehran Conference dispersed, a cloud, no larger than Poland, dulled the seven colors of the rainbow. The Big Three, with their foreign secretaries, ambassadors, and interpreters lunched at 1 P.M. in the Soviet Embassy, as usual, for Roosevelt's convenience. Again they discussed Turkey's entry into the war. Churchill was hopeful. "But the entire question," he mused, "is that I do not know whether Inonu [the President of Turkey] will or will not come to Cairo."

Stalin: "Might not Inonu become ill?"

Churchill: "He well might. . . ." The Prime Minister, in that event, promised to go to Ankara.

Harry Hopkins indicated U.S. reluctance to sidetrack military operations toward the Eastern Mediterranean. Stalin took the same position, but did not object to the Turks joining the war provided they fought Germany.[36]

32. *Tegeran, Yalta, Potsdam,* p. 41. Churchill's words do not occur in his memoirs or anywhere else. I have therefore translated them from the Russian.
33. *F.R.,* p. 581.
34. Sherwood, p. 793.
35. *F.R.,* pp. 469 and 585.
36. *Tegeran, Yalta, Potsdam,* pp. 42–46.

Turkey, of course, never entered the second world war. She was not "mad." She feared Germany during the fighting and Russia after it. She kept her powder dry and her men alive.

The company at lunch then came to the question of Finland. Churchill said "the first consideration" was the security of Leningrad. And "the position of the Soviet Union as the leading naval and air power in the Baltic Sea should likewise be secure." But he would regret anything done "to impair the independence of Finland, and would therefore welcome the Marshal's statement on that point." The Prime Minister also said Finland was too poor to pay reparations.

Stalin made no statement on the impairment of Finnish independence. He disagreed, however, on indemnities. Finland could render timber, paper, and other goods to Russia and he "intended to demand such reparations."

Churchill recalled the original Bolshevik slogan during the first world war: "No Annexations and No Indemnities."

Stalin laughed. "I have told you I am becoming a conservative," he announced. He had long been a conservative. Lenin's slogans had no meaning for Stalin. Except in name, he had never been a Bolshevik or communist. In power he believed in what Lenin in office believed: "practicality," and practicality when opportunity knocked meant annexations and indemnities. In the instance of Finland annexations meant the cession to Russia, according to the Armistice Agreement of September 19, 1944, of the territories taken by the Soviet Union in 1940 (Viborg and the Karelian Isthmus) as well as the transfer to Russia of nickel-bearing Petsamo in the north instead of Hanko in the south ("A fair exchange," Roosevelt commented) and the lease to Moscow for fifty years of the Porkkala Peninsula near Helsinki as a naval base. Indemnities meant the payment of 300 million prewar dollars in goods to be delivered in six years by a country of a little over four million inhabitants.[37]

After lunch Roosevelt, accompanied by Harriman and Bohlen, conferred with Stalin and Molotov. The President thought he might give the Marshal a lesson in the ways of American democracy. He told Stalin he did not wish to run again but might have to if the war was still on. Now there were six or seven million Americans of Polish ancestry "and as a practical man, he did not wish to lose their vote." Therefore he could not participate in any decision, until after the election in November, 1944, regarding Polish boundaries although "personally he agreed with Marshal Stalin" about Russia's annexing the eastern half of Poland and giving the Poles German territory in the west to the Oder River.

Stalin said he understood.

37. Max Jakobson, *Finnish Neutrality. A Study of Finnish Foreign Policy Since the Second World War*, p. 20.

Roosevelt then alluded to the Americans of Estonian, Latvian, and Lithuanian origin; he needed their votes too. He therefore recommended "a referendum and the right of self-determination . . . some day," and "he personally was confident that the people would vote to join the Soviet Union."

No doubt the new Russian settlers brought in to replace deported Balts, and natives sufficiently cowed, would do as F.D.R. believed. Stalin, knowing his own system, did not see why propaganda in the United States could not create the proper mental attitude in these American citizens. Moreover, under the Soviet Constitution "there would be lots of opportunities" for the "expression of the will of the people," but he could not tolerate "any form of international control."

"The President replied it would be helpful for him personally if some public declaration in regard to future elections . . . could be made."[38]

Stalin now understood something about U.S. democracy.

The final meeting of the Tehran Conference was called at 6 P.M. December 1 to discuss the fateful problems of Poland and Germany. Roosevelt urged the restoration of diplomatic relations between Moscow and the Polish government-in-exile in London.

Stalin: "The agents of the Polish government who operate in Poland are connected with the Germans. They kill partisans. You cannot imagine what they are doing there."[39]

Churchill, clad in radiant romantic armor, rode forth with a lance dipped in the ink of recent history to do battle for Poland. England, he said, had gone to war on September 3, 1939, to rescue her from Hitler's rapacity, and "the Polish question was important for us." But he fell from his horse without striking a blow when he proclaimed that "One of the main objects of the Allies was to achieve the security of the Soviet western frontier, and so to prevent an attack by Germany in the near future."

This being the case, Poland had to be sacrificed to Russia's defense, and therefore Poland could not be saved though Britain had gone to war to save her. A Poland that was forced to surrender her eastern half to Russia and take German territory in compensation would fear Germany and depend on Moscow for safety. Stalin was right in refusing to resume relations with a Polish government in London, and not because of the false charge that it collaborated with the Nazis, it fought the Nazis, or because of the Katyn Forest "slander," but because no independent Polish government would consent to border changes that put the country at Russia's mercy. The only possible Polish government in these circumstances was a Moscow puppet government or, in current terminology, a communist Poland. That is what Stalin got by Churchill's three-matches

38. *F.R.*, pp. 594–595.
39. *Tegeran, Yalta, Potsdam*, p. 48.

maneuver. Roosevelt agreed. This was the essence. But Stalin did not put it that way. As Churchill sallied forth to charge, Stalin raised the shield of self-determination. He wanted no Poles, and when Mr. Bohlen unrolled a map and a debate ensued about Poland's eastern boundary—should it be the Curzon Line or the Ribbentrop-Molotov line?—Stalin marked the map with red lines to indicate the division between regions inhabited by Poles and regions inhabited by Ukrainians and ethnic White Russians (Byelorussians). The latter would be annexed by Russia. On the other hand, the city of Lvov, he admitted, was predominately Polish, but its hinterland was Ukrainian and hence must go to Russia. Self-determination by Kremlin fiat is flexible. Churchill writes, "I was not prepared to make a great squawk about Lvov."[40] Self-determination is flexible outside the Kremlin too.

Poland's fate as a satellite was sealed at Tehran. In fact, however, it was determined by the Red Army's impending conquest of Poland on its way to crush Germany. Given this prospect, what could Roosevelt and Churchill have done? What they did was to beg Stalin to be merciful. He obviously had no intention of being anything of the kind. An alternative western policy might have taken the shape of an ultimatum: Britain and America insist on a Poland intact, not robbed of her eastern provinces and ruled by the Polish government in London returned to Warsaw after the Russian army had expelled the Germans. Such an ultimatum would have had to be accompanied by a threat: no more Lend-Lease; no invasion of France; an end to the Three-Power coalition. Any person proposing such a policy would have been considered insane. Either Russia would have occupied all of Poland and all of Germany and France and become mistress of Europe or Germany might have defeated Russia or made a pact with Russia, and one or both would have controlled the entire continent. Russia or Germany or both might then have supported Japan against the U.S. and the U.K.

Poland was doomed irrespective of Tehran. With all their power Roosevelt and Churchill were powerless to oppose Stalin. Their only feasible strategy would have been to delay Overlord, to penetrate into the Balkans, Austria, and Czechoslovakia, to let Russia bleed and weaken, and to confront the Russian army with an Anglo-American army somewhere in eastern Europe. Was this in Churchill's mind? He denied it in his memoirs.

Without some such wild gamble the independence of Poland was a lost cause, and neither Churchill nor, much less, Roosevelt was ready to risk all to make Polish sovereignty inviolable. Roosevelt in particular had his mind set on postwar collaboration with Russia, and he did not intend at

40. *F.R.*, pp. 596–601. Churchill, pp. 394–397. *Tegeran, Yalta, Potsdam,* pp. 48–50.

Tehran to antagonize one of his Four Policemen for the sake of Poland, whose future he saw, in part, in terms of his fourth election as President.

In its last gasp the Tehran Conference grappled tentatively with the German problem. All three heads of governments favored the dismemberment of Germany. Roosevelt began by saying that Germany should be split into five parts. Stalin, "with a grin, interrupted and suggested that Churchill was not listening because he was not inclined to see Germany broken up." Churchill replied he considered Prussia, the Prussian army, and the General Staff "the root of the evil." Continuing, the President outlined his plan for five separate, independent German states: (1) Prussia, (2) Hanover and the northwestern part of Germany, (3) Saxony and the Leipzig area, (4) Hesse, Darmstadt, Cassel and the region south of the Rhine River, (5) Bavaria, Baden, and Wuerttemberg. In addition, two regions should be under international control: (1) the Kiel Canal and the city of Hamburg and (2) the Ruhr and the Saar, "the latter for the benefit of all Europe."

Churchill: "The President has said a mouthful." This did not signify agreement. The Prime Minister proposed the separation of Prussia from the Reich. He would treat Prussia "sternly," but the people of Bavaria, Wuerttemberg, Saxony, Baden, and the Palatinate were "not the most ferocious" and "I would make things easier for them and allow them to unite in a Danubian Confederation" with Austria and Hungary.[41]

Stalin: "I do not like the plan of new united states. If it is decided to divide Germany then it is not necessary to create new unions. Whether it be five or six states and two regions [under international control] into which Roosevelt proposed to dismember Germany, this Roosevelt plan for the weakening of Germany can be studied. Soon Churchill will have to deal with the same kind of large masses of Germans we have been dealing with. Churchill will then see that not only Prussians are fighting in the German army but also Germans from other German provinces. Only Austrians, in surrendering, shout 'I am an Austrian,' and our soldiers accept them. As far as the Germans of other German provinces are concerned, they fight with equal ferocity. No matter how we approach the question of dismembering Germany, it is not necessary to create new, nonviable combinations of Danubian states. Hungary and Austria should exist separately. Austria existed as an independent state as long as it was left untouched."

Roosevelt: "I agree with Marshal Stalin, in part, on the point that there is no difference between Germans from various German provinces. Fifty years ago this difference existed, but now all German soldiers are alike. True, this does not apply to Prussian officers."

41. Churchill, pp. 400–401; *F.R.*, pp. 600–602; Sherwood, pp. 797–798.

Churchill said he did not oppose the division of Germany, but if the country was divided into several parts and the parts were not united, a time would come when they would unite.

Stalin: "There are no measures that would exclude the possibility of the unification of Germany."

Churchill: "Does Marshal Stalin prefer the splintering of Europe?"

Stalin: "Why bring up Europe? I don't know whether it is necessary to establish four, five or six independent German states. This matter should be discussed."

It was decided to put the problem of Germany in the hands of the London Commission where the three powers were represented.[42]

"I then," writes Churchill, "brought the discussion back to Poland." He would have to face the Polish officials in London and wanted to minimize their complaints. He accordingly proposed a new Poland stretching from the Curzon Line to the Oder River and including East Prussia and Oppeln.[43]

Stalin offered an amendment: "The Russians have no ice-free ports on the Baltic Sea. Therefore the Russians need the ice-free ports of Koenigsberg and Memel and a corresponding part of the territory of East Prussia. All the more since historically this is age-long Slav soil. If the British agree to the transfer of the territories mentioned to us, then we will agree with the formula proposed by Churchill."[44]

Nothing was left on the agenda but the communiqué, and it was signed on December 1, 1943, by "Roosevelt, Stalin, Churchill" in that order. "We have concerted our plans," it declared, "for the destruction of the German forces" by operations from the east, west, and south, and it added, "With our diplomatic advisers we have surveyed the problems of the future. We shall seek the cooperation and active participation of all nations, large and small, whose peoples in heart and mind are dedicated, as are our own peoples, to the elimination of tyranny and slavery, oppression and intolerance. We will welcome them, as they may choose to come, into a world family of democratic nations."[45]

What price words?

*   *   *

President Roosevelt opened the Tehran Conference by welcoming Stalin into the "family circle." Stalin murdered many members of his family.

42. *Tegeran, Yalta, Potsdam,* pp. 51–52.
43. Churchill, p. 403.
44. *Tegeran, Yalta, Potsdam,* p. 53. The U.S. minutes, *F.R.,* p. 604, note that Stalin also asked for Tilsit.
45. *F.R.,* pp. 640–641.

Toward the end of the conference, Sherwood reports, Roosevelt said he "felt sure Stalin was getatable." He was as getatable as a hungry tiger. F.D.R. failed to understand the animal. It was not wrong to try to charm him into eating oats out of the American's hand. The mistake was to believe that the tiger would prefer the proffered fodder when the air reeked with the smell of red meat.

Stalin was a consummate actor. He fooled many foreigners. He could be mild, moderate, soft-spoken, and accommodating. His pipe-smoking enhanced the impression of serenity. His penchant for ridicule and destruction were in abeyance. At Tehran he was on stage, he asked for little though indicating, ever so gently, that at the proper time he might ask for more—power over Poland, rights in the Turkish Straits, a "bite" out of Germany, a bit of East Prussia, and "friendly" neighbors. He thus appeared "getatable." As a result Roosevelt and Churchill were eating out of his hand.

Given the character of the communist regime and Tsarist Russia's history of expansion and attempts at expansion, Roosevelt deluded himself if he thought he could convert the carnivore to vegetarianism. Stalin's appetite for territory has been amply documented in the provisions of the Soviet-Nazi pact and secret protocol of 1939 and in Molotov's meetings with Hitler in 1940. To suppose that the partition of Germany into impotence and the planned elimination of France as a power factor would not drive Moscow into making a bid for European hegemony was naïve.

Lenin laid down the proposition that a developed capitalist country must be imperialistic even if it owned no colonies. Though he himself warned that a victorious proletariat "might ride on somebody else's back," many persons assumed that socialism precluded imperialism. The fact is, however, that the Soviet Union possesses an empire and behaves like an empire. This proves either that socialism is compatible with imperialism or that Russia is not socialist. She is actually capitalist, state capitalist, and her state capitalism has displayed all the expansionist, exploitative proclivities of robber-baron monopoly private capitalism.

Theory apart, the record shows that Russia meant to retain every square foot of non-Russian territory the Red Army conquered in defeating Germany and to hold it by crushing the active resistance of the populations, communists included, of those lands. Witness East Germany, Poland, Hungary, and Czechoslovakia. Only Bulgaria has not risen against the Soviet intruders. Rumania rebels in her own way. Yugoslavia won independence.

U.S. State Department officials could have warned Roosevelt of the menace of Soviet imperialism. But F.D.R. was not in the habit of listening to subordinates or reading their meticulous memoranda. He was his own State Department—he and, at the time of Tehran, Harry Hopkins; before that, he and Sumner Welles.

Economic determinists can dig to the roots of Soviet imperialism. Its causes are known. Power yearns to be used when opportunity beckons. Certain groups benefit, others pay. James Mill, quoted in J. A. Hobson's *Imperialism,* called the British colonies "a vast system of outdoor relief for the upper classes." When the beneficiaries lost strength and the payers gained strength the game came to an end. In the Soviet Union the military and the bureaucracy get political and social nourishment from empire. It guarantees their tenure by perpetuating the dictatorship.

After the first world war the West built a cordon sanitaire around Russia to keep communism in. After the second world war Stalin built a cordon sanitaire around Russia to keep the West out. If eastern Europe were free, prosperous, and democratic, Russia would be infected. Her people might demand liberty and more groceries; a national minority like the Ukrainians might ask independence. The Soviet Empire is designed to prevent Russia's neighbors from living better than Russians.

Russia is Eastern. Her church and part of her elite always sought to erect a wall against the corrosive influence of western ideas and institutions of democracy. This was tsarism. This is communism. The two are different and alike. The one was, the other is, conservative, obscurantist, intolerant, rigid, repressive, fear-ridden, dogma-ridden, dull, and dominated by absolute autocrats or oligarchs. There was the "Little Father" in the palace, there is Big Brother in the Kremlin. The monarchy's Okhrana was a kindergarten compared to the Cheka, GPU, and NKVD. Red Moscow knows better the methods of mind manipulation. The Tsars enslaved men but the human spirit eluded them and soared; Russia in the nineteenth century gave the world its best literature. Communism, being more pervasive, kills creativity. It has forged a new jargon to replace language. It invents formulas to disguise facts: democratic centralism is the disguise for dictatorship and dictatorship of the proletariat a synonym for working-class impotence; proletarian internationalism is Kremlinese for Russian imperialism; an imperialist is anybody Moscow dislikes.

Stalin's nationalism fostered Soviet imperialism. Imperialism, in turn, nurtures Russian nationalism. Both bolster the governing oligarchs who exploit patriotism to extract more underpaid work from the masses and use glory won abroad to brighten the bleakness at home. The worst criticism of the Lenin-Trotsky revolution is that it has ended in boredom. Stalin wanted empire for circuses. It was the people's reward for the blood they shed so profusely. He hoped political power outside would conceal economic failures inside. He sold empire as a patent medicine for security. It is an old story. Churchill knew it well. Roosevelt dreamt of a new world order.

When the President, on the afternoon of November 29, outlined to Marshal Stalin a United Nations whose executive organization would consist of "Four Policemen," Stalin objected that "a European state would probably resent China having the right to apply certain machinery to it. And in any event, he did not think China would be very powerful after the war." He preferred a European Commission consisting of the United States, Great Britain, the Soviet Union, "and possibly one other European state." But Roosevelt "doubted if the United States Congress would agree to United States' participation in an exclusively European Committee which might be able to force the dispatch of American troops to Europe." He envisaged sending only "American planes and ships to Europe." England and the Soviet Union would have to provide the land armies in the event of a threat to peace.[46]

Roosevelt's concept of the Four Policemen ignored the world's major problem: who will police the policemen? Big powers, not little countries, cause most of humanity's troubles. Little countries make little difficulties, and even they cannot be policed or penalized when they enjoy the protection of a big power. But how is Russia or America to be policed except by a nuclear war tantamount to global suicide? The alternative is for each superpower to recognize the other's sphere of influence and shut an eye to the depredations of each in its segment of the planet.

Roosevelt's new world order implied this tacit bargain. Stalin saw through to its core: Britain could not, America would not, interfere. He equated a friendly Roosevelt, thrice elected President, with a friendly America, and why would such an America, ready to cut down Germany and mark down France, bother about Poland and remote, little-known countries in eastern Europe? He returned to Moscow a happy man. The Soviet press reflected his pleasure. If he had the power he could have an empire.

Politically, that was the Tehran total.

At Tehran Stalin invariably spoke of "Russia" and "we Russians." After the dissolution of the Comintern in May, 1943, this sounded reassuring to western ears: Moscow, now nationalistic, no longer dreamt of world revolution. Roosevelt apparently forgot that communist revolution never extended the Soviet Union's frontiers whereas the imperialistic pact and protocol with Hitler had. Imperialism, once fed, hungers for more food.

It is possible to judge the Tehran Conference as a tragedy of errors, a

46. *Ibid.,* pp. 530–531.

new act of appeasement of another aggressive dictatorship. But this would be a verdict based on hindsight. At the time it may have been an experiment in faith, an investment in hope. Without Russia the second world war would have become a massacre of American and British young manhood. With the Red Army bearing the brunt of the fighting, victory had appeared on the horizon. In gratitude Roosevelt and Churchill buried their anticommunism, Churchill forgot some of his anti-Russianism. Both had been long in politics, so neither was an innocent. Yet in their eagerness to keep Russia as an ally in the postwar they gambled on her friendship. They forgot the millennial striving of Russia to be an ever-greater land mass. Under Lenin the Soviets were weak and therefore anti-imperialist, but even at the nadir of power they tried to regain Poland, Finland, Estonia, Latvia, and Lithuania, and did conquer Georgia. Under Stalin they had lurched, in addition, toward Rumania, Bulgaria, and the Straits. What would they do when Europe was prostrate? This apparently never crossed the mind of Roosevelt and flashed only once through Churchill's, when he asked whether Stalin wished to splinter Europe.

At Tehran the West began whetting Stalin's appetite. No clairvoyance, only statesmanship, was necessary to foresee the result. It would have been far better if Roosevelt and Churchill had sent their military commanders to Moscow to concert plans with Stalin for the next offensive campaigns and left the final decisions to the heads of government calmly assessing the political connotations of that strategy while sitting in Washington or London, not in the diplomatic hothouse of Tehran. But Roosevelt pre-eminently, and Churchill too, loved the drama of a great confrontation, especially with so powerful, and at that time so enigmatic, a figure as Stalin. Few leaders can resist the limelight when there seems to be a chance to remake the world or at least to make history.

XVI OF COMMUNISTS AND KINGS

The contours of the postwar world began to appear at Tehran. That unattractive world would have three prominent features: a British, a Soviet, and an American sphere of influence. Whether a sphere of influence was an empire depended on the measure of control the superpower exercised over weaker states.

The Big Three powers seemed to welcome spheres of influence. Stalin said at Tehran he hoped England would retain, even enlarge, her empire. Roosevelt and Churchill, according to the Tehran minutes, encouraged Russia to expand. The Big Three behaved as if the existence of one sphere of influence lent legitimacy to the existence of the others.

The American sphere of influence was nebulous. No one mentioned, therefore no one questioned, U.S. pre-eminence in Latin America; the interest of American companies in Arabian oil was common knowledge. Would China be a policeman or a piece of the American sphere of influence? The matter was not broached.

Large regions in other continents were left unassigned. If France was to lose her colonies, as Stalin suggested, if Indochina must not revert to France, as Roosevelt urged, what was to be their future?

Roosevelt wanted India free; this was in the liberal American tradition of the President and the men nearest him. But in his first talk with Stalin in Tehran F.D.R. cautioned the Marshal never to mention the subject, the mere thought of losing India enraged Churchill. There is no fact or hint to support the suspicion that America wanted to replace England in India or France in Indochina and Africa.

The biggest uncertainty was Europe. What of Germany? France? Italy? The Balkans? Which superpower would dominate where? Here was material for conflict. These crucial issues remained unresolved when the Big Three leaders parted at Tehran on December 1, 1943. The armies would decide.

A great Russian army was on the move westward. A growing Anglo-American army was poised to move onto the continent. Military mobility actuates political mobility. The European weather prediction read: variable winds and unstable conditions. Political geography might be changed by external force or by a realignment of internal political power.

Italy was the first European country to erupt. Benito Mussolini, genius of misjudgment, had an inferior intellect. He advised Hitler on January 3, 1940, to invade Russia. He hoped thereby to keep the war away from Italy, whose energy and resources had been wasted in Ethiopia and Spain. When France, whose military strength Stalin and Hitler overestimated, was on the verge of surrender, Mussolini, convinced it would all end soon, took Italy to war to earn a share of the loot. But the war was only then beginning. On March 8, 1943, after the German catastrophe at Stalingrad and when Italy was feeling the blood drain of fighting in North Africa, Mussolini begged Hitler to leave Russia and turn west: "I ask myself whether it is not too risky to repeat the struggle against the boundless space of Russia, which is practically impossible to reach and grasp, while at the same time in the west, the Anglo-Saxon peril mounts."[1]

Mussolini was thinking with his skin; he wanted to save it. He knew he was gravely ill and that Italian fascism was dying. But he showed lack of political understanding. The Soviet-Nazi war could end only in the total defeat of one of the belligerents, for if Hitler proposed a peace, Stalin would sense victory and pursue the struggle, and if Stalin sued for peace, Hitler, concluding that Russia teetered on the lip of collapse, would strike to kill. As Hitler once said, "It is childish and naïve to expect that at a moment of grave military defeats the time for political dealings has arrived. Such moments come when you are having successes." But since one man's successes are the other man's defeats, the moment for "deals" never arrives. Only surrender satisfies.

Mussolini's letter of March 8, 1943, reads in retrospect like a premonition of disaster. For on July 25 the King ordered the Duce imprisoned. Italian fascism disintegrated as though the twenty black years had been a zero in history. Marshal Badoglio, the new Prime Minister, the monarch's appointee, dissembled. He assured the Germans, whose legions occupied much of the peninsula, that Italy remained loyal to the Axis, and then established secret contacts with the Anglo-Americans. Moscow justly resented its exclusion from the talks, for as a member of the warring coalition Russia was entitled to a role in peacemaking. The circumstances, however, were unusual. Italy's double game had to be hidden from the Nazis. Their diplomatic representative signaled his presence in Lisbon, the spy capital of the western world. A Russian negotiator there would have stuck out like an obelisk in the desert. General Walter Bedell Smith, Eisenhower's Chief of Staff in the Mediterranean theater, who had lived in military uniform for many years, and Brigadier Kenneth Strong of the British army acquired strange collections of civilian costumes to conceal their identity for their prearranged rendezvous with Badoglio's emissary. Every move and message was conspiratorial. General Smith traveled on a British civilian passport. In Lisbon, Smith and Strong immediately clarified the position: the Allies expected unconditional surrender; no negotiations. The Italian protested. Italy did not wish to quit the war, Badoglio intended to switch sides and join the Big Three powers.[2]

The Allies, having ousted the Germans from Sicily, now planned a landing in the vicinity of Naples, and it would save lives to execute this operation with Italy's cooperation rather than against her resistance. General George C. Marshall had explained at Tehran that "the failure of a river crossing is a reverse, while the failure of a landing operation from

1. F. W. Deakin, *The Brutal Friendship,* p. 247.
2. Harold Macmillan, *The Blast of War,* pp. 310–314.

the sea is a catastrophe, because failure in the latter case means the almost utter destruction of the landing craft and personnel involved."[3] Hence the eagerness to sign with the Italians before the descent on Italy's western shore. The armistice was concluded on September 3, 1943, and announced on September 8. Badoglio declared war on Germany on October 15. But Germany was so much in command in Rome that the King and Badoglio fled by cruiser to Brindisi, on the heel of Italy.

The future of Italy was at stake. On July 28, 1943, Roosevelt said in a radio broadcast, "Eventually Italy will reconstitute herself." Harry Hopkins remarked aboard the *Iowa,* en route to Tehran, that Churchill "evidently desires a status quo as regards monarchies."[4] The movement in Italy for a republic was running strong, especially in the north and especially among communists who were resisting the German occupiers.

Badoglio was a conservative soldier. He informed General Eisenhower on Malta on September 29 that the King and he hoped to have as their Foreign Minister not Count Carlo Sforza, an antifascist exile long resident in the United States whom the U.S. preferred for the post, but Count Dino Grandi, Mussolini's ambassador in London who precipitated the fall of the Duce by calling for a vote of no confidence at the July 24, 1943, Grand Fascist Council meeting.[5] King Victor Emmanuel had indeed put an end to Mussolini's role as dictator, but only after adjusting to his whims for two decades. Neither Badoglio nor the King, therefore, lent the new government popularity or stability. The public demanded a republic. The communists demanded the King's abdication. Deputy Soviet Foreign Commissar Andrei Y. Vyshinsky told Ambassador Harriman in Cairo on November 23, 1943, "he was predisposed not to favor the retention of the King."[6]

Nevertheless, Stalin, smarting under Russia's exclusion from the secret armistice talks with Italy and determined to have a foot in the door to the politics of the peninsula, accredited an ambassador on March 14, 1944, to the rickety authority in Brindisi, and Palmiro Togliatti, the secretary general of the Italian Communist Party, returned to Italy late in March, 1944, after long years of exile in the U.S.S.R., announced, "I am ready to participate in the government, even with the King."[7] Badoglio, anticommunist to his core, welcomed this communist stance because it gave him a little leverage with the British and Americans whose guns dominated the government at Brindisi. The communists entered the Ba-

3. U.S. Department of State, *Foreign Relations of the United States. Diplomatic Papers. The Conferences of Cairo and Tehran 1943.* pp. 527–528.
4. *Ibid.,* p. 197.
5. *Ibid.,* p. 593.
6. *Ibid.,* p. 309.
7. Quoted by Carlo Sforza, cited by André Fontaine, *Histoire de la Guerre Froide.* Vol. I: *de la Révolution d'octobre à la Guerre de Corée. 1917–1950,* p. 228.

doglio Cabinet in the name, they stated, of "national unity," rarely a communist preoccupation in capitalist countries.

The war had bisected Italy: in the north the Germans, using Mussolini, whom they had lifted out of prison in a spectacular commando raid, as their shrunken, pitiful puppet; in the south the King and Badoglio by grace of the western Allies. In the north, now officially a "social republic," the communists fought the Germans and Mussolini and ultimately captured him and Clara Petacci, his mistress, shot them, and hanged both head down; in the south the communists made common cause with the diminutive Victor Emmanuel and Badoglio, Mussolini's marshal in Ethiopia. The Anglo-Americans, who might have exercised a veto over Badoglio's appointment of a communist Cabinet minister, presumably hesitated to offend Moscow, where Togliatti had got his instructions.

After Italy capitulated, her ships were seized by the Allies. Moscow, on October 23, 1943, claimed a share of the prize: one battleship, one cruiser, eight destroyers, and four submarines "to be dispatched right away" to Soviet northern ports because the Montreux Treaty prohibited the passage of warships through the Turkish Straits in time of war, and 40,000 tons of merchant vessels "for immediate dispatch to the Black Sea."[8]

Roosevelt ruled that all Italian ships were to be used where they could render "the best service" to the Allied cause.[9] He later interpreted this to mean that the U.S.S.R. would receive one third of all Italian shipping.[10] At the Tehran Conference Roosevelt, Churchill, and Stalin decided that the Russian share of Italian vessels "pass over to Soviet command sometime around the end of January, 1944."[11] But on November 30, 1943, when Italy had been recognized by the western powers and the Soviet Union as a cobelligerent, Admiral William D. Leahy, Chief of Staff of the U.S. navy, feared that the Italian crews, now cooperating with the Allies in the Mediterranean, might scuttle their ships rather than surrender them to Russia and remain idle. Leahy also questioned whether the Soviets could man so many additional ships and modernize them, "especially as regards antiaircraft armament, which the U.S.S.R. has no means of effecting."[12]

Because Italian units had fought the Red Army, Russia demanded her slice of pie. Roosevelt informed Harriman in Moscow on December 21, 1943, that the transfer would commence "about February first." At present, he said, the Italian fleet was employed "in the Allied war effort."[13]

A multiple conversation followed between Roosevelt and Churchill

8. *F.R.,* pp. 112–113.
9. *Ibid.,* p. 120.
10. *Ibid.,* p. 129.
11. *Ibid.,* p. 597.
12. *Ibid.,* p. 597.
13. *Ibid.,* pp. 852–853.

and between Roosevelt and Ambassador Harriman about the western pledge: was it one third of all Italian shipping, as the President had stated publicly, or one battleship, one cruiser, eight destroyers, four submarines, and 40,000 tons of freighters? Churchill contended, correctly, that the one-third slice had never been promised. Harriman corroborated Churchill. This having been established, the Prime Minister agreed with Leahy that there were "dangers" in surrendering the Italian ships. Instead he proposed giving the Soviets the British battleship *Royal Sovereign,* which recently completed refitting in the United States. Roosevelt offered an American cruiser, the *Milwaukee.* The U.S. and the U.K. also provided the U.S.S.R. with 40,000 tons of merchant shipping—all these, the freighters and the warships, until title to the Italian vessels could be given the Russians. After the successful landing on the Normandy beaches (Overlord) Britain transferred to the Soviets four of her modern submarines and eight destroyers. Stalin acquiesced.[14]

Most of the correspondence about the Italian fleet occurred while Churchill was away from home and ill. He had not felt well in Tehran. He was worn out after Tehran and the subsequent talks in Cairo. "I am completely at the end of my tether," he announced on arrival by air in Tunis. There, in neighboring Carthage, he took to his bed with pneumonia and a fever. "Take it easy," Roosevelt wired. Shortly thereafter Roosevelt himself was smitten with the flu. The Italian campaign was in full heat, preparations for Overlord proceeded apace, and Churchill lay "prostrate," as he put it, reading Jane Austen. On recovering he flew to Marrakesh in Morocco for convalescence but was too limp to paint. Franco and Tito telegraphed good-health wishes. The patient exchanged telegrams with Eden, Deputy Prime Minister Attlee, Stalin, Roosevelt, generals, admirals; the war waited for no man. Eden said on December 20 that Churchill was "displaying great vitality by sending ever more frequent and fierce dispatches." He returned to London late in January, 1944.

Once at No. 10, Downing Street Churchill was awash with historic tasks: military strategy, war production, relations with allies, domestic politics. The war at sea was going well, he reported to Roosevelt on March 2, 1944: German U-boats sank 659,000 tons in February, 1942, 378,000 tons in February, 1943, and 70,000 tons in February, 1944. This buoyed his spirits and sharpened his eyesight. "Just below the Foreign Office," he wrote Lord Portal, Minister of Works, on March 7, "on the grass opposite St. James's Park Lane, there's a very untidy sack with holes in it and sand leaking out. . . . Such a conspicuous place ought not to look untidy." The same day he sent a note to the Minister of Supply:

14. Winston S. Churchill, *The Second World War. Closing the Ring,* pp. 457–460.

"Just off the main road between Amersham and Uxbridge, at a place called Chalfont St. Giles, there is a rubbish heap where for the last three years work has been going on. I pass it every time I go to Chequers. Are tins and metal objects being recovered from what was a dump in past years, or are they being thrown there together with other rubbish?" Master of the English language whose verbs worked and whose nouns were images, he questioned the Director of Military Intelligence: "Why must you write 'intensive' here? 'Intense' is the right word. You should read Fowler's *Modern English Usage* on the use of the two words." Again, to the Minister of Works: ". . . we must have a better word than 'prefabricated.' Why not 'ready-made'?"

Churchill's ingrained anticommunism, lulled into dormancy by Stalin's low-key behavior at Tehran, had revived. A purge was in progress. "You will remember," he reminded Sir Alexander Cadogan, Permanent Under Secretary of the Foreign Office, "that we are purging all our secret establishments of Communists because we know they owe no allegiance to us or our cause and will always betray secrets to the Soviet, even while we are working together." The Prime Minister's old irritations with the Soviet Union were dominant again. Russia, fully occupied by Hitler, wanted no trouble with Japan. Japan, hard-pressed by America and England, did not wish to add Russia to her enemies. She had made concessions to the Kremlin. Eden and Cadogan thought this "good." Churchill reproved them in a note dated April 23, 1944. ". . . personally," he said, "I thought the business looked rather suspicious. . . . They are getting their own quarrels with Japan settled. This will put them in a better position to drive a hard bargain with us when Hitler is defeated before they embark upon hostilities with Japan. It may of course be part of a deception scheme to lull the Japanese into a false sense of security. Personally I do not like it." He liked it less when it happened at Yalta.

In Churchill's heart the honeymoon with Moscow had ended. He ordered Eden on May 4 to draft a one-page paper for the Cabinet and possibly for the Imperial Conference setting forth "the brute issues between us and the Soviet government which are developing in Italy, in Rumania, in Bulgaria, in Yugoslavia, and above all in Greece. . . . Broadly speaking, the issue is, Are we going to acquiesce in the Communization of the Balkans and perhaps of Italy?" He proposed that Britain resist "Communist infusion and invasion, and we should put it to them pretty plainly at the best moment that military events permit. We should of course have to consult the United States first." As a preliminary step he suggested recalling the British Ambassador from Moscow. He wanted Eden's opinion on this drastic step. "I am not very clear on it myself, but evidently we are approaching a showdown with the Russians about their Communist intrigues in Italy, Yugoslavia, and Greece. . . . I must say I think their attitude becomes more difficult every day."

While Ambassador Clark Kerr remained in Moscow, Churchill instructed him to use new methods. It was unnecessary for the Ambassador to deliver every telegram in person to Stalin or Molotov and wait several days "if these potentates are away or do not choose to give audience," he explained to Eden on May 7. "It seems to me that it would be much better, for instance when we send a very stiff message, not to have our man waiting about to be bulldozed and afterwards sometimes offer deprecatory observations which weaken the force of what it has been decided to say." The Prime Minister was disturbed by Soviet manners. "They treat our people like dogs," he exclaimed in a note to the military chiefs at home. He was much more distressed by Russian intentions in France and the Balkans. Yet Soviet crudity in personal relations made him irate. This manifested itself with special vehemence when the British government, at considerable inconvenience to itself, gave the Russians vessels from its own navy and mercantile fleet in lieu of the Italian ships. "Do not hesitate to be blunt with these Russians when they become unduly truculent. . . . Not one word of thanks has ever been expressed to us," he wrote the First Sea Lord on May 28, 1944, "for this transfer of ships. We have borne the brunt of meeting their requests for shipping. There are all sorts of ways of making people feel you resent their insults. If however their conduct improves, you should neglect nothing which will encourage this amendment."[15]

The Russians undoubtedly felt they were bearing the brunt of the fighting, and as to the ships—Russia's right to them had been recognized. Nevertheless, the British made a special effort to implement the agreement, and a "Thank You" never hurts. But there are many shortages in the Soviet Union and one of the most trying is the shortage of courtesy among communist bureaucrats from the top down.

Churchill, the anticommunist, nevertheless favored Tito, the communist leader of the Yugoslav Partisans, over anticommunist General Draza Mihailovic, supporter of young King Peter. Ideology was in deepfreeze because Tito mauled more German divisions than Mihailovic. The British were bigger givers than the Russians to Tito's guerrillas, yet Churchill tried to marry Tito to Peter politically. So did Moscow. If this is confusion, so were the policies. They often are. The confusion looks like what was later called "convergence." Roosevelt believed in convergence. He said to Under Secretary Sumner Welles "that American democracy and Soviet Communism could never meet. But he told me he did believe that if one took the figure 100 as representing the difference between American democracy and Soviet Communism in 1917, with the United

15. *Ibid.*, pp. 696–715.

States at 100 and the Soviet Union at 0, American democracy might eventually reach 60 and the Soviet system might reach the figure of 40."[16] This was a misreading at least of Soviet history. Churchill and Stalin, however, thought not of convergence but of coalition when they wished to meld Peter with Tito. Churchill's case is clear: he loved kings, and it is not that he loved communists, he hated them, but he hated Hitler more, and Tito was effectively anti-Hitler.

The story of Peter, Tito, Stalin, and Churchill begins on March 27, 1941, when Yugoslav officers, mostly Serbs, overthrew the government of Prince Regent Paul because it acceded to the Nazi-made Tripartite Pact, and proclaimed Peter, age seventeen, king. The Soviets immediately recognized the new regime. The Germans immediately occupied Yugoslavia. Mussolini, dreaming of easy annexations of the Dalmatian coast across the Adriatic, also sent troops. Peter fled to England.

The many thousands of Yugoslavs who joined anti-invader guerrilla bands split into two camps: one, led by Mihailovic, Peter's Minister of War, was largely Serb, largely urban, and largely favorable to the monarchy; the other, led by Josip Broz, a Croat, whose communist party name was Tito, consisted of Croats, Bosnians, Montenegrins, Macedonians, and Herzegovinians, and some Serbs and Slovenes. The division ran, roughly, along ethnic lines, Serbs versus Croats and the other minorities of Yugoslavia; along political lines, monarchists versus antimonarchists; and along social lines, city folk against hardy mountaineers and tough hillside peasants eager to get land in the plains. This was thus a war within a war: two armies of guerrillas against Germans and Italians and against one another. At genesis, only a tiny percentage of Tito's Partisans—the leadership—was communist. They joined Tito for ethnic, political, and social reasons, and, having joined and endured common sufferings, and won and lost battles, they identified with communism.

The Chetniks were first in the field. Tito began to fight several months later, in July, 1941, after the Nazi invasion of the Soviet Union. But the Chetniks were cautious, they built up their organization and harassed the invaders without challenging them and tried, at the same time, to curb Tito's Partisans, who lusted for enemy blood. The British had cloak-and-dagger liaison officers with Mihailovic only. "By the autumn [of 1942], the position had to be reviewed," writes an official British historian of the war. "Support could no longer be confined to the Chetniks. The Partisans were by now a powerful force, perhaps of over 100,000 men, which was fighting the enemy at least as effectively as the Serbs."[17]

In the spring of 1943 the British government accordingly decided to

16. Sumner Welles, *Where Are We Heading?* p. 37.
17. J. R. M. Butler (Ed.), *History of the Second World War. Grand Strategy.* Vol, V. John Ehrman, *August 1943-September 1944,* p. 78.

establish contact with the Partisans and continue helping Mihailovic but to warn him "that the British would withdraw their support unless he ceased to collaborate with the Italians and with Nedic [the Prime Minister of the puppet Yugoslav government set up by the Germans in Belgrade], unless he stopped fighting the Partisans."[18] At the end of May, Captain F. W. Deakin, an Oxford don "who," Churchill writes, "had helped me for five years before the war in my literary work," was dropped by parachute with a small party into Montenegro to serve as liaison officer with Tito. On June 6 the British Chiefs of Staff reported: "It is clear from information available to the War Office that the Cetniks are hopelessly compromised in their relations with the Axis in Herzegovina and Montenegro. During the recent fighting in the latter area, it has been the well-organized partisans rather than the Cetniks who have been holding down the Axis forces." Churchill bubbled over with enthusiasm for Tito's followers: while "Serbian resistance" to the German terror had become "only a shadow," the common people sustained the national struggle. "A wild and furious war for existence against the Germans broke into flame among the partisans. Among these Tito stood forth, pre-eminent and soon dominant. Tito . . . was a Soviet-trained Communist. . . . But once he united in his breast and brain his Communist doctrine with his burning ardour for his native land in her extreme torment, he became a leader, with adherents who had little to lose but their lives, who were ready to die, and if to die to kill." That sufficed to muffle Churchill's anticommunism. "The partisans under Tito," the Prime Minister continued, "wrested weapons from German hands. They grew rapidly in numbers. No reprisals, however bloody, upon hostages or villages, deterred them. For them it was death or freedom."[19]

So impressed was Churchill with the Partisans that he decided in July, 1943, to send an outstanding personality to work among them: Fitzroy Maclean, a witty Scot wielding a brilliant pen, who had written entrancing tales of visits to exotic places like Samarkand, Soviet Bokhara, and Afghanistan. In 1939, at war's beginning, he joined the Foreign Office, but finding life dull he went into Conservative politics and was elected to Parliament. This too seemed tame and he volunteered for adventurous behind-the-enemy-lines parachute jumps in North Africa. Churchill told him to drop from an airplane on to Tito's stronghold in Bosnia. The Partisans fell in love with the tall, lanky, smiling, stubborn, audacious, learned Scotsman. Parcels of arms were parachuted to the Tito bands by British planes based in Egypt and Italy.

However, Tito, Edward Kardelj, Milovan Djilas, Mosha Piyade, and a growing number of Partisans were communists; in the second half of

18. *Ibid.*, p. 78.
19. Churchill, pp. 462–463.

1941, throughout 1942, and in 1943 they were compelling Hitler to keep at least a dozen divisions in Yugoslavia which would otherwise have been transferred to the Russian front. They felt, therefore, that they had a right to expect some assistance, or at a minimum, some moral support from their Soviet brothers-in-ideology. The Yugoslav communists must have blushed unseen at the thought that while the British "imperialists" were at their side no Russian comrades had appeared or helped. In February, 1942, having established radio contact with "Grand-dad"—that is, Moscow—Tito received a telegram: "There is possibility of our sending men to you in the immediate future. . . . Give us details as to where our aircraft can come down. What reception signals can you make to ensure accurate and easy landing? Have you any aviation spirit?"

All excitement and faith, Tito radioed Grand-dad the information requested and added a list of his needs: medicines, automatic arms, munitions, boots, explosives, submachine guns, and pistols. "If you send us sufficient military equipment we can mobilize 100,000 more men."[20] The watch for the Soviet aircraft was maintained day and night. But "the immediate future" did not arrive in February, 1942, or at any time in 1942 or 1943. Grand-dad pleaded "technical difficulties." No aid in any form and no military mission came to Tito's Partisans from the Soviet Union during that entire period. Instead the Kremlin offered advice and acted in a way to show that the "difficulties" were not "technical." Early in March, 1942, Tito received a telegram from Grand-dad telling him to "Take into account that the Soviet Union has treaty relations with the Yugoslav King and Government, and that taking an open stand against these would create new difficulties in the joint war efforts and the relations between the Soviet Union on the one hand and Britain and America on the other." In August, 1942, the Soviets raised the Royal Yugoslav Legation in Russia to the rank of embassy.[21]

Tito told Grand-dad on November 12, 1942, of the formation of new Partisan divisions and brigades. "We shall now," he announced, "set up something like a government, which is to be called the National Liberation Committee of Yugoslavia." Grand-dad shot back, "Do not look upon the committee as a sort of government. . . . Do not put it in opposition to the Yugoslav government in London. At the present stage, do not raise the question of the abolition of the monarchy. Do not put forward any slogan of a republic."[22]

20. Mosha Piyade, *About the Legend That the Yugoslav Uprising Owed Its Existence to Soviet Assistance,* pp. 6–9. Piyade was a member of the Politburo of the Yugoslav Communist Party. His article was published in English in 1950 and distributed as a 24-page pamphlet by the Yugoslav Information Center in New York City.
21. *Ibid.,* pp. 11 and 16.
22. *Ibid.,* p. 20.

Tito radioed his Russian "grandfather" on June 12, 1943: "The enemy is again trying to surround us. . . . We are at present feeding on horseflesh, with no bread. Our position is hard, but we shall get out of it, even though with heavy losses. . . . We request your support in this supreme trial." Piyade comments: "But even in that difficult situation we got nothing beyond fine words and compliments. Nor would they send us a Military Mission."[23]

Fate smiled on the hungry, embattled Partisans. Italy having surrendered in September, 1943, Tito's valiant men speedily deprived six Italian divisions in Yugoslavia of their arms and equipment and persuaded two other Italian divisions to join the fight against the Germans.[24] Shortly thereafter the United States delivered to the Partisans 400 tons of uniforms, medical supplies, ammunition, and other essential commodities.[25]

At the beginning of October, 1943, the Partisans, reinforced by volunteers who could now be armed, had "gained control, in varying degrees, of over half of Yugoslavia. By the end of that month, Maclean reported that they disposed of twenty-six divisions, comprising some 200,000 men."[26] Emboldened by success, eager to strike while their triumphs were hot, Tito defied Moscow and convened a meeting of the Anti-Fascist Council of the National Liberation of Yugoslavia at Jajce, in Bosnia, where on November 29 a National Committee was chosen to function as a Cabinet. The same assembly decided to deprive the royal Yugoslav government in London of its right to govern the country, cautioned King Peter and all members of his dynasty not to set foot on Yugoslav soil, and ruled that the issue of monarchy or republic would be resolved after victory.[27]

"Early in December," writes Churchill, "we withdrew official support from Mihailovic and recalled the British mission operating in his territory."[28]

Monarchist, anticommunist Churchill and the British government now limited their support in Yugoslavia to antimonarchist, communist Tito. But Moscow was wroth. "Moscow's first reaction [to the Jajce decisions] was furious. The 'Free Yugoslavia' radio station [on Soviet territory] had orders not to broadcast the resolution prohibiting the King's return. Yugoslavia's representative in Moscow, Veljko Vlahovic, was reprimanded and his broadcasts for 'Radio Free Yugoslavia' and the Moscow

23. *Ibid.,* p. 22.
24. Churchill, p. 465. Vladimir Dedijer, in *Tito,* p. 201, puts the number of disarmed Italian divisions at 11.
25. Dedijer, p. 202.
26. Ehrman, p. 80.
27. Dedijer, p. 207.
28. *Closing the Ring,* p. 467.

radio were censored. Manuilsky [former effective chief of the Comintern] delivered Stalin's message: 'The Hazyahyin [the Boss, Stalin's nickname] is extremely angry. He says this is a stab in the back of the Soviet Union.' "[29]

"It was only later," writes Dedijer, "that Stalin's opposition became clear: he opposed the principle of Yugoslavia for the Yugoslavs; he wished the country to be a 'sphere of influence' for one big power or another." Stalin was incensed because a foreign communist leader had disobeyed him, because that leader and his communist friends had, for all practical purposes, declared Yugoslavia a republic although Moscow still recognized the monarchy.

But "the Boss" rarely retreated without a fight. The Soviet Ambassador in London handed Foreign Secretary Eden a note on December 21, 1943, saying the Soviet government thinks "it is necessary to make efforts to find a basis for collaboration between the two sides." On the other hand, "The British Ambassador to the Royal Yugoslav Government, Mr. Stevenson," in Cairo, where King Peter now resided, "telegraphed the Foreign Office on December 25: '. . . the partisans will be the rulers of Yugoslavia. . . . It is extremely doubtful whether we can any longer regard the Monarchy as a unifying element in Yugoslavia.' "[30]

Churchill was nevertheless eager to reconcile the Partisans to King Peter, and so wrote Tito. Tito remained adamant. "The [Yugoslav] Government in Cairo," he replied on February 9, 1944, "must be suppressed" and Peter must "submit" to the Anti-Fascist Council, heavily communist, which had met at Jajce. Churchill now referred to Peter's "bedraggled Government" and added, "Unless he acts promptly . . . his chances of regaining his throne will, in my opinion, be lost."

Churchill had conceived an affection for Tito. He informed the Marshal that his son, Major Randolph Churchill, a Member of Parliament, would parachute to Tito's headquarters, and added, "I wish I could come myself, but I am too old and heavy to jump out on a parachute."[31]

The British observed and drew the right conclusions: the King was no king. The monarchy was finished. The two camps were irreconcilable. The Soviet communists, with all their ideological equipment, their historical materialism, Marxism-Leninism, and dialectics, were incapable of making a correct analysis of the Yugoslav situation and believed they could force Tito and his passionately nationalistic communists into a coalition with their enemies. Moscow had no representatives in Yugoslavia. It did not know the facts. It went by the rules and went wrong.

29. Dedijer, p. 209. Dedijer, a close friend of Tito, wrote his book, *Tito*, in collaboration with the subject and it is, in effect, an autobiography.

30. Churchill, p. 468.

31. *Ibid.*, pp. 474–478.

XVII YE SHALL BE DEVOURED
WITH THE SWORD

The anti-German forces expected to win the second world war in 1944. Russia's brilliant triumphs over the Wehrmacht in 1943, the fall of Mussolini, the imminence of the Anglo-American descent on the shores of northern France, and the heavy bombings of Germany by British and American planes seemed to portend early victory. In Nazi-occupied territories this prospect gave wings of courage to the secret resistance units who fought the occupiers with all the stratagems and inadequate weapons at their disposal. Communists usually dominated these resistance movements. It is not that the communists were a special breed of human being. Most twentieth-century communists are Leninists, not Marxists. Lenin's philosophy was violent revolution, his ideology was organization. He believed that a well-organized minority, well led, employing force, could seize political power. He also believed in war as the crucible of communism; he proved it in Russia. Leninists were told to think in universal terms: if it happened in backward Russia in the first world war it could happen in France, or Italy, in the second. It was this conviction that made them brave. During the Spanish Civil War Loyalist soldiers would ask, as they lay on the ground at night knowing they were to attack at dawn, "Will this be important?" Men in certain moods are ready to die if their death will change something significantly, but if the result of the morning action might be a War Ministry bulletin saying, "On the X front today, Y battalion succeeded in straightening a segment of the line," it could not be regarded as worth the loss of all the soldier had—his life. The communists in Nazi territories felt in 1944 that everything was at stake, that it was revolution now or not now, perhaps not for a long time or ever. The social chaos, political anarchy, and economic privations following in the wake of war might, they speculated, open the door to the fulfillment of the heart's desire: the reign of communists. Faith was their spear, hope their buckler.

In Yugoslavia the western powers helped the communists. "It was only at the close of 1943 that British and American aid began to come in greater volume—but still no Russian aid," writes Mosha Piyade,[1] transla-

---

1. *About the Legend That the Yugoslav Uprising Owed Its Existence to Soviet Assistance,* p. 24.

tor of Marx into Serbo-Croat who had spent fourteen years in the monarchy's prisons. In Greece, Italy, and France, however, Churchill feared the communists and blamed Moscow. The Prime Minister was for assisting any organization that fought the Nazis. In Yugoslavia he had favored a kind of political hermaphrodite, half-monarchist, half-communist. But when royalists collaborated with the Axis enemy he took only Tito to his heart. Could he have sensed that Yugoslavia would someday defect from the Soviet Empire? In his *Conversations with Stalin,* Milovan Djilas quotes Tito as saying in February, 1943, "Our first duty is to look after our own army and our own people." Djilas, then No. 2 or 3 in the Yugoslav communist hierarchy, comments, "This was the first time that anyone on the Central Committee openly formulated our disparateness from Moscow." Did Churchill know or guess?

But the communists of Greece, Italy, and France were also fighting Germans. That was different. I had tea alone on January 18, 1944, in the British Embassy in Washington with Lord Halifax, former Foreign Secretary and Viceroy in India. "Tell me," the Ambassador asked, "how far do you think the Russians will go in Europe?"

"As far as they can," I replied.

He began biting the fingernails of his one hand. (The other hand was artificial.)

That morning American newspapers reproduced a strange tale from yesterday's *Pravda. Pravda*'s "own correspondent" in Cairo, where, it subsequently developed, *Pravda* had no correspondent, reported from "Greek and Yugoslav" resources that "two leading British personalities" were negotiating with Nazi Foreign Minister Joachim von Ribbentrop "in the Iberian peninsula" about a separate peace. "Tell me," Halifax wondered, "what are the Russians up to? Why do they accuse the British Government of wanting a separate peace with Germany?" Secretary Hull, Under Secretary of State Edward R. Stettinius, Jr., Assistant Secretary of State Adolf A. Berle, and other American diplomats whom I saw in the following days were equally puzzled.

Perhaps the British and Americans deserved their anguished perplexity for having excluded Russia from the secret talks with Marshal Badoglio's emissary in the Iberian Peninsula. Perhaps the Soviets spread the story of an Anglo-American separate peace because they knew they were suspected in Washington and London of being susceptible to a separate peace with Hitler. There was apparently no truth in either suspicion. As the war seemed to near its end the Soviets as well as the British and Americans grew more nervous, more bellicose toward one another, and more curious about their relations when peace dawned. Lord Halifax was worried, only nine weeks after the apparent sweetness, light, and unity of Tehran, where in Europe the Russians would stop.

They had once attained Paris. Americans were also worried. General Charles de Gaulle too. The anti-Russian Poles as well. Stalin himself probably could not have answered a question about the limit of his reach. He proclaimed on May 1, 1942, "It is not our purpose to invade foreign countries or subjugate foreign peoples. Our aim is clear and noble. We wish to liberate our Soviet soil from the German-Fascist scoundrels. . . . We have no other goals." Few then doubted his word. He proclaimed on May 1, 1944, that three-fourths of Soviet lands previously held by the conqueror had been regained and soon all of Russia would be free of foreign armies. "But our aims," he added, "cannot be limited to the expulsion of enemy troops from our fatherland." The Red Army, he said, must pursue the enemy and release "our brother Poles and Czechs" and other peoples from Nazi slavery.

Appetite comes with success.

Czechoslovakia and Poland, fateful patches on the crazy quilt of Europe before the second world war, were again in focus. For whereas the French underground resistance had been alerted to meet and succor the Anglo-American invaders on D Day, the anti-Soviet London Polish government devised a complicated double strategy for their underground Home Army in Poland: it was to cut off the German retreat when the Russians entered Poland and hack the Wehrmacht to pieces. At the same time it would entrench itself where the Nazis had ruled, thus preventing a communist take-over. The result was a grim tragedy.

A revealing colloquy took place in London on November 13, 1943, between President Eduard Beneš of the Czechoslovak government-in-exile and Stanislaw Mikolajczyk, Prime Minister of the Polish government-in-exile in succession to General Wladyslaw Sikorski, killed when his airplane fell near Gibraltar. Beneš, small of stature, had a vivid mind and, despite decades of political experience, a gullible one. Between the two wars he believed in the League of Nations as the guarantor of Czechoslovakia's safety and the guardian of world peace. He was anticommunist. I had met him in Moscow in the 1930's and talked with him in London on September 23, 1941. As usual, he felt optimistic. Inevitably, he harked back to the vivisection of his country at Munich in 1938: Czechoslovakia could have fought at that time. The Soviets promised planes; they had already delivered 300 to Czechoslovak airfields. But England and France did not wish him to resist and he could not defy them. "I did not want my country to become a second Spain," he said. "If we had accepted Soviet aid and gone to war, I would have been called a Bolshevik."[2]

When I met President Beneš on May 17, 1943, in Blair House in Washington, D.C., he again saw the future in rosy colors. His relations with

2. Louis Fischer, *The Great Challenge,* pp. 72–73.

Moscow, he predicted, would be cordial. He thought he had dissuaded the Soviets from taking the Carpatho-Russ, an underdeveloped sliver of Czechoslovakia populated by several hundred thousand Ukrainians. He underestimated Stalin. He always underestimated danger. Russia annexed Carpatho-Russ on June 29, 1945.[3]

Beneš had invited Mikolajczyk to his London home on that day in November, 1943, and began the conversation with an exposé that lasted two hours. "He thought that although Russia had abandoned her imperialistic designs," reads the official Polish account of this encounter, "she continued to feel endangered." America, he foresaw, would be disinclined to "commit herself actively in the domestic affairs of Europe," and British policy would be "never to act against Russia." He did not say, but the conclusion follows ineluctably, that the Soviets could do very much as they pleased on the continent, and why they should feel imperiled he did not explain. Presumably, a defeated Germany, disarmed, divided into five or more sections, and robbed of certain territories in the east would constitute the menace.

Beneš proceeded to tell Mikolajczyk that he had discussed the future of Czechoslovakia with Soviet Ambassador in London Ivan M. Maisky. What would the Soviet government prefer, he had asked Maisky: that Czechoslovak communists join the Czechoslovak government when Germany is defeated or that "Czechoslovak opinion shift towards the Left"? A more Leftist Czechoslovakia, Beneš felt, "will provide you with a much better opportunity for cooperating with us." The practical Maisky replied: ". . . the Soviet Government opted for the participation of Communists in the governments of neighboring countries."

Maisky, of course, was a diplomat and not privy to Stalin's plans. But he understood that the Kremlin was interested primarily in having its minions in positions of power in the governments of Russia's neighbors (and elsewhere too; in Italy, for instance). Communists serving in the Cabinets of Czechoslovakia, Rumania, and other neighbors would see to it that the "Left" flourished.

Beneš seemed not to comprehend the implications of Maisky's preference. He proposed to Ambassador Maisky a Czecho-Soviet treaty "directed against Germany" which would contain "a clause guaranteeing the full independence of Czechoslovakia," a pledge of "mutual non-interference in domestic affairs," and the conclusion of a similar Soviet-Polish treaty.

Prime Minister Mikolajczyk, a stocky man and staunch Polish nationalist from his sparse blond hair to his toes (the mere presence of Alexander F. Kerensky, a Russian nationalist, in a New York living room one

3. *Ibid.,* p. 185.

afternoon sent searing electric shock waves between them), took a glum view of the Beneš analysis. How could there be a Soviet-Polish treaty without Soviet-Polish diplomatic relations? When the Russians spoke of an independent Poland, he said, "They had in mind either half of Poland or a Poland constituting the 17th Republic of the USSR. In these circumstances," he told Beneš, "Czechoslovakia could only become a tool of Communism."[4]

The pessimist Mikolajczyk was nearer the truth.

The "Delegate Plenipotentiary of the Polish Government in Poland"—meaning the Pole representing the Polish government in London—had already issued orders to the inhabitants of the eastern provinces of Poland to take possession when the German armies retreated. "There exists . . . no force in the world," he proclaimed, "which could permanently separate and partition the Polish nation."[5]

Such a force existed, the Soviet government. "Permanent" can be debated. What is permanent in politics? Decades have already passed. Mikolajczyk regarded the surrender of 72,000 square miles in the eastern half of Poland as an inadmissible sacrifice. The annexation of 32,000 square miles of German lands in Silesia, East Prussia, and Pomerania was no compensation. He hoped that an Anglo-American mission would enter Poland when the Russian army entered and assure Poland's future. But he knew, and all pro-London Poles knew, that no Anglo-American mission, certainly no argument about justice, could save their cause. When armies are on the march the only argument is an army. The London Poles had an army in Poland, the Home Army, and they planned to use it to win the argument. It would seize control before the Russians came. Here was another demonstration of the romantic side of the Poles. The Czechs let the Germans roll over them. The Poles fought in September, 1939, and thought they could win. Now, too, they thought they could win.

Prime Minister Mikolajczyk and his colleagues, however, were not altogether impractical. They had their feet on the ground in Washington and London, where they waged mighty battles in the approaches to the White House and No. 10, Downing Street and finally inside those lofty precincts. Mikolajczyk made no secret of his highest hopes. In a conversation in London on December 1, 1943, the day of the adjournment of the Tehran Conference where, in principle, the fate of Poland was sealed according to Churchill's three matches, he told U.S. Ambassador to Poland Anthony Drexel Biddle that even if by the end of the war the Soviet armies had crossed the width of Poland, "the Allied Nations [Britain and

4. General Sikorski Historical Institute, *Documents on Polish-Soviet Relations 1939–1945.* Vol. II: *1943–1945,* pp. 78–80.
5. *Ibid.,* pp. 82–83.

America] would be standing on the corpse of Germany. Then there would be no possibility of blackmail with a Soviet-German agreement because the German armies would have been destroyed. Two armies would face each other: on the one side the exhausted Soviet armies and Russia entirely dependent on food supplies from the United Nations, on the other side a very powerful Allied air force and 300–400 unimpaired British and American divisions. Although unfortunately," the Polish Prime Minister added, "I could not expect a clash between the two armies at that time either, I considered that the Soviets would have to reckon with such a force, just as the Allies had to reckon with the advancing and victorious Soviet armies."[6]

This was evil, cynical, realistic, and, as events proved, unrealizable, therefore romantic. Mikolajczyk was fighting for the freedom of his Poland and he knew the only way this could be achieved. If indeed the Anglo-American armies had conquered all of Germany before the Russians reached the German frontier, Poland might have remained noncommunist. That is not what happened.

Prime Minister Mikolajczyk was received by Churchill at No. 10, Downing Street on January 20, 1944. Churchill pleaded with the Pole to accept the Polish boundary solution proposed at Tehran. He understood that it was "hard," but as a friend he considered it the best they could obtain. "Personally, he thought it fair. . . . Poland would obtain valuable [German] territory in exchange for a region including the Pripet Marshes, which could be of little value to them." And if Poland accepted she would be "rendering a great service to the future of Europe." All unwanted Germans could be transferred out of the acquired lands, Churchill declared, and the United Nations would safeguard Poland against German vengeance. In fact, Germany would be so "disarmed and mutilated" as to lack the capacity for "any further aggression against Poland. It was unthinkable that this country [Britain] should go to war with the Soviet Union over Poland's eastern frontier, and the United States would certainly never do so."

This last sentence contains the quintessence of the kind of argument by which the government of Neville Chamberlain coerced President Beneš into submission to Hitler in 1938–1939.

"What, after all, is the alternative?" Churchill demanded. It would surely be better to accept the proposal of the Big Three at Tehran than to wait until the Russian army rolled on and gave Moscow the power to make a unilateral decision.

Mikolajczyk contended that Poland might relinquish her eastern marshes yet fail to receive compensation in the west.

6. *Ibid.,* pp. 101–103.

In that case, Churchill explained, Poland would not be bound by the agreement to cede her eastern half to Russia. The British Prime Minister promised to put this point to Stalin in a telegram and to add a strong protest against Moscow's questioning the authority of the Polish government in London. Moreover, "no government had the right to dictate to another regarding its composition." In his dispatch, Churchill said, he would also press Stalin to negotiate with Mikolajczyk.[7]

Even according to this official Polish record of the interview, Mikolajczyk had a weak case and Churchill an unanswerable one. What indeed was the Polish alternative? The news from Poland augmented Mikolajczyk's anguish. Trouble began in December, 1943, when Soviet guerrilla bands started to filter across Poland's 1939 frontier and collided with Home Army units loyal to the government-in-exile in London. In January, 1944, the vanguards of Rokossovsky's mighty legions entered the same territory. Among them marched the Tadeusz Kosciuszko Brigade, child of the Kremlin-made Union of Polish Patriots, commanded by Major General Zygmunt Berling. Members of the Home Army captured by the Russians were, according to news from eastern Poland, being conscripted into the Kosciuszko Brigade consisting of their fellow countrymen and political enemies.

True to his promise, Churchill on February 1, 1944, telegraphed Stalin a long summary of his talk with Mikolajczyk. Britain went to war not for any particular Polish frontier "but for the existence of a strong, free, independent Poland which Marshal Stalin declared himself as supporting," he had told the Pole. He had also explained that from what happened at Tehran he believed the Soviet government "would be willing to agree to the eastern frontiers of Poland conforming to the Curzon Line subject to the discussion of ethnographic considerations [a reference to the surrender of Lvov though the city was heavily Polish] and the cession to Poland, in compensation, of German territory to the Oder River and also East Prussia. But here," Churchill added, "I did not mention the point about Koenigsberg." (The point was that Stalin, at Tehran, had claimed the East Prussian city of Koenigsberg for Russia.) Mr. Churchill then told Stalin of the Polish desire to "be allowed to go back and form a more broad-based government in accordance with the popular wish and allowed to function in the liberated areas [liberated by the Soviet army]. . . . In particular they are deeply concerned about the relations between the Polish underground movement and the advancing Soviet forces." Next the British statesman raised the question of the Kremlin's attitude to the Polish government in London. ". . . do you not agree," he asked Stalin, "that to advocate changes within a foreign government

7. *Ibid.*, pp. 144–149.

comes near to interference in internal sovereignty . . . ? I may mention," he added, "that this view is strongly held by His Majesty's Government."[8]

Stalin had no reason to be disturbed. He was in command of the situation because he was in command of Rokossovsky's advancing army. He insisted, in his February 4 reply to Churchill, that the Poles must accept the Curzon Line which diminished pre-1939 Poland by half. He agreed that Poland receive German territory but not the ice-free port of Koenigsberg. Nevertheless, "we cannot re-establish relations with the present Polish Government. Indeed," he argued, "what would be the use of re-establishing relations with it when we are certain that tomorrow we shall not be compelled to sever those relations again on account of another fascist provocation on its part, such as the 'Katyn Affair'? . . . no good can be expected," Stalin declared, "unless the composition of the Polish Government is thoroughly improved . . . the removal from it of pro-fascist imperialist elements and the inclusion of democratic-minded people, one is entitled to hope, create the proper conditions for normal Soviet-Polish relations, for solving the problem of the Soviet-Polish frontier and, in general, for the rebirth of a strong, free and independent state."[9]

Stalin's rejoinder is a masterpiece of clarity. Everything, including the boundaries settlement, depended on a new "democratically-minded"—read communist or fellow traveler—Polish government purified of "pro-fascist imperialist elements" who might go so far as to protest another "Katyn Affair." That was Moscow's definition of a "friendly" government. Stalin specifically rejected Churchill's proposal to abstain from "interference in internal sovereignty." Superpower respect for small nations had become an anachronism. Stalin and Hitler proved this in tandem in 1939 and 1940. Stalin was about to prove it again in Poland and eastern Europe.

Poland was only Poland and Roosevelt and Churchill had, in principle, thrown her to the Russians at Tehran. Yet thousands of Polish soldiers and airmen were fighting in Allied units in the Middle East and Italy and from airfields in the United Kingdom and Italy. The Poles had a powerful lobby in London and Washington. The British public was particularly sensitive to the fate of Poland because they had gone to war when Hitler's threat to that country seemed to portend a bleak future for a large part of the European continent. Now, in quite different circumstances, the curtain was apparently going up on a similar drama. Communist aspirations in Italy and the Balkans troubled Churchill. He had no qualms about rendering the eastern half of Poland to the Soviets in exchange for German lands. If this contravened the almost forgotten Atlantic Charter, so did his resolve to hold India. He was an avowed imperialist. But he

8. *Correspondence*, Vol. I, pp. 192–195.
9. *Ibid.*, pp. 195–197.

hoped to save Poland from communism. He did not appear to grasp what Mikolajczyk and company knew by instinct: that territorial readjustments would make Poland a helpless Soviet satellite which could only be ruled by the Moscow puppets already packing their bags and ready to follow in the footsteps of General Berling's brigade and the treads of Marshal Rokossovsky's tanks. Yet Stalin had told him the truth: the next Polish government would have to be "democratically-minded."

At Chequers on February 6, 1944, Churchill dropped the other shoe: he told Mikolajczyk that Stalin had demanded Koenigsberg and the surrounding East Prussian territory. Mikolajczyk was shocked. This meant, he said, that Stalin's claims grew with every yielding to his wishes. First he wanted half of Poland up to the Curzon Line, now half of East Prussia. If this was historically incorrect—Stalin at Tehran had asked for both simultaneously—Mikolajczyk's evaluation of western appeasement, this time of Russia, was prescient. Impressed by Soviet military power and eager to buy its continued cooperation, intent on winning Moscow for postwar peace-keeping, the Anglo-Americans allowed Stalin to drive a bulldozer through western diplomacy at Tehran, Yalta, and Potsdam and shatter it. Hitler had adopted a similar policy: thinking the French army formidable and the task of reducing France enormous, he paid Russia heavily, in the Ribbentrop-Molotov pact and secret protocols, for Soviet neutrality although neutrality was the main goal of Soviet foreign policy. In each case Poland was the first of several victims. In each case war followed: hot in 1939, cold in the midst of the second world war and after its close. But the start of both the hot and cold wars goes back to August 23, 1939, when Hitler yielded the eastern half of Poland, the Baltic States, and Finland to Stalin. At Tehran Roosevelt and Churchill in effect reaffirmed the Stalin-Hitler arrangement on Poland. Now the London Poles and their supporters in Poland rejected it.

The Polish government's position was considerably weakened when Molotov roundly rebuffed an offer by Secretary of State Hull on January 22, 1944, to mediate the dispute. The Foreign Commissar declared that mediation was "doomed to fail" because the London Poles sought to "aggravate the conflict" and by mediation "involve the Allies in it."[10] Thereafter, despite strenuous Polish efforts, Washington remained on the diplomatic sidelines and left it to Churchill to fight the Polish cause.

Churchill, however, had no intention of taking on Stalin in single combat. He urged Mikolajczyk to compromise. The Curzon Line, he told the Pole at Chequers on February 6, was the best that could be expected from the Kremlin. The Curzon Line, Mikolajczyk replied, stopped north of eastern Galicia. Now Stalin wished to extend it southward through Gal-

10. *Documents on Polish-Soviet Relations 1939–1945*, p. 152.

icia so as to give Lvov—and Vilna—to Russia. What Stalin was demanding, accordingly, was not the Curzon Line of 1919 but the Ribbentrop-Molotov line of 1939, only it was more politic in dealing with the British, and less embarrassing generally, to invoke Curzon's name rather than Ribbentrop's. Churchill then pressed the Polish Prime Minister-in-exile to make his government more acceptable in Moscow by reconstituting it. Mikolajczyk said Moscow had already laid plans to launch a Polish government of its own making.

The upshot was: stalemate.

In desperation, Mikolajczyk requested an invitation to visit President Roosevelt. Back came the reply that such a visit "might be misconstrued."[11] Presumably in Moscow. Mikolajczyk therefore asked to see Churchill and Eden again. He met them for several hours on February 16. It was a sad affair. Churchill declared himself "the Polish counsel trying to win their case." If Moscow decided to have nothing to do with the Polish government this would "create a great cause of difficulties between the Soviet Union and Great Britain and the United States of America." Yet he justified Stalin's claim to the eastern half of Poland, including Lvov, and "would support this at the peace settlement." After all, he had little to offer the Soviets "except to invest with a show of right arrangements acceptable to Russian strength. The Polish government would then drop out of the picture."

This sounded like a threat, it was in fact a plausible preview. Mikolajczyk could only hope "that Great Britain would live up to its reputation of protecting the weak." The British Prime Minister said he thought "the Russian claim to be the Curzon Line right."[12]

Thus was might clothed in right.

Once more Mikolajczyk turned to Roosevelt. The President pleaded ill health and commitments as reasons for postponing the interview at least until May. F.D.R. had not been well for months after Tehran and was occasionally away from the White House for long periods of rest. But Secretary Hull gave the true explanation of Roosevelt's reluctance to receive Mikolajczyk. "Spring of 1944 was the period of preparation for the greatest military campaign in American history—the landing in Normandy. That landing had to be coordinated with Russian military movements in the east. . . . We could not afford to become partisan in the Polish question to the extent of alienating Russia at that critical moment."[13]

Roosevelt and Churchill kept Stalin informed about their Polish policies. The Soviet leader therefore expected no trouble from those quarters. But he knew the Poles. He had been in Poland in 1920 as chief political

11. *Ibid.*, pp. 177–178.
12. *Ibid.*, pp. 180–187.
13. Cordell Hull, *The Memoirs of Cordell Hull,* Vol. II, pp. 1441–1442.

commissar of one of the Russian armies defeated, in Lenin's own admission, by Polish nationalism raised on tsarism's history of partitions and persecutions. Bolshevik atheism added another feeding stream to the fervent anti-Russian sentiments of the predominantly Catholic Polish people. The latest partition of Poland pursuant to the 1939 Soviet-Nazi pact and secret protocols, the Katyn massacre, the execution and banishment to death camps of Poles, some of them socialists who had escaped from Nazi occupation into the U.S.S.R., swelled the torrent of anti-Soviet hatred in Poland. In 1938 Stalin had had most of the Polish communist leaders in Russia shot. He would have to depend on second-string communists to govern a recalcitrant Poland after the Red Army conquered her. He needed recruits. He aimed to mollify.

During the month of March, 1944, Stalin invited Professor Oscar Lange, an economist at the University of Chicago, and Father Stanislaw Orlemanski, of Springfield, Massachusetts, both of Polish origin, to consult with him in Moscow. They arrived by Soviet transport facilities in April. Lange later became a high official of communist Poland. "I am a Menshevik, not a Bolshevik," he explained in a private conversation. "But I assume that relations between America and Russia will be friendly and I can then play a useful role in minimizing Moscow's interference in Polish affairs." His assumption proved wrong, his hope vain.

Orlemanski, a priest in a small parish, suddenly saw himself a figure on the world stage, advising Stalin, ameliorating the lot of his people in Poland. Molotov had told Ambassador Harriman that the Kremlin envisaged a reconstructed Polish government which might include Lange, Orlemanski, and Leo Krzycki, national chairman of the American Slav Congress and vice-president of the Amalgamated Clothing Workers of America—as well as Mikolajczyk.[14] This was a triple-targeted device designed to win support among American Poles and other American Catholics, reassure Roosevelt, if that was necessary, of Moscow's moderation, and above all create the impression in Poland that her inhabitants had nothing to fear from the Soviets. Father Orlemanski, innocent of politics, did his best. *Pravda* of April 28 published his photograph standing with Stalin and Molotov who had granted him a two-hour interview. He then spoke on the Soviet radio: "I want to make the historic statement that the future will prove that Stalin is a friend of the Roman Catholic Church. . . . Stalin is a friend of the Poles. He wants to see a strong, powerful, independent and democratic Poland. . . . Stalin does not intend to interfere in internal Polish affairs."[15]

14. U.S. Department of State, *Foreign Relations [F.R.] of the United States. Diplomatic Papers. 1944.* Vol. III: *The British Commonwealth and Europe,* pp. 1230–1231.
15. Alexander Werth, *Russia at War,* pp. 844–846.

The Red Army, striking south, occupied Bessarabia in February and March, 1944, and, crossing the Pruth River, seized additional Rumanian territory in the vicinity of the city of Jassy. Molotov, on April 2, told a press conference that the Soviet government did not intend to annex Rumanian lands or change the social system of Rumania. The same Molotov had stated in an address on October 31, 1939, that the mutual aid treaties Moscow signed with Estonia, Latvia, and Lithuania in September and October, 1939, "firmly stipulate the inviolability of the sovereignty of the signatory nations as well as the principle of noninterference in the affairs of the other nation."[16] As is well known, the Soviets violated the sovereignty of Estonia, Latvia, and Lithuania and converted them into captive Soviet republics. As is equally well known, the Soviets annexed Rumanian Bessarabia (which the Rumanians, communists and noncommunists, cannot forgive to this day) and changed the social system of Rumania. Molotov's statement on Rumania was calculated to calm Rumanian apprehensions, and Orlemanski's radio performance to pacify the Poles until they were powerless to protest. The Kremlin acts on the assumption that foreigners are stupid, else why would they continue to live under capitalism, and that its own people have either trained their memories to forget or actually cannot compare and recall because declarations and facts uncomfortable to the regime never appear in history books. Socialist realism is not only for novelists and playwrights, Soviet politicians apply it with impunity in their fictional utterances. It scrambles the tenses: the past is out, the present is perfect, the future pluperfect.

Prime Minister Mikolajczyk was not beguiled by Molotov's semantic legerdemain. In a letter dated March 18, 1944, to Roosevelt replete with compliments ("Mr. President, your name is revered by every Pole") and with vehemence, Mikolajczyk characterized Soviet policy as "a combination of old Russian imperialism and communist totalitarianism" and said, "Will not Poland, and later Europe, be overwhelmed against their will by a new wave of communist totalitarianism? Can the nations condemned to the rule of such a new totalitarianism agree to accept its tyranny? Never, as far as Poland is concerned." And to appeal to F.D.R.'s capitalist ideology he added, "The masses of Polish small farmers anxious to build their prosperity not in collectivized farms but in individual farmsteads will never agree to it. . . . All the classes of the Polish nation want to build a better future for the country and its citizens on a basis of private enterprise." The Polish government, moreover, could not hand over "at least 5 million Poles" in eastern Poland to Russia.[17]

The President acknowledged the letter, he could see Mikolajczyk "no sooner than the early part of May."

16. Louis Fischer, *Russia's Road from Peace to War*, p. 372.
17. *Documents on Polish-Soviet Relations 1939–1945*, pp. 207–211.

Unfortunately for Mikolajczyk, he had to fight his diplomatic battles in London and Washington offices whereas Stalin was winning his diplomatic battles on the battlefield. The Red Army opened a series of spectacular victories on January 27, 1944, when it drove the besieging Nazis away from the great city of Leningrad whose inhabitants had for 880 days endured pains of starvation, shelling, bombing, frost, and fear that shrink man's daily cares to irrelevancies.[18] The March penetration into Rumania was followed in April and May by the recapture of the Crimea. Only a small fraction of Hitler conquests in Russia remained. The day had dawned on Stalin's conquests outside Russia.

Moscow already regarded eastern Poland to the Curzon Line as inside Russia, and behaved accordingly. When Rokossovsky's Russian army and Berling's Polish brigade advanced into it during March and April, elements of the Home Army, on instructions from the Polish government in London, offered their cooperation against the Germans. Submission was demanded instead. News came to Mikolajczyk that twenty soldiers of the Home Army had been hanged and commanding officers shot. He gave the information to Churchill. He put his faith in Roosevelt, and finally he flew to Washington in a U.S. government plane as a guest of the President, arrived on June 6, and stayed nine days. Mikolajczyk, by prior agreement, saw no Polish-Americans and made no effort to influence American public opinion. Though F.D.R., needless to say, was busy, he received the Polish Prime Minister four times in the nine days.

It is interesting to speculate on the motives of Roosevelt, and of Churchill, in giving so much of their valuable time to Mikolajczyk. They knew full well that they could not break Stalin's determination to have half of Poland and half of East Prussia, the more so since they had acquiesced in this surgery at Tehran. They therefore could do little for Mikolajczyk who, as he reiterated in Washington as well as in London, possessed neither the wish nor the authority to approve these amputations and would be out of office if he did. It is not likely that they had pangs of conscience; most statesmen, most politicians, most human beings are disinclined to be critical of their important acts. Both Roosevelt and Churchill, knowing that politics is the art of compromise, hoped they could induce Stalin to accept an accommodation with Mikolajczyk. Roosevelt did not quite comprehend that totalitarian politics is allergic to compromise and that what appeared to be compromise was the Stalin tactic of postponing death while sharpening the knife. Stalin anticipated difficulties in taking over Poland and intended to achieve it by the install-

18. Harrison E. Salisbury, *The 900 Days, The Siege of Leningrad,* is more than a magnificent achievement of research and writing, and more than a meticulous account of the crucifixion of a city. The book carries a philosophic impact by compelling a comparison between the horrors the besieged citizens experienced and what preoccupies most of us.

ment plan. Under certain conditions he would do business temporarily with Mikolajczyk. This left a little room in which Roosevelt and Churchill could maneuver.

In his first conversation with Mikolajczyk on June 7 President Roosevelt said, "Poland must be free and independent."

"What about Stalin?" the Pole asked.

"Stalin is a realist," F.D.R. replied. ". . . Stalin is not an imperialist."

The President told Mikolajczyk that he had gotten along "famously" with Stalin at Tehran, better than Churchill had. "In all our dealings with Stalin we must keep our fingers crossed. And you Poles must find an understanding with Russia. On your own, you'd have no chance to beat Russia, and, let me tell you now, the British and Americans have no intention of fighting Russia. But don't worry. Stalin doesn't intend to take freedom from Poland. He wouldn't dare to do that, because he knows that the United States Government stands solidly behind you. I will see to it that Poland does not come out of this war injured."

"But there is every indication at the present that we will," the Polish Premier objected.

"I'm sure," Roosevelt assured him, "I'll be able to manage an agreement in which Poland gets Silesia, East Prussia, Koenigsberg, Lvov, the region of Tarnopol and the oil and potash area of Drohobycz. But I don't believe I can secure the city of Vilna for you." [19]

These seemed like the statements of a man suffering from delusions of grandeur and divorce from reality. Or was it all in tune with Roosevelt's customary wish to make every visitor happy? His report to Stalin pleased the recipient. Mikolajczyk's "visit," the President wired the Marshal on June 19, 1944, "was not connected with any attempt on my part to inject myself into the merits of the differences which exist between the Polish Government in Exile and the Soviet Government. . . . I can assure you that no specific plan or proposal in any way affecting Polish-Soviet relations was drawn up. . . . Mr. Mikolajczyk impressed me as a very sincere and reasonable man whose sole desire is to do the best for his country. He is fully cognizant that the whole future of Poland depends upon the establishment of genuinely good relations with the Soviet Union. . . . He believes that coordination between your armies and the organized Polish underground is a military factor of the highest importance. . . . In fact it is my belief that he would not hesitate to go to Moscow, if he felt that you would welcome such a step."[20]

Stalin replied by wire on June 24 saying Polish-Soviet military collaboration "is vital to the defeat of our common enemy." The Soviet government desires "to see Poland strong, independent and democratic" but a

19. Stanislaw Mikolajczyk, *The Pattern of Soviet Domination,* pp. 65–68.
20. *Correspondence,* Vol. II, pp. 146–147.

prior condition of "good-neighborly" relations with Poland "is a reconstruction of the Polish émigré Government." At the moment, therefore, "I find it hard to express an opinion about a visit to Moscow by Mr. Mikolajczyk."[21]

It was Mikolajczyk's misfortune that the Anglo-Americans were late. They did not capture Rome until June 4, 1944, when U.S. troops drove into the Piazza Venezia. They did not land in Normandy until June 6 when he, by symbolic coincidence, landed in America. Had the western powers yielded to Stalin and launched the second front in 1942 or 1943 and had it been successful, Mikolajczyk would have been content and Stalin might have been cheated of Poland.

The Anglo-American cross-Channel invasion made surprising progress and the Wehrmacht, thanks to ingenious western deception, made surprising blunders, first in misjudging the date of the landing (Rommel, commander of part of the western front, was at home in Germany on vacation) and in misjudging the place and distributing its forces all along the coast from France to Holland; second in delaying the deployment of its Panzer divisions. When that powerful arm was finally thrown into the confused battle, British and American tank divisions blocked the blow. At the end of June the German military were in a quandary, not to say panic. Field Marshal Wilhelm Keitel, Hitler's Chief of Staff, on July 1 telephoned Field Marshal Gerd von Rundstedt, commander of the front, and asked what should be done. "Make peace, you fools," he replied.[22]

This was one of the numbers on the roulette wheel of history, including Poland's history. Keitel, Rundstedt, and Rommel and a few more field marshals in collusion could have removed Hitler and sued for peace. But Keitel reported the conversation to Hitler; the same night Rundstedt was relieved by Field Marshal Gunther von Kluge.

The German armies' decisive defeats on the eastern and western fronts cannot but have influenced the choice of a date for the attempt to kill Hitler. The conspiracy, assassination followed by a military-civilian coup d'état, had been long in preparation. Many marshals and generals hesitated to join because of their personal oath of allegiance to Hitler. When Rundstedt was approached by one of the plotters, he said, "In my position I naturally cannot participate in such a plan. But should it succeed do not forget that I hold the highest rank among the generals."[23] The July 20, 1944, attempt on Hitler's life failed. War raged east and west for nine and a half more months. The Anglo-American flood did not pour

21. *Ibid.,* p. 148.
22. *Grand Strategy.* Vol. V. John Ehrman. *August 1943–September 1944,* p. 342. This is part of the semiofficial British *History of the Second World War,* edited by J. R. M. Butler.
23. Rainer Hildebrandt, *Wir Waren die Letzten,* p. 99. Hildebrandt, a friend of Albrecht Haushofer, participated in the plot yet survived.

into Germany until 1945. But Marshal Konstantin K. Rokossovsky's army smashed through eastern Poland, and in the fourth week of July he crossed the Curzon-Molotov-Ribbentrop Line into what the Kremlin called Poland, thus officially proclaiming the annexation by Russia of all territory east of that line. Rokossovsky first took the small town of Chelm in the southeastern corner of the new Poland where Polish communists on July 22 launched the "Chelm Committee," which, after coopting several noncommunists, announced itself the government of Poland. Ever since, July 22 has been celebrated as the Polish national day. The next day Rokossovsky captured the somewhat larger university town of Lublin and the "Chelm Committee" became the "Lublin Committee." Moscow recognized the committee as the legal government of the country yet to be conquered.

Rokossovsky raced on. The anti-Soviet Poles knew that every day's delay in the west and every kilometer's advance in the east whittled away a slice of their independence and a sliver of their dreams. On July 31 Rokossovsky's advance units reached Praga, a suburb of Warsaw across the Vistula River from the central city. There he stopped.

Now commenced one of the most gruesome and misunderstood episodes of the second world war: the Warsaw Uprising, in which at least 250,000 Poles lost their lives. Most of the city was laid waste.

XVIII THE WARSAW UPRISING

Somehow it seems that war, always the supreme horror, has an added inhuman dimension when it is fought inside a city. A battle connotes a battlefield, and battlefield conjures up a picture of meadows, farms, brooks and beaches, woods, ridges, rivers, roads. A city is not a field and ought not to become a battlefield. During the long siege of Leningrad the Russian army engaged the German army in its outlying districts and the inhabitants were passive victims. That was tragic enough. In Warsaw the people, in their tens of thousands, armed with rifles, a limited number of machine guns, and milk bottles and soft drink bottles full of gasoline, fought war-hardened Nazi divisions using cannon, tanks, planes, heavy machine guns, and rifles, fought them for many weeks, from every window in a street, from the ruins when artillery had leveled the houses, from cellars under the ruins, from sewers under the streets where a German and a Pole would wrestle in knee-high muck until one or both drowned in it. At first it was a battle for a Polish victory, then it became a battle for sure death and history. When so many are dead it is ignoble not to fight on and die too. Yet commingled with undoubted death was the undimmed hope that somebody from the outside would come and help save Warsaw. No one came. A city of a million is a big place, and when every avenue and alley has to be taken by close-in fighting the battle is long. There was plenty of time for assistance to arrive. None arrived.

The Warsaw Uprising was a desperate political gamble. For five years less two months the Poles had been waiting to avenge themselves on the Germans for invading their country on September 1, 1939. Dreams and whispers grew into an organization and finally into the Home Army in daily touch with, and responding to orders from, the Polish government in London. The Anglo-American landing in Normandy encouraged them to think that action could turn hopes into reality. The Russian army's progress westward was read as helpful, and menacing. Helpful because it hurt the Wehrmacht, menacing because if Moscow captured Warsaw, Poland would become communist. The London Poles and the Home Army expected, perhaps naïvely, that if they ousted the Nazis and took possession of the capital before the Russians arrived they could save their country from Soviet embraces.

The usual version of the Warsaw Uprising holds that Stalin, shrewdly divining the Home Army's purpose, urged Warsaw to rise but prevented Rokossovsky's army, which had reached the bank of the Vistula River opposite Warsaw, from going to the aid of the insurrection, thus allowing Hitler to win and the city to die so that ultimately he could make Poland a Russian colony. The truth is more involuted and far more fascinating.

Stalin, true to his promise to Roosevelt and Churchill at Tehran, launched a mighty offensive in Byelorussia on June 23, 1944. The Red Army, enjoying a numerical superiority in men, guns, planes, tanks, and trucks, trounced the Germans worse than at Stalingrad. It tore a 250-mile gap in the German front and swept toward Warsaw and East Prussia. Minsk, the capital of Byelorussia, was captured on July 3; the Russians rushed in the direction of Vilna. Anticipating events, the Home Army in and around Vilna, numbering 6,000, attacked the Germans on July 7. The battle lasted a week and closed on July 14 when the Russians, who had given arms to the Home Army and coordinated their operation with it, drove the Germans away. With victory assured, Colonel Wilk-Kryzanowskis, the commander of the Home Army detachments, and his staff were arrested and transported to Russia. He died in a Soviet prison in 1951.[1] Similar acts of drama and deceit were enacted at Lvov and other Polish cities.

1. Joseph Czapski, *Unmenschliche Erde,* p. 405.

The Red Army continued its invincible offensive, which had already cost the Germans 350,000 men killed and captured. Panic seized the Germans in Warsaw. The Home Army oiled its old weapons.

Hitler was at Rastenburg in East Prussia, in the path of the advancing Soviet forces. At 12:30 P.M. on July 20, 1944, twenty-one members of his military staff including Field Marshal Wilhelm Keitel and Colonel General Alfred Jodl, and two stenographers joined Hitler in his Wolf's Lair, as it was officially called, for a routine military conference. At 12:50 P.M. the bomb in a briefcase, which Colonel Claus Schenk von Stauffenberg, a badly mutilated Roman Catholic count, had placed under the conference table, exploded. An air force general sitting two removed from Hitler died of the wounds he received from the bomb. Likewise a colonel who sat three removed from Hitler. A stenographer sitting diagonally across the table from Hitler was killed immediately. An army lieutenant general who occupied a seat at the short side of the table to the right of Hitler died of wounds. Several others were slightly wounded. Hitler was among those. His right arm was partly paralyzed. His right leg suffered burns. His hair took fire. His hearing was impaired. His trouser legs were blown off. A block of wood dropped from the roof and hurt his back. At 5 P.M. he entertained Mussolini at tea.

The panic caused among Germans in Warsaw by the Russian advance turned to rout when news came of the attempt on Hitler's life. The post office closed down. Daily papers published by the occupying power did not print. The Gestapo began burning its files. High German officials packed and left in haste. The Home Army signaled its men to stand by.

A few minutes after midnight on July 20 Hitler spoke by radio to the German people. An attempt had been made to assassinate him. A coup d'état was to have followed. Several persons were severely wounded. "I myself," he added, "sustained only some very minor scratches, bruises, and burns. I regard this as a confirmation of the task imposed upon me by Providence."

The task, needless to say, was not to go down to defeat but to win and perpetuate the Third Reich. Reinforced in his faith that he had been killing millions to fulfill God's mission, he forthwith ordered the Wehrmacht to assume the offensive in the west and stop the retreat in the east. The situation in and around Warsaw changed drastically. On July 28 Rokossovsky had taken Brest Litovsk and moved on the capital. "On the 31st . . . he was within fifteen miles of the city. . . . This was temporarily the high water mark of the Russians' advance. . . . In the first half of August, the Germans managed to stabilize the front on the borders of East Prussia, on the Vistula and near Warsaw. They counter-attacked, indeed, in Poland with some success, halting Rokossovski until the middle of September."[2]

Moscow reported on July 29: "In Central Poland, Marshal Rokossovski's tanks, motorized infantry, and Cossack cavalry, powerfully supported by the Red Air Force, pressed on towards Warsaw and were heavily engaged about 20 miles southeast [of the city] with German lorry-borne reinforcements rushed to the front to stem the advance. Praga, the industrial suburb on the East bank of the Vistula, came under Russian artillery fire."[3]

The same day, July 29, the Polish-language Kosciuszko radio station in Moscow broadcast a call to Warsaw to stage the long-desired insurrection. "No doubt," it began, "Warsaw already hears the guns of the battle which is soon to bring her liberation. Those who have never bowed their heads to the Hitlerite power will, as in 1939, join battle with the Germans, this time for the decisive action."[4]

It has been suggested that the Kosciuszko call was intended to provoke the Home Army into revolting prematurely so the Nazis could suppress it. There is no basis for such a suspicion. Jubilant to the point of euphoria over the Red Army's headlong dash out of Byelorussia into Poland, Moscow assumed that nothing could stop Rokossovsky from taking Warsaw. It summoned the city's underground forces to strike the first blow. The Polish communists had their own underground in Warsaw. It was much smaller than the Home Army. But communists are congenital exaggerators who habitually give Moscow extravagant reports of their strength and prospects. The Kosciuszko broadcast was directed to the communist underground in Warsaw, not to the Home Army. "The Polish Army now entering Polish territory, trained in the U.S.S.R.," its text reads, "is now joined to the People's Army to form the corps of the Polish Armed Forces, the armed arm of our nation in its struggle for independence."[5]

The Polish army trained in Russia was the communist brigade of General Berling. The People's Army, originally the People's Guard, which General Tadeusz Bor-Komorowski, commander of the Home Army, called the "Polish Communist partisan groups," was renamed the People's Army in July, 1943.[6] General Bor estimated its strength "at a few hundred men in all."

Their number did not matter. Rokossovsky had the numbers and the guns. The Kosciuszko appeal to the People's Army to rise was calculated to give the Warsaw communist underground a role in the conquest of the capital and the Polish Communist Party a place in the political future of

2. John Ehrman, *August 1943–September 1944*, p. 344.
3. Stanislaw Mikolajczyk, *The Pattern of Soviet Domination*, p. 75.
4. *Ibid.*, p. 76.
5. *Ibid.*
6. T. Bor-Komorowski, *The Secret Army*, p. 135.

the country. It made the People's Army a rival of the Home Army. Rivalry led to lies. Shortly before the uprising, scrawls chalked on Warsaw walls alleged that the leaders of the Home Army had fled Warsaw.[7] They and their men and women fighters were very much in Warsaw.

For many months the German occupational forces had been at war with the Home Army. Throughout Poland executions and imprisonment were the order of the day. The underground struck back with assassinations. It had its own munitions works, hospitals, training quarters, radio monitoring studios, and political offices. General Bor and his staff waited impatiently for the order to stage a large-scale uprising. The Polish government in London was of two minds: General Kazimierz Sosnkowski, commander in chief of Polish armed forces in and outside of Poland, opposed a bold, open attack on the Germans. Russia's purpose, he felt, was to swallow Poland as she had the Baltic countries. Sacrifices resulting from an insurrection would therefore be in vain without the certainty that Moscow intended Poland to be truly independent. Mikolajczyk still harbored hopes of an accommodation with Stalin. Churchill shared this view. It was in accordance with the Mikolajczyk policy that the Home Army offered to help the invading Russian army and was paid in persecution for services rendered. Nevertheless, the Mikolajczyk government voted on July 25 to permit Bor to "proclaim the insurrection at the moment which you will decide is most opportune."[8]

Bor consulted the Council of National Unity, an underground parliament. It ruled unanimously that Warsaw must be captured before the Red Army entered. The Home Army and the home political apparatus would then, so the underground anticipated, act as host to the Russians and prove to the world that it had ousted the Germans, thereby earning the right to rule. Logic cannot be expected of massed men in a tense emotional situation. The simple fact is that the advance of the Russians and the retreat of the Germans dissolved restraint and eliminated all alternatives except blind heroism ending in self-immolation. "Let me die with the Philistines."

July 29, 1944, Mikolajczyk left London for Moscow. Stalin had promised Churchill to receive him. Having heard the Moscow Kosciuszko call to the minuscule communist underground to launch an insurrection and fearing communist usurpation, the Home Army went into action against the Germans on August 1 at 5 P.M. when its volunteers could mix with the crowds going home from work and reach their designated stations without being detected.

The previous evening Mikolajczyk was received by Molotov. "Why did you come here?" Molotov demanded. "What have you got to say?"

7. Czapski, p. 402.
8. Mikolajczyk, p. 204.

"I came here to see Stalin," the Polish Premier replied.

"We'll take Warsaw soon," Molotov declared. "We are already six miles from Warsaw."[9]

This meant there was no longer anything to discuss.

Stalin saw Mikolajczyk late on August 3. The interview was bound to be unsatisfactory. Stalin was polite. "Won't you sit down?" he said. Then he gestured Mikolajczyk to begin. The Pole asked that arms be supplied to the Warsaw fighters. Stalin: "I cannot trust the Poles. They suspect me of wanting to occupy Poland again. They're making a lot of trouble for me. . . . You must realize that nothing can be done for Poland if you do not recognize the Curzon Line . . . first you must reach an agreement with the Lublin Poles. Hereafter I intend to deal with only one Polish Government, not two."

There was nothing more to discuss; Stalin had appointed the Lublin Poles as the new government of Poland and invited Mikolajczyk to make peace with it. Mikolajczyk met the Lublin Poles on August 6 in Moscow. Wanda Wassilewska, whom Mikolajczyk characterized as a "horse-faced fanatic," was their leader. He appealed to them to supply munitions to the Polish underground battling the Nazis.

"There is no fighting in Warsaw," Wanda announced. Translation: the communists in Warsaw are not fighting.

Mikolajczyk took from his pocket dispatches dated August 2, 3, and 4 and showed them to her: "We are engaged in heavy fighting with the Germans in the whole city of Warsaw. We defeated part of their forces with the use of armaments captured from the enemy, but we have difficulty securing ammunition. Extremely urgent that mass dropping of ammunition and weapons be carried out today. . . . Disastrous lack of ammunition. . . . Request categorically immediate assistance in ammunition and anti-tank weapons today and on following days."

Mikolajczyk returned to London empty-handed.

Revolt raged in Warsaw. "Our strength," General Bor writes, "amounted to nearly 40,000 Underground soldiers and about 4,200 women." They were short of arms. At the Kammler factory, for instance, which was Bor's headquarters, 33 men had 15 rifles, some 40 grenades, and a few homemade grenades called filipinki. The insurgents, however, were not limited to members of the Home Army. Once the fighting began, teen-age boys and girls and older men and women joined the fray. Rags dipped in gasoline or kerosene were dropped on German tanks from roofs or upper floors. Bottles containing inflammable liquid were hurled at trucks carrying Germans to the multiple scenes of battle. There was no front. The entire city was the front. The central post office was captured

9. *Ibid.*, p. 78.

by the Home Army on August 2. The gasworks too. And the electric power station. The main railway terminal was taken and lost. The Germans shelled the electric plant with 88-mm. guns. General Bor wirelessed his London superiors to parachute munitions and antitank weapons on Napoleon Square and the Jewish cemetery. He also asked that the Polish parachute brigade of the British army be dropped in Warsaw and indicated where. By the evening of the second day the guerrillas had knocked out twelve German tanks. They controlled several city districts and the town center. The next day they captured a tank and immediately found an experienced crew. They then seized three truckloads of ammunition. Morale was high. But on the fourth day Bor and his comrades were perturbed. Across the river in Praga the battle seemed to have died; the Moscow radio was silent about the uprising and about Rokossovsky's progress. Bor had reckoned on seven to ten days of fighting for the city before the Russians came over the Vistula. But by August 4 the Germans were bombing Warsaw and the Russian air force had vanished from the skies. The Germans took the initiative on the ground too. Two British Halifax machines parachuted supplies early in the morning of August 5.

Among Americans and more particularly among Britons the events in Warsaw aroused admiration and anxiety. Newspapers lauded the Polish underground yet feared for its fate. Poles in the British Royal Air Force volunteered to fly from bases in Italy to Warsaw—a distance of 700 to 900 miles, most of it over Nazi territory—to deliver supplies. On August 4 Churchill telegraphed Stalin: "At the urgent request of the Polish underground army we are dropping subject to weather about sixty tons of equipment and ammunition into the south-western quarter of Warsaw where it is said a Polish revolt against the Germans is in fierce struggle. They are being attacked by one and a half German divisions. This may be of help to your operations."[10]

Stalin replied the next day: "I think that the information given to you by the Poles is greatly exaggerated and unreliable. . . . The Home Army consists of a few detachments misnamed divisions. They have neither guns, aircraft nor tanks. I cannot imagine detachments like those taking Warsaw, which the Germans are defending with four armoured divisions, including the Hermann Goering Division."[11] Churchill wired Stalin again on August 12: "I have seen a distressing message from the Poles in Warsaw, who after ten days are still fighting against considerable German forces which have cut the city into three. They implore machine-guns and ammunition. Can you not give them some further help as the distance from Italy is so very great?"[12]

10. *Correspondence,* Vol. I, p. 248.
11. *Ibid.,* p. 249.
12. *Ibid.,* p. 252.

Stalin remained adamant. "I have come to the conclusion," he told Churchill on August 16, "that the Warsaw action is a reckless and fearful gamble, taking a heavy toll of the population. This would not have been the case had Soviet headquarters been informed beforehand about the Warsaw action. . . . Things being what they are, Soviet headquarters have decided that they must dissociate themselves from the Warsaw adventure since they cannot assume either direct or indirect responsibility for it."[13]

The British government was under heavy, unceasing pressure to airlift supplies to Warsaw. Polish pilots in the RAF in Italy insisted on manning these flights. Things went so far that Poles at Bari, Italy, responding to the appeals of the Polish government in London, were ready to take their planes up despite an explicit order to the contrary from Air Marshal Sir John Slessor, RAF commander in Italy. Pressure continued. Slessor resisted. "For two days I stuck to my guns and refused to play," Slessor writes. "Then on the 7th I made a decision, which has always rather weighed on my conscience, but was I think inevitable." On the night of August 8 three Polish crews flew in as many machines to Warsaw; on the night of the 9th four crews. "The fact that all seven aircraft had the luck to get away with it and that some of their containers reached the right hands was really a misfortune," Slessor lamented in 1957. It compelled him to dispatch British and South African crews. Between August 12 and 17, 93 planes sallied forth from Italy to Warsaw; 17 did not return. Three others, having been hit by flak while over enemy territory, crash-landed. Some of the men were wounded. Churchill, who had an irresistible urge to get away from London to the fighting fronts, was in Italy. Slessor told him on August 17 that "unless supplies could be sent in from England or by the Russians, Bor's army was beyond help."[14]

A day later Churchill wired Roosevelt from Italy: "An episode of profound and far-reaching gravity is created by the Russian refusal to permit American aircraft to bring succour to the heroic insurgents in Warsaw, aggravated by their own complete neglect to provide supplies by air when only a few score of miles away." Churchill did not believe Stalin who said a Russian officer dropped into Warsaw had been killed by the Germans. And it "is quite untrue," Churchill writes, that the Soviets had dropped arms on Warsaw. He therefore pleaded with Roosevelt to join him in an appeal for help to Stalin "even at the risk" of his resenting it.[15]

Roosevelt consented on August 20 and he and the Prime Minister

13. *Ibid.,* p. 254.

14. Sir John Slessor, *The Central Blue: The Autobiography of Sir John Slessor, Marshal of the RAF,* pp. 613–617.

15. Winston S. Churchill, *Triumph and Tragedy,* p. 135.

signed this telegram to Stalin: "We are thinking of world opinion if anti-Nazis in Warsaw are in effect abandoned. We believe that all three of us should do the utmost to save as many of the patriots there as possible. We hope that you will drop immediate supplies and munitions to the patriot Poles in Warsaw, or will you agree to help our planes in doing it very quickly? We hope you will approve. The time element is of extreme importance."[16]

The words "or will you agree to help our planes in doing it?" were a reference to the shuttle air base at Poltava in the Ukraine. During the Tehran Conference the President gave Stalin a memorandum on the American proposal at the Moscow Conference to make available to the U.S. Air Force Soviet airdromes where planes from Italian and British bases, which had been bombing Germany and the Rumanian oil fields, could refuel, receive repairs, and reload with bombs for the return flights. This promised multiple advantages: targets in eastern Germany, now immune to attack because of distance would come into range. Damaged bombers, which might not be able to make it back to home base, could limp to the closer Soviet fields. On the return trip U.S. planes could bomb military objectives of interest to Russia. At Moscow the Soviet delegation had agreed "in principle." But there is many a slip between a Russian agreement "in principle" and its implementation. At Tehran in November, 1943, Stalin promised Roosevelt to look into the matter. Two months passed before Stalin informed Ambassador Harriman on February 2, 1944, that the proposal had his approval. Four more months passed in nerve-consuming combat between Americans and the Soviet bureaucracy. The first American planes landed on June 2 at the Soviet air base near Poltava, east of Kiev and some 600 miles east of Warsaw. In their joint message of August 20 Roosevelt and Churchill were asking Stalin to open Poltava, or a Soviet field farther west, to Anglo-American air force planes after they had dropped supplies on Warsaw. They felt they needed his permission to do so.

Stalin's reply of August 22 was crude but shrewd. "Sooner or later," he telegraphed, "the truth about the handful of power-seeking criminals who launched the Warsaw adventure will out. Those elements, playing on the credulity of the inhabitants of Warsaw, exposed practically unarmed people to German guns, armour, and aircraft. The result is a situation in which every day is used, not by the Poles for freeing Warsaw, but by the Hitlerites, who are cruelly exterminating the civil population.

"From the military point of view the situation, which keeps German attention riveted to Warsaw, is highly unfavourable both to the Red Army and to the Poles. Nevertheless, the Soviet troops, who of late have

16. *Correspondence,* Vol. II, p. 294.

had to face renewed counterattacks, are doing all they can to repulse the Hitlerite sallies and go over to a new large-scale offensive near Warsaw. I can assure you that the Red Army will stint no effort to crush the Germans at Warsaw and liberate it for the Poles. That will be the best, really effective, help to the anti-Nazi Poles."[17]

Thus Stalin refused to help Warsaw and refused to help the Americans and British do something for the people of the city. At the same time, however, he proclaimed his humanitarian feelings and undertook to help the Poles who were anti-Nazi until August 23, 1939, and since June 22, 1941. One man's patriots are another man's criminals; one man's heroes are another man's adventurers.

Stalin's rebuff to the Roosevelt-Churchill request disarmed the President. Although he had wired Ambassador Harriman in Moscow on August 23, 1944, apparently before receiving the Marshal's message, "We must continue to hope for agreement by the Soviet to our desire to assist the Poles in Warsaw," the moment he read Stalin's No, he capitulated. Churchill had sent him on August 24 an eyewitness account of the Warsaw Uprising. (He gave a copy to the Soviet Ambassador in London.) "The morale of the Home Army and of the civilian population," he commented, "is of the highest standard. . . . Despite lack of weapons, the Polish forces continue to hold the initiative. . . . In some places they have broken into German strongholds and captured much-needed arms and ammunition. On August 12, 11,000 rounds of rifle ammunition, five machine-guns, 8500 [rounds of] small arms ammunition, twenty pistols, thirty anti-tank weapons, and transports were captured. The German forces are fighting desperately. . . . During the night of August 12–13, the Home Army received some weapons from Allied aircraft. . . . The German forces brutally murdered wounded and sick people, both men and women, who were lying in the SS Lazarus and Karol and Marsa hospitals."

Churchill adds in his book, "I thought that some of this tale of villainy and horror should reach the world." He called the behavior of the Russians "strange and sinister." He was obviously boiling with rage.

Roosevelt read the eyewitness account and the same day wired the Prime Minister coolly: "The supply by us of the Warsaw Poles is, I am informed, impossible unless we are permitted to land and take off from Soviet airfields. Their use for the relief of Warsaw is at present prohibited by the Russian authorities. I do not see what further steps we can take at the present time that promise results."

Churchill did. His indignation bred daring. On August 25 he cabled Roosevelt the draft of a message both would dispatch to Stalin. Since the

17. *Ibid.,* p. 255.

Russian dictator did not wish to be associated with aid to Warsaw, the British and Americans would send such aid and land behind the Russian lines at "the refuelling ground assigned to us" without informing Moscow of the mission they had carried out on the way. "We therefore propose," he and the President would tell Stalin, "to send the aircraft unless you directly forbid it." If Stalin did not reply, Churchill added, "we ought to send the planes and see what happens. I cannot believe that they would be ill-treated or detained."

Roosevelt's answer was negative: "I do not consider it would prove advantageous to the long-range general war prospect for me to join with you in the proposed message to Stalin." The President did not object to Churchill's making the proposal to Stalin "if you consider it advisable to do so."

Churchill was furious. Although he had a touch of fever he attended the British Cabinet meeting on September 4. "I do not remember," he writes, "when such deep anger was shown by all members, Tory, Labour, Liberal, alike. I should have liked to say, 'We are sending our aeroplanes to land in your territory, after delivering supplies to Warsaw. If you do not treat them properly all convoys will be stopped from this moment by us.' " But, he explains, in crises "terrible and even humbling submissions must at times be made to the general aim." Yet the "drastic step" might have been effective because the men in the Kremlin "were governed by calculation and not by emotion," and although they "did not mean to let the spirit of Poland rise again at Warsaw," their only interest being the Lublin Poles, the stopping of the convoys during the great Russian advance "would perhaps have bulked in their minds as much as considerations of honour, humanity, decent common good faith, usually count with ordinary people." In other words, Churchill believed Stalin would yield. And well he might have, by closing his eyes, if Roosevelt had concurred. Churchill again wired Roosevelt on September 4, when Warsaw was nearing its last gasp, urging the President to reconsider. "Could you not authorise your air forces to carry out this operation, landing if necessary on Russian airfields without their formal consent? In view of our great successes in the West, I cannot think that the Russians would reject this fait accompli." In a second cable the same day the Prime Minister, customarily courteous in dealing with Roosevelt, invoked the War Cabinet's views to press the President with unconcealed rigor: "The War Cabinet themselves find it hard to understand your Government's refusal to take account of the obligations of the British and American Governments to help the Poles in Warsaw." Invoking "obligations" was a harsh reproach.

The President replied on September 5 that he was informed the Germans were in full control of Warsaw.[18] They were not.

18. Churchill, pp. 136–144.

Churchill's audacity highlights Roosevelt's irresolution, his passion is in contrast with Roosevelt's penchant to appease. Although America was wading deep in the salt waters of war, some vestiges of isolationism and neutralism still clung to her skirts, and Washington did not wish to become involved in Russia's quarrel with Poland and thereby imperil the friendship which the White House regarded as the firm foundation of the future peace. Moreover, Stalin must have found Churchill's sentiments for Warsaw incomprehensible after the Big Three had, in effect, agreed at Tehran to recarve the map so that Poland became a Soviet dependency. Roosevelt may have shared Stalin's puzzlement. Above all, Roosevelt did not wish to irritate Stalin. "I do not believe it would be goodfor our long range war prospects," he telegraphed Ambasssador Winant on August 25, "to make a further endeavor to induce Stalin to reverse his present attitude in regard to the use of Soviet airfields to assist Warsaw."[19]

When news of the Warsaw Uprising came to the areas recently conquered by the Soviets, Home Army units prepared to march to the assistance of the capital. The Russians stopped and disarmed them. As the fighting grew in intensity inside the city, the underground Poles made increasingly effective use of the sewers for communications and transportation of supplies. The efficacy of these foul, murky, narrow passages had been discovered in April-May, 1943, when the Germans, in a special "Final Solution" operation, demolished the large Jewish Ghetto of Warsaw. But the more they were forced into cellars and sewers the more the Poles lifted their eyes to the skies whence they expected the manna of war to rain down on them. Throughout the telegraphic discussions conducted by the Big Three, American and British planes in limited numbers and with limited tonnage flew in from Italy and Britain, dropped their precious gifts, and flew back again. The price in crews and planes was enormous, particularly on the long, weary return flight. German airplanes bombed Polish positions in Warsaw with impunity. Not a dozen miles away lay the inert Soviet army which might, at the least, have used its artillery to batter the Germans in the city. Rokossovsky rejected all offers of contact with General Bor.

On September 5, when the picturesque Old Town had been flattened and refugees and fighting were concentrated in the center of Warsaw, the German command sent a message across the barricades suggesting a parley. Bor agreed but dragged out the talks in the hope, now faint, of Soviet intervention. On September 10, writes General Bor, "something occurred for which we had been waiting for forty-two days. From across the Vistula came the thunder of powerful Soviet artillery. At the same time, the first Soviet planes appeared over the city." The Russian army took Praga on September 15. There they stopped.

19. This and the August 23 telegram to Harriman were seen at Hyde Park.

Churchill writes, "My efforts to get American aid led to one isolated but large-scale operation. On September 18 a hundred and four heavy bombers flew over the capital, dropping supplies."[20]

The heavy U.S. bombers did drop supplies on Warsaw. Moscow now let them use the American base at Poltava. One wonders whether Roosevelt had undergone a sudden conversion to Churchill's viewpoint. The reason for the American action may have been totally different. The Lublin Committee broadcast a statement on the evening of September 14 which was picked up by Bor's wireless. It said: "To fighting Warsaw: The hour of liberation for heroic Warsaw is near. Your sufferings and martyrdom will soon be over. The Germans will pay dearly for the ruins and blood of Warsaw. The first Polish Division Kosciuszko has entered Praga. It is fighting side by side with the heroic Red Army. Relief is coming. Keep fighting. Whatever may have been the motives of those who started the rising prematurely, without agreement with the High Command of the Red Army, we are with you with all our hearts. . . . A decisive fight is now taking place on the banks of the Vistula. Help is coming. Victory is near. Keep fighting."[21]

During the nights of September 15, 16 and 17, Soviet planes dropped supplies. During the night of September 17–18, the U.S. Air Force dropped supplies. The Russian strategy now was to encourage the Home Army to keep fighting until the Russians could cross the Vistula. The water level of the river was seasonally low. General Berling, commanding the Kosciuszko Division in Praga, ordered a battalion of some 500 men to ford the Vistula. They got over and joined the battle inside Warsaw. Apparently Berling's patriotism or political calculation took the upper hand. But at that juncture the Russian artillery barrage from Praga ceased. Berling was returned to Moscow for "further training."[22] Therewith hope perished.

Bor capitulated on October 2 after 62 blood-soaked days of heroism betrayed.

Those who fought in Warsaw lost a military and political battle.

Those who did not fight in Warsaw won.

Roosevelt dropped a tear. "I have been deeply distressed," his September 5 telegram to Churchill reads, "by our inability to give adequate assistance to the heroic defenders of Warsaw and I hope that we may together still be able to help Poland be among the victors in our war with the Nazis."[23]

Poland became a Russian satellite.

20. Churchill, p. 144.
21. Bor-Komorowski, p. 343.
22. Mikolajczyk, p. 94, and Bor-Komorowski, pp. 347–348.
23. President's Map Room Papers, 052. *Polish-Russian Relations 1944 (September-December)*. Seen at Hyde Park.

XIX TWO IMPERIALISTS

Churchill arrived in Moscow on the afternoon of October 9, 1944, and at 10 P.M. he and Eden and Ambassador Harriman conferred with Stalin and Molotov. The Prime Minister went briskly to business. "Let us settle about our affairs in the Balkans," he urged. "Your armies are in Rumania and Bulgaria. We have interests, missions, and agents there. Don't let us get at cross-purposes in small ways. So far as Britain and Russia are concerned, how would it do for you to have ninety percent predominance in Rumania, for us to have ninety percent of the say in Greece, and go fifty-fifty about Yugoslavia?"

During the time it took Pavlov, the Russians' interpreter, to translate these remarks, Churchill elaborated his scheme on a half-sheet of paper:

Rumania	
Russia	90%
The others	10%
Greece	
Great Britain (in accord with the U.S.)	90%
Russia	10%
Yugoslavia	50-50%
Hungary	50-50%
Bulgaria	
Russia	75%
The others	25%

The Prime Minister pushed the paper across the table to Stalin, who took his blue pencil, made a large tick on the paper, and passed it back toward Churchill and Eden. Churchill had a moment of doubt, not about the transaction but about the evidence. "Might it not be thought rather cynical," he said, "if it seemed we had disposed of the issues, so fateful to millions of people, in such an offhand manner? Let us burn the paper."

"No, keep it," Stalin advised.[1]

Stalin was not worried about the deal or the document. Both have been kept from the Soviet public as completely as the secret Soviet-Nazi protocol of August 23, 1939, also an arbitrary disposal of the lives of millions

1. Winston S. Churchill, *The Second World War. Triumph and Tragedy*, pp. 226–228.

of people. Nor was Stalin troubled by the arithmetic. Russia has had great mathematicians. The new communist mathematics, however, has a preference for 100 and zero. In Hungary, for example, Moscow permitted a free national election in 1945 in the presence of the Red Army. The communists received 17 percent of the votes, the Small Holders' or Peasant Party 57 percent. On February 26, 1947, the secret police altered the percentages. Bela Kovacs, the general secretary of the Small Holders' Party, was arrested and disappeared forever; later the party was suppressed. The Hungarian communists now had 100 percent of the political power, all other parties none. Stalin had burned the content of his paper agreement with Churchill. And, indeed, what could be the Rumanian reality of 10 percent for noncommunists when the communists held 90 percent? Even 50 equals 100 in communist arithmetic. Churchill feared the appearance of cynicism. Stalin boldly practiced realism.

Churchill was not totally lacking in realism. From Russia's behavior in Poland he knew she would not be gainsaid in the Balkans. He accordingly concluded that a few slices of the peninsula were better than none. His eyes were on the Mediterranean, the English channel to empire, and on Italy. If Britain had Greece and a foothold in Yugoslavia, Italy could be protected against Soviet inroads. Like Halifax, Churchill apparently did not know how far Stalin would go in Europe. He wondered whether Poland was a lost cause.

At their first session Churchill obtained Stalin's permission to bring Polish Prime Minister Mikolajczyk to Moscow. He thereupon telephoned Mikolajczyk in London and "under dire threats" "persuaded" him to come. Mikolajczyk realized that this was an invitation to his political beheading, but like a good Pole he would go down fighting. He arrived in the Soviet capital on October 12, ten days after the collapse of the uprising in Warsaw. Failure there had deprived him of most of his cards and, as he soon learned, of Churchill's support. Mikolajczyk, in the nature of his circumstances, was constrained to tilt at windmills.

The British Prime Minister had not been completely well since Tehran; illness made him irascible. One day in Moscow he had diarrhea. His temperature rose. He suspected he was getting pneumonia again, asked that specialists be flown from Britain, thought he should send for his wife, and hinted that he needed two male nurses.[2] The Poles suffered.

Churchill had made up his mind not to quarrel with Stalin on account of the Poles. Mikolajczyk therefore fought a lone battle at his first meeting in Moscow on October 13, 1944, with Stalin, Molotov, Fyodor Gusev, the new Soviet Ambassador in London, Churchill, Eden, Sir Archibald

2. Lord Moran, *Churchill. Taken from the Diaries of Lord Moran. The Struggle for Survival 1940–1945*, p. 216. Lord Moran was the Prime Minister's personal physician and usually traveled with him.

Clark Kerr, Ambassador Harriman, and their interpreters. They faced two issues: boundaries and the composition of the future Polish government. Stalin made any relationship with Mikolajczyk dependent on Polish recognition of the Curzon Line as the boundary between Russia and Poland. Churchill concurred.

Mikolajczyk: "I disagree both with Premier Stalin and Prime Minister Churchill. I cannot decide this problem, for the decision lies with the Polish Nation."

It took courage to say this. Nobody ever defied Stalin without suffering dire consequences. However, there was one bright spot in the Pole's situation, and he could not have been unaware of it. Stalin needed Mikolajczyk. The dictator of all the Russias had gone out of his way to bring from America and to court a Chicago economics professor and Father Orlemanski, a priest unknown outside his little parish in Springfield, Massachusetts, because he expected to encounter mountainous obstacles before Poland, largely Catholic and largely peasant, submitted to communist harness. Mikolajczyk, leader of the massive Polish Peasant Party, could be an enormous asset if only he would play the Kremlin's game.

The name of the game was Coalition.

The Soviet government had recognized the Lublin Committee as the government of Poland, and that committee was conscripting Poles into its army. The result was flight into the forests and armed fights. Stalin, assessing the immediate and grim future, was ready to appoint Mikolajczyk head of a new Polish government. Churchill put it this way: on October 22, "at my request, Stalin saw Mikolajczyk and had an hour and a half's very friendly talk. Stalin promised to help him, and Mikolajczyk promised to form and conduct a Government thoroughly friendly to the Russians. He explained his plan, but Stalin made it clear that the Lublin Poles must have the majority." The same day Churchill "bluntly" told Stalin the new Polish government should be a 50–50 affair, half Lublin Poles, half London Poles, plus Mikolajczyk as prime minister. Stalin accepted, then quickly changed his mind and urged a 75–25 majority for his Lubliners. Churchill, nevertheless, did not think "the composition of the Government will prove an insuperable obstacle if all else is settled," and so he wired Roosevelt. F.D.R. wired back asking to be consulted about the announcement of any compromise reached. He wanted publication delayed "for about two weeks. You will understand."[3] That meant until after November 7, 1944, the day of the U.S. presidential elections. (Roosevelt won a fourth term by a large majority which probably included many Polish-American votes.)

During his October, 1944, fortnight in Moscow Churchill lost much

3. Churchill, pp. 240–242.

time and, frequently, his temper discussing the Polish problem. The British Prime Minister had gone to the Soviet capital to cultivate friendship with Stalin, and it would be charitable to assume that what he said to Stalin was designed to serve that purpose without being sincerely meant. Churchill must be acquitted of political innocence. Hence one is entitled to wonder what he intended by his statement at the Soviet-British-Polish conference on October 13: "I feel it is Russia's intention that Poland should again rise free, independent and sovereign, and that this is her intention not because she feels strong but because she considers that she is right. But no Government could suffer an unfriendly attitude on the part of a neighbor if it had been through what Russia has in this war."

Stalin nodded his head in approval. Later he declared that the Poles would, if they relinquished their eastern half to Russia, get Danzig as well as Stettin. Mikolajczyk was not appeased: "May we be told what is actually considered as the Curzon Line?"

Churchill: "We will let you have a map showing it."

Mikolajczyk: "Is the Curzon Line identical with the demarcation line introduced in 1939?"

Stalin, stung by this reminder of the Soviet-Nazi pact, exclaimed, "No, not by any means. The Curzon Line gives you Bialystok, Lomza, and Przemysl." Mikolajczyk wanted Vilna and Lvov with the nearby oil field.

Thus ended a fruitless meeting.

The next day, October 14, Churchill spent from 11:45 A.M. to 2 P.M. with Mikolajczyk and his colleagues. The Polish Prime Minister was adamant, the British Prime Minister angry to the point of being rude. The Curzon Line, fixed by Curzon and Clemenceau in 1919, again served as the bone of contention. Mikolajczyk scorned this loathsome demarcation. "Should I sign a death sentence against myself?" he asked.

Eden remarked that if the Curzon Line was accepted "it will be possible to get from Stalin full guarantees of the independence of Poland."

Mikolajczyk: "The problem of frontiers is of such a nature that all the Polish people should express their opinion."

Churchill: "I wash my hands; as far as I am concerned we shall give the business up. Because of quarrels between Poles we are not going to wreck the peace of Europe. In your obstinacy you do not see what is at stake. It is not in friendship that we shall part. We shall tell the world how unreasonable you are. You will start another war in which 25 million lives will be lost. But you don't care."

Mikolajczyk, unmoved, said: "I know that our fate was sealed at Tehran."

Churchill, with frenzy: "It was saved at Tehran . . . we are preserving you from disappearance, but you will not play. You are absolutely crazy."

Mikolajczyk, still cool: "But this solution does not change anything."

Churchill: "Unless you accept the frontier you are out of business forever. The Russians will sweep through your country and your people will be liquidated. You are on the verge of annihilation."

Here Churchill spoke the truth and it was quite different from his saying in Stalin's presence that Russia acted not because she was strong but because she considered herself right.

Mikolajczyk, seeking a solution, wondered: "Would it not be possible to proclaim that the big three Powers have decided on the frontiers of Poland without our presence?"

Churchill: "We will be sick and tired of you if you go on arguing."

Eden, eager to pour water on the rising flame, suggested that the Pole agree to the Curzon Line declaration of the British and Soviet governments under protest. "I quite see the difficulty of your saying it of your own volition."

Churchill, apparently realizing that he had overstepped the bounds of courteous discourse, sought to mollify Mikolajczyk by reverting to the question of coalition. He said he might get him 60 percent against Lublin's 40. And after the war the U.S.A. "will take a great interest in the rehabilitation of Poland and may grant you a big loan . . . possibly without interest."

Mikolajczyk repeated his refrain: "We lose all authority in Poland if we accept the Curzon Line."

Before adjourning, Churchill expressed sympathy for the London Poles who had to deal with Russia's puppets in Lublin. "I don't envy you," he said, addressing Mikolajczyk. "I took a considerable dislike to them."[4]

Churchill had met his match in stubbornness and did not like it. He confessed to Lord Moran that "I was pretty rough with Mikolajczyk. He was obstinate and I lost my temper." He still thought Mikolajczyk wrong. ". . . if the Poles are sensible I shall be able to help while they are bargaining with the Russians." Subsequent events proved Churchill wrong. It is always difficult to know the future. It was not so difficult to know Stalin's power-acquisitive proclivities. They were a matter of record. The Russians were strong, and Stalin applied their strength against Poland and against Mikolajczyk.

Mikolajczyk took his stand on high principle because he had no other ground on which to stand: the Red Army had already pre-empted part of Polish soil and would soon hold the remainder. He nursed one last hope: help from Roosevelt. Only the United States had the power, if she had the

4. *Documents on Polish-Soviet Relations 1939–1945.* Vol. II: *1943–1945,* pp. 405–422.

will, to block Stalin's Russia. With this dream buzzing in his troubled head he returned to London, where Churchill told him in another acrimonious session that he should have gone to Lublin instead. Then came the final dismaying blow. Roosevelt, ten days after his re-election, wrote Mikolajczyk a letter and gave it to Ambassador Harriman to deliver on his way back to Moscow. The U.S. government, the President declared, "stands unequivocally for a strong, free and independent Polish state with the untrammeled right of the Polish people to order their internal existence as they see fit." After this ringing assertion, a retreat. If the Polish, Soviet, and British governments reached an agreement on frontiers, "including the proposed compensation for Poland from Germany," the United States "would offer no objection." The clause about compensation from Germany implied approval of that which called for compensation: Russia's annexation of eastern Poland. But the President's administration, in accordance with the American tradition, "cannot give a guarantee for any specific frontiers." And the U.S. government "is working for the establishment of a world security organization [the United Nations] through which the United States together with member states will assume responsibility for general security which, of course, includes the inviolability of agreed frontiers." Scant comfort for Mikolajczyk, who felt the knife at his throat. Further, F.D.R. promised aid to Poland in her postwar reconstruction and in the transfer of populations "in connection with the new frontiers."[5] Another indication that Roosevelt expected boundaries to be changed.

This was a skillfully drafted document. Without saying so for the record, Roosevelt joined Stalin and Churchill at the Curzon Line, thus sanctioning the amputation of eastern Poland because Moscow wished it. No plebiscite, no elections, no self-determination. The imposition by the Kremlin on Poland of a handful of men whom Churchill himself called "those horrible Lublin Poles," "a kind of Quislings," and, to Stalin in Moscow, "only an expression of the Soviet will." It augured ill for the postwar world. The decision on Poland meant that the security of powerful nations took precedence over the security of weak nations, although it should be the other way around.

Having read Roosevelt's letter, Mikolajczyk felt that "my own usefulness as Prime Minister was ended." Deprived of American and British support, he came to the conclusion that his government should accept the Curzon Line as Poland's eastern boundary even though it meant the loss of between 40 and 50 percent of the nation's territory. The Cabinet disagreed. He warned his colleagues that "they were on the verge of being cut off from the Polish people by the threatened recognition of the Lublin

5. *Ibid.*, p. 468.

group by all the major powers."[6] They were not impressed. He resigned on November 24, 1944. But eternal optimist and eternal Pole, he would act out still another tragic role on the political stage inside Poland.

It is easy to understand Mikolajczyk. He was an anticommunist, anti-Russian Polish patriot and politician. But how explain Churchill? And Roosevelt? Both were anticommunist and procapitalist, and Churchill, being upper-class British to boot, was reared on fear of Russian territorial expansion. Why, then, should he have put such heavy pressure on Mikolajczyk to give Russia almost half of Poland?

The Prime Minister and President were quite conscious of their differences with Stalin. In fact it was this knowledge that induced them to make concessions to him. Thus Churchill, defending his percentages agreement with Stalin about the lands from Rumania to Greece, wrote F.D.R. on October 11: "It is absolutely necessary we should try to get a common mind about the Balkans, so that we may prevent civil war breaking out in several countries, when probably you and I would be in sympathy with one side and U.J. [Uncle Joe] with the other."[7]

The gratification of Stalin's wishes was the price paid for unity. And half a loaf is better than bloodshed. Even two slices are. But it was more complicated than that. The western leaders' conduct cannot be ascribed solely to their inability to influence the course of events in countries contiguous to Russia. Churchill believed he could. Two days after his percentage deal with Stalin he set down "an authentic account of my thought" on the arrangement. He wrote it as a letter for the Marshal but changed his mind, "deeming it wiser to let well alone." Published in his memoirs more than a decade later, it must be accounted a true reflection of the Prime Minister's ideas at the time even though developments had made them look ridiculous. "We certainly do not wish to force on any Balkan State monarchic or Republican institutions," Churchill told Stalin in the undelivered letter. When peace comes they "should have a free and fair chance of choosing." Apart from institutions, there was "the ideological issue between totalitarian forms of government and those we call free enterprise controlled by universal suffrage. We are very glad that you have declared yourself against trying to change by force or by Communist propaganda the established systems in the various Balkan countries. Let them work out their own fortunes during the years that lie ahead. . . . Great Britain and Russia should feel easy about the internal government of these countries, and not worry about them or interfere with them once conditions of tranquillity have been restored." Hitler, the Prime Minister recalled, had used the fear of communism in western Europe and he would be destroyed. "But, as you know well, this fear

6. Stanislaw Mikolajczyk, *The Pattern of Soviet Domination*, pp. 117–118.
7. Churchill, p. 229.

exists in every country, because, whatever the merits of our different systems, no country wishes to go through the bloody revolution which will certainly be necessary in nearly every case before so drastic a change could be made in the life, habits, and outlook of their society."

How Stalin would have laughed had he been permitted to read the letter. How little Churchill understood of Stalin and his methods and his attitude to "bloody revolution." Preaching freedom of choice to a dictator was ludicrous. Preaching noninterference in the affairs of other countries to a ruler who had already intervened in the Baltic nations and Poland and who was about to intervene in the Balkans and central Europe would be comic if it were not so grimly tragic. "We feel we were right," Churchill's letter continued, "in interpreting your dissolution of the Comintern as a decision of the Soviet Government not to interfere in the internal affairs of other countries." Is there no limit to the naïveté of a great statesman? Growing philosophical, the Prime Minister ended on an evangelical note: "the differences between our systems will tend to get smaller, and the great common ground which we share of making life richer and happier for the mass of the people is growing every year."[8]

Stalin contributed to the intellectual meanderings of the innocents abroad. Mikolajczyk said to Stalin on October 22, "As you know, Marshal, there are very few communists in Poland; do you think, consequently, that the Polish Constitution will not be Communist?"

"Of course not," Stalin replied. "Poland must have a democratic rule. Private ownership and a free economy should be maintained. It is understood that Capitalism will be under State control. There are no conditions in Poland for a Communist system."[9] There were none. But there were the guns of the Red Army and the NKVD behind the transparent façade of quaking Quislings who had survived Stalin's purges of the 1930's. Empires ineluctably create colonial regimes in their own image. The British tolerated Gandhi, who unhorsed them. The Soviets removed Dubcek though he could not have done so if he had wished.

Mikolajczyk knew enough about conditions in the Soviet-conquered parts of Poland not to believe Stalin. Churchill, on the other hand, wrote of tolerance and the convergence of social systems. Convergence may come if the democracies move away from freedom much faster than the dictatorships are capable of moving toward it. Because John Bull and Mother Russia could converge in Moscow to accomplish the ruin of Germany, their mutual national foe, one of them drew the false conclusion that imperial appetites were no more. Perhaps the profundity of this error explains the later vehemence of his Cold War rhetoric. He had been to the zoo, as the old Russian saying goes, and not seen the elephant.

8. *Ibid.,* pp. 231–233.
9. *Documents on Polish-Soviet Relations,* p. 432.

Suffused by the warm atmosphere with which Moscow, and especially Stalin, could surround visiting dignitaries, Churchill did not realize that the Cold War already was in the making. In the midst of unity, disunity. While uniting to destroy an enemy a new enemy had been born out of ambition by annexations.

At the root of it lay the internal weakness of the Soviet regime.

A little scene out of Churchill's fortnight in Moscow: Lord Moran, the solicitous guardian of the P.M.'s health, asked him on October 17 what he was doing today. Churchill replied he had nothing on except seeing Stalin at 10 P.M. Moran: "Couldn't 10 P.M. be altered to 6 P.M.?"

Churchill: "No, Stalin specially said it would be more convenient for him at ten o'clock."

Moran: "You do all the travelling. Surely he could make this slight alteration." Churchill: "Stalin isn't as safe in his capital as I am in mine. When he came to the ballet it was all very secretive."[10] This offers a tiny glimpse of a major Soviet phenomenon.

Stalin knew that the Red Army soldiers were not imbued with Soviet ideals. He said to Ambassador Harriman in September, 1941, "that he was under no illusions, the Russian people were fighting as they always had 'for their homeland, not for us,' meaning the Communist Party."[11]

In May, 1941, on a visit to England, I visited John Strachey, an old friend, at Bath where he was serving as adjutant of a Royal Air Force squadron. Strachey, tall and aristocratic looking and member of a famous family of intellectuals, had a big room at the base lined with books by Marx, Engels, and Lenin. He introduced me to some of his officers, the men who had saved Britain during the Blitz, and took me to lunch in the mess. After the meal many of the blue-clad fliers went out into a lobby for coffee and to listen on the radio to "Lord Haw Haw," an Englishman who had joined the Germans and regularly broadcast denunciatory diatribes filled with wit and satire against the "doomed" British Isles. The officers laughed. Strachey's Red library on a military airfield and Lord Haw Haw's gay audience were a mirror of British democracy. The state trusted its people. Moscow does not tolerate such phenomena in peacetime. It has no confidence in the Soviet people. The ubiquity of the secret police, the one-sidedness of the press, radio, television, and education, the leaden official hand on art and literature, the restrictions on travel outside the Soviet sphere, the constant rewriting of history are proof that the Soviet government, mighty though it be, is weak from lack of a popular base. A government which banishes to Siberia five dissidents who quietly protest on the Red Square against the invasion of Czechoslovakia must

10. Lord Moran, p. 219.
11. *Foreign Relations of the United States. Diplomatic Papers 1945.* Vol. V: *Europe,* p. 923.

be afraid of what the others would do if left unwatched and unchained. Throughout the second world war Stalin was aware of this failure of communism in Russia. "All the more monstrous are the acts whose initiator was Stalin and which are rude violations of the basic Leninist principles of the nationality policy of the Soviet state," Chairman Nikita S. Khrushchev said on February 24, 1956, in his secret speech. "We refer to the mass deportations from their native places of whole nations, together with all Communists and Komsomols without any exception; this was not dictated by any military considerations."

Obviously by a political consideration.

In a radio speech on May 9, 1945, Stalin made no mention of communism or Marxism or of the virtues of the Soviet system. He said: "The centuries-old struggle of the Slav peoples for their existence and their independence has been concluded by victory over the German invaders and over German tyranny." Slavism, not socialism. At a victory banquet in the Kremlin to Red Army officers on May 24, 1945, Stalin admitted that "Our government made not a few blunders; there were moments of desperation in 1941 and 1942 when our army retreated, abandoned our native villages and cities in the Ukraine, White Russia, Moldavia, Leningrad province, the Baltic region, the Karelian Republic, abandoned them because it had no choice. Another nation might have said to the government: You have not justified our hopes, get out; we will set up a new government that will sign a peace with Germany and give us tranquillity. But the Russian people did not take that road because it had faith in the policy of the government. . . . Thank you, Russian people, for your trust."

A totalitarian state is deliberately so constructed as to make it impossible for the people to tell the government to get out. But the people whom the dictator thanked were the Russian people, then slightly over 50 percent of the Soviet population. (The remainder were the national minorities like the Byelorussians and the Ukrainians and non-Slav ethnic races such as the Armenians, Georgians, Kazaks, Uzbeks together now outnumbering the Great Russians.) Stalin thanked the Russian people, not the Soviet peoples or the entire Soviet population. Apparently the non-Russians had not earned his gratitude or deserved his courtship. Like Tsarist Russia, the Soviet Union was—and is—a country broken up into islands of castes and ethnic units floating in a vast polluted ocean of political ignorance, impotence, and indifference. Beginning in 1934 Stalin undertook the herculean task of welding this archipelago into a continent. But his purges and intensified labor exploitation as a means of rapid industrialization did just the opposite, and when the Nazis erupted into Russia her weakness was manifest. Stalin then appealed to patriotism; the people responded. The Russians fought for Russia. The Ukrainians had less interest in fighting for Russia, the non-Slav minorities still less. This does not mean that Kirghiz, Buryat, Azerbaijan, Georgian, Tadjik soldiers and officers did not fight bravely. There are many reasons why men fight well in wars. Love of the government is not frequently one of them.

A totalitarian system like the Soviet Union seeks to identify the government with the nation because it is conscious of the gulf between them. Stalin hoped to close the chasm by retrieving for the Russians all the territories Russia had lost since 1917 and gaining for the Ukrainians all the East European territories inhabited by Ukrainians. He could then make a claim on their loyalty by pointing to what he had done for them. And by creating an empire beyond the old Tsarist frontiers he could boast of having made Russia mighty among the nations of the earth and earn the popular support denied the government in the past. Thus the Soviet regime's social weakness stood at the cradle of Soviet imperialism. Other factors contributed to the yearning for empire: the mistaken notion, for instance, that in the modern age territory is a source of strength, although even oceans would no longer protect national territories in a full-scale nuclear war, and one engaging the Soviet Union would soon become that. The wish of the Soviet military caste for political power is another circumstance making for imperialism. And, too, the essential fact that, despite all its fantastic industrial development in numerous areas, the Soviet Union is an underdeveloped country governed by men with nineteenth-century minds dragging a nineteenth-century dogma. Twentieth-century nations, approaching the threshold to internationalism, do not need empires. The European peoples that have sloughed off their empires are living better without them. This is why Churchill, who brilliantly led Britain to victory over Germany, was voted out of office immediately thereafter by a politically astute British electorate which knew that England had to be liberated from India and that Churchill would not do it.

It was fitting that Churchill and Stalin should meet and agree on sharing the Balkans and bisecting Poland. Their practical imperial minds met. Churchill realized that if tired Britain was to hold her own empire she would have to be reconciled to Stalin's acquiring his. The Prime Minister was left only with the timorous hope of Moscow's noninterference in the affairs of British colonies and of achieving, with American assistance, a live-and-let-live Anglo-Soviet compact: peaceful imperial coexistence.

XX FRANKLIN D. ROOSEVELT
AND THE MILITARY

President Roosevelt in 1942 recommended me to Secretary of State Cordell Hull. This conduced to friendly treatment and frank talk in numerous meetings until Mr. Hull resigned on November 21, 1944, because he was physically ill and sick of being ignored in policy making. The Secretary was a soft-spoken Tennessean with a waxen face that lent him an appearance of translucence. During our chats he sat in front of his roll-top desk. I was seated a few paces away. At my feet stood a high, gently rounded brass spittoon. Every time he spat I instinctively drew back my feet. But he was a champion marksman. His tastes, habits, and views were simple. "My best friends," he said to me in his office on May 19, 1943, "have always been the people back home in the mountains of Tennessee."

"For Christ's sake!" he exclaimed as I advocated independence for India. "When I was a young fellow I raised a regiment [in 1898] to fight for the independence of Cuba." He favored freedom for Indochina too. His attitude toward Russia was literally earthy: "When I was a boy I had to handle a number of mules in plowing on my father's farm in Tennessee. One of them could outkick any three mules. When he did I would lay my whip on him. That just gave him fuel, and he would kick all the more. I therefore had to give up and let him cool off. Then I would start quietly moving forward in the plow, whereupon he agreed to work. But whenever he kicked and I fought him with the whip he kicked all the more." He applied this boyhood lesson to relations with Stalin: "We cannot settle questions with Russia by threats. We must use friendly methods."[1]

But Hull displayed the stubbornness of his father's mules as soon as one of his basic political principles was in jeopardy. He not only opposed empires. He abhorred spheres of influence. "I was not, and am not, a believer in the idea of a balance of power or spheres of influence as a means of keeping the peace. During the First World War I had made an intensive study of the system of spheres of influence and balance of power, and I was grounded to the taproots in their iniquitous consequences. The conclusions I then formed in total opposition to this system stayed with me."[2]

1. *The Memoirs of Cordell Hull,* Vol. II, p. 1465.
2. *Ibid.,* pp. 1452–1453.

With the emergence, therefore, of spheres of influence in 1944 Hull commenced kicking. For the Secretary the Soviet campaign of annexation-and-deception began on April 1, 1944, when Soviet Ambassador Andrei A. Gromyko came to see him to state that the Red Army's advance into Rumania would re-establish the 1940 Soviet-Rumanian frontier [demarcated with Hitler's acquiescence]. Gromyko added that the Soviet government "did not aim at acquiring any part of Rumanian territory or at changing Rumania's social regime."

Hull comments: "A stir of speculation now arose in the press of many countries as to whether Russia's aim was liberation or acquisition." Here the Wilsonian Secretary revealed the origins of the Churchill-Stalin percentages deal in Moscow in October: "Suddenly British Ambassador Halifax inquired of me on May 30, 1944, how this Government would feel about an arrangement between the British and Russians whereby Russia would have a controlling influence in Rumania, and Britain a controlling influence in Greece."

Hull condemned this betrayal of "our broad basic declarations on policy, principles, and practice." He "bluntly opposed" any division of Europe into spheres of influence. Dean Acheson calls Hull "slow, circuitous, cautious." Slow he was, and at times circuitous, but when internationalist principles were threatened his shots traveled as straight as a mountaineer's bullets.

Informed by Halifax of Hull's hostility, Churchill telegraphed Roosevelt direct. An exchange of messages followed in which the Prime Minister, seeking to make his gambit more palatable, declared that what he intended was a wartime *modus vivendi.* Would not F.D.R. sanction a three months' trial? Hull remained skeptical: "regardless of Churchill's statement that the agreement would be limited to military matters" the bargain would soon extend into political and economic fields and inevitably result in "the division of the Balkans into spheres of influence without diminishing the tensions between the contracting powers."

Wisdom and even prophecy often stem from loyalty to principle.

Roosevelt, however, yielded to Churchill's importunings. He hated to disagree with friends. He told Churchill on June 12 to go ahead "without," Hull writes, "consulting me or the State Department." The Secretary consequently continued his feud by diplomatic notes with the British government until U.S. Ambassador in Cairo Lincoln MacVeagh wired the Secretary on June 26 that he had heard from the British Ambassador there of a change in U.S. policy toward the proposed percentage deal. On June 29 Hull asked Roosevelt what happened. On June 30 F.D.R. revealed to Hull what he had done on June 12.

This was not an isolated instance of Roosevelt's mistreatment of his State Department. At the November-December, 1943, Tehran Conference, the U.S. minutes were recorded by the Joint Chiefs of Staff and by Charles E. Bohlen of the State Department. But Bohlen's minutes went to the White House and the Department remained ignorant of the Tehran decisions on Poland, Germany, and the projected Anglo-American landing in Normandy because, presumably, it was too diffuse to keep secrets.

The State Department suffered from the virus disease of institutionitis to which few institutions, whether governmental, business, philanthropic, or academic, are immune. The bigger they are the harder they fall. The State Department, big and growing bigger each year, with many thousands of employees at home and abroad, was racked by jealousies and rivalries at all levels, including the highest. Roosevelt made a contribution to some of these. His mind moved like a speedboat—fast and half out of water. Increasingly, therefore, he bypassed the plowing Secretary and operated through Under Secretary Sumner Welles, a tall, distinguished-looking, meticulously groomed diplomat with a throaty voice, long face, and brilliant brain full of the facts of the world and an understanding that bridged boundaries and seas. On fundamentals he and Hull seldom differed. But intellectual agreement does not preclude personal or political conflict. Welles spoke the President's shorthand which left Hull panting. The Secretary resented being nominally first and functionally second. Hull's fury was fed by Welles's "malign enemy, William Christian Bullitt, a singularly ironic middle name," in Dean Acheson's cutting phrase.[3] Bullitt, rich, intelligent, emotionally unstable, and former ambassador to Moscow and Paris, coveted Welles's pre-eminence, which he felt should be his. He regarded himself an intimate of the Roosevelt family and fawned on the President. "I think you know what a joy it is to me to be able to work with you and under your orders," Bullitt wrote the President on December 6, 1933. "I know you refuse to admit it —especially to yourself—but the fact is you are a very great human being and a great President." Bullitt was then on his way to Moscow to open the U.S. Embassy. He expressed gratitude for the assignment but added, "The only regret I have is that I shall not be able to work with you in Washington. I would rather do that than any job anywhere." Again, on Easter Day, 1934, from Moscow, Bullitt wrote F.D.R.: "I am a bit homesick . . . in the past year you and Mrs. Roosevelt and Miss Le Hand have made me feel that I was a member of the family."[4] But after Roosevelt died Bullitt attacked him in two articles in *Life* magazine (August 30, 1948, and September 6, 1948), just as he attacked Woodrow Wilson in an

3. Dean Acheson, *Present at the Creation. My Years in the State Department*, p. 46.
4. From the secret files of the Franklin D. Roosevelt Library at Hyde Park, N.Y.

imitation of a book to which the dying Freud lent his illustrious name. Bullitt suffered from an irrepressible desire for revenge. Hull therefore found him an eager collaborator in the plan to ride Welles out of office into private life by spreading, as Acheson puts it, "rumors of a personal nature" which, even if true, in no way impaired his public usefulness. Welles resigned on September 25, 1943, and was succeeded by Edward R. Stettinius, Jr., strikingly handsome and startlingly ill-equipped for the post.

"It's wonderful," Benjamin Franklin remarked in 1785, "how preposterously the affairs of this world are managed." The centuries roll on and it does not become less preposterous.

The American management of the German problem was a tragedy of errors. The question of what to do with Germany in defeat, under discussion in 1943 and demanding decisions when victory came into view in the second half of 1944, disclosed broad differences of opinion between the State Department and other branches of the U.S. government and between the U.S. government and the British government. For a time President Roosevelt was so intent on his dispute with Britain that he lost sight of the Soviet aspect of the problem. The crucial matter of Berlin was neglected. "It is a striking fact," writes the State Department historian, "that during the entire period from January 1944 to February 1945, during which the tripartite [Anglo-American-Soviet] protocol [on Germany] was drafted, amended, and finally approved, the question of access to Berlin had never once been raised with the Russians in a forthright manner."[5]

The explanation of this lapse must be sought in the widespread official and popular belief in Soviet-American friendship. Even granting that this attitude promoted the war effort and gave promise of postwar peace, it is the first law of international politics that nothing in it is permanent except its impermanence. Attention should therefore have been paid to the contingency that relations between Moscow and Washington might so change as to necessitate precise provisions for access to Berlin. This was overlooked.

The same misconception of lasting friendship with the Soviets and eternal hostility to Germans lay at the root of the Roosevelt-Churchill-Stalin desire to dismember Germany. Whether such friendship with Russia was attainable and whether such hostility to Germans was justified is not germane. The point is that the friendship did not endure and the hostility, in practical politics if not in personal emotions, quickly dissolved into Moscow's close embrace of one part of Germany and An-

5. William M. Franklin, *World Politics,* October, 1963, p. 24.

glo-American collaboration with the other, thus dividing postwar Europe.

With dismemberment axiomatic, it followed inexorably that Germany would be split into three zones of occupation: American, British, and Soviet. A French zone was subsequently created surgically, like Eve, out of the U.S. and U.K. zones. No thought was given to a national government of a united Germany disarmed and totally occupied by the victors. Thus the idea of dismemberment led to zonal partitions, and zonal partitions led to deep divisions between West and East which have reverberated throughout the world ever since.

Exactly how the zonal boundaries were fixed the State Department did not know because, writes its historian, "the Department does not have all the pertinent records, since the Department was not included in all the negotiations on this subject."[6] In part this was due to Roosevelt's affection for the military. After Pearl Harbor, Secretary Hull asserts, F.D.R. preferred to be called Commander in Chief rather than President. "He relished the title. . . . At a Cabinet dinner, probably in 1942, where I was to propose a toast, the President asked me before I rose to speak: 'Please try to address me as Commander-in-Chief, not as President.' "

Until Pearl Harbor Hull had been a member of the War Council consisting of the President, the Secretaries of State, War, and Navy, the Chief of Staff, and the Chief of Naval Operations. After America was bombed into war, Hull no longer attended War Council sessions. "I feel it is a serious mistake," Hull complains, "for the Secretary of State not to be present at important military meetings . . . some development of a military character . . . also had a strong foreign policy angle. . . . The President did not take me with him to the Casablanca, Cairo, or Tehran conference . . . nor did I take part in discussions with Prime Minister Churchill in Washington, some of which had widespread diplomatic repercussions."[7] British Foreign Secretary Eden almost always accompanied Churchill to international conferences.

A major reason for the President's exclusion of Hull was the Secretary's unbending opposition to the postwar dismemberment of Germany. At the Quebec Conference in August, 1943—the only meeting Hull attended with Roosevelt, Churchill, and Eden—he told Eden that he and his colleagues at the State Department thought "an imposed dismemberment of Germany might merely create a German slogan for union. A German economy must exist for the support of the people of Germany, and toward this end such national systems as canals, railroads, post offices, and telegraph must exist as units." Hull gathered the impression that Eden, but not all members of the British Cabinet, agreed with him

6. *Ibid.,* p. 1.
7. Hull, pp. 1109–1111.

on dismemberment "largely because of the impracticability of carrying it out."[8]

Secretary of War Henry L. Stimson, who had served as Secretary of State from 1929 to 1933, was more zealous than Hull in his opposition to reducing Germany to a congeries of separate states or to a nation of farmers. Roosevelt's Cabinet now split on the future of Germany: it was Stimson versus Secretary of the Treasury Henry Morgenthau, Jr. Stimson stated his views in a memorandum dated September 5, 1944: "The position frankly taken by some of my colleagues [in the Cabinet] was that the great industrial areas of Germany known as the Saar and the Ruhr with their very important deposits of coal and ore should be totally transferred into a nonindustrialized area of agricultural land."

This referred to the Morgenthau Plan for the "pastoralization" of Germany.[9]

"I cannot," Stimson argued, "conceive of such a proposition being either possible or effective and I can see enormous general evils coming from an attempt to so treat it. . . . I cannot treat as realistic the suggestion that such an area in the present economic condition of the world should be turned into a nonproductive 'ghost territory.' . . . I cannot conceive of turning such a gift of nature into a dust heap. . . . Such methods . . . tend to breed war."[10]

The battle over the Morgenthau Plan was "the most violent single interdepartmental struggle of Stimson's career"—a long career in high public office that began in 1911. He communicated his basic idea orally to President Roosevelt on December 18, 1943: ". . . not to divide Europe up into separate pieces which could not each of them feed itself on its own land."

A wartime military consideration hampered Roosevelt's thinking about postwar Germany: the cross-Channel invasion of the continent and Germany was so mapped, and executed, that the British army would be on the left and the American army on the right. This meant that the British army would move into northern and northwestern Germany, the American into southern and southeastern Germany. Roosevelt nevertheless wanted northwestern Germany as the U.S. zone of occupation because in that position the Americans would control the great harbors of Hamburg and Bremen through which U.S. divisions were to be shipped to the Far East for the final struggle against Japan. Further, he anticipated that if America got the southern zone bordering on France he would have trouble with General Charles de Gaulle, whom he abomi-

8. *Ibid.,* p. 1233.
9. Full text of Plan in Henry Morgenthau, Jr., *Germany Is Our Problem,* pp. 1–4.
10. Henry L. Stimson and McGeorge Bundy, *On Active Service in Peace and War,* pp. 571–573.

nated as a "prima donna," and involvement in the French civil war of his imagination.

The British military, however, foresaw endless confusion if, after debouching into Germany according to plan, the huge British army would be obliged to leave its stations in the conquered land and exchange zones with a million armed Americans. Nevertheless, F.D.R. raised this issue whenever his officials came to him to discuss the future of Germany. The President's concentration on the immediate may explain his vacillation on the ultimate. To delay a decision he resorted to a common device, he appointed a committee. It consisted of Stimson, Hull, Morgenthau, Hopkins. Morgenthau proved to be a minority of one. Each side prepared its memorandum for the President: the State Department, on September 1, 1944, in behalf of Hull, Hopkins, and Stimson; the Treasury on September 2 on behalf of Morgenthau, aided in the drafting by Assistant Secretary of the Treasury Harry Dexter White.

Thus briefed, F.D.R. proceeded to the second Quebec Conference with Churchill, September 11–16. Both were served by large staffs but the President had no top-level adviser, neither Hull, nor Stimson, nor Hopkins, except Morgenthau, and the man present enjoyed an enormous advantage. On September 15, at Quebec, the President and the Prime Minister approved a declaration that the metallurgical, chemical, and electric industries of Germany in the Ruhr and the Saar be "necessarily put out of action and closed down." The two districts "should be put under some body under the world organization which would supervise the dismantling of these industries and make sure that they were not started up again by some subterfuge."[11]

One of the conferees, presumably Roosevelt, inserted into the statement a reference to the German destruction of industries in Russia and her neighbors and added that "it is only in accordance with justice that these injured countries should be entitled to remove the machinery they require in order to repair the losses they have suffered." In the light of the experience with German reparations after the first world war, no one, least of all Morgenthau, placed much trust in monetary indemnities. His Plan provided for none. Reparations would take the form of territory, industrial equipment, "forced German labor outside Germany," and confiscation of all German assets abroad.

Stalin was invited to the conference but pleaded the pressure of leadership. Had he been present he could only have welcomed the Morgenthau Plan; it projected a further weakening of Germany and reparations in kind for Russia. But Churchill's acceptance of pastoralization has provoked considerable conjecture. The Prime Minister himself sheds help-

11. William Hardy McNeill, *America, Britain, and Russia. Their Cooperation and Conflict 1941–1946,* p. 489.

ful light on the matter. He was surprised, he writes, to see Morgenthau at the conference yet glad "as we were anxious to discuss financial arrangements between our two countries for the period between the conquest of Germany and the defeat of the Japanese." Roosevelt and Morgenthau tried to convince Churchill that Germany pastoralized would not only pluck the nettle of future wars, British exports would rise if German industry crumbled. "At first [as was to be expected from everything known about him] I violently opposed this idea. But the President, with Mr. Morgenthau—from whom we had much to ask—were so insistent that in the end we agreed to consider it."[12] The hint is blunt. It prompts one to conclude that dollars triumphed over his better sense. Says William Hardy McNeill, "Morgenthau arrived full of ardour for his plan to destroy German industry. He was also prepared to offer the British the prospect of a large American loan." Morgenthau proposed in addition to give England three and a half billion dollars in Lend-Lease help.[13]

Eden was aghast and remonstrated with his Prime Minister when he arrived in Quebec one day after Churchill had concurred in Morgenthau's ideas. But the act had been done. However, Roosevelt felt the cold wind of dissent on his return to Hyde Park and Washington. On September 17 Stimson decided to send the President yet another memorandum criticizing the Morgenthau project: "The question is not whether we want the Germans to suffer for their sins. Many of us would like to see them suffer the tortures they have inflicted on others. The only question is whether over the years a group of seventy million educated, efficient and imaginative people can be kept within bounds at such a low level of subsistence as the Treasury proposals contemplate. I do not believe that is humanly possible."[14]

The Germans were undoubtedly efficient. The real issue was whether history's worst wartime crimes could or should be requited by a peacetime crime against the hungry, naked, homeless, and hopeless of a world in dire need of everything man's ingenuity can produce.

News of the Stimson démarche, buttressed by Hull's stand, alarmed the Treasury, which drafted a rebuttal. This leaked through Drew Pearson, the columnist. A storm broke. Influential newspapers condemned the Morgenthau Plan. So did Governor Thomas E. Dewey, who charged—the presidential campaign was in high gear and he was the Republican candidate—that the Plan prolonged the war.

Roosevelt retreated. He not only dropped the Morgenthau Plan, he refused for many months to consider an alternative. "I dislike making

12. Winston S. Churchill, *The Second World War. Triumph and Tragedy,* p. 156.
13. McNeill, p. 489.
14. Stimson and Bundy, pp. 578–579.

detailed plans for a country which we do not yet occupy," he wrote Hull on October 20, 1944.[15] This mollified Hull. This reflected a politician's caution. This reflected Roosevelt's dislike of being disliked. "Henry Morgenthau pulled a boner," he told Stimson, a Republican, at lunch on October 3. And he confessed that he had evidently approved the Morgenthau Plan "without much thought."[16] It was he who had pulled the "boner" by deciding such a question frivolously.

Remained the task of charting the zones of occupation in Germany. It was assigned to the military. But at the October, 1943, Moscow tripartite conference Hull, Eden, and Molotov had agreed on creating a civilian European Advisory Commission (EAC), with seat in London, to tackle the same task. The dual arrangement invited confusion.

The EAC members were Ambassador Winant for the United States, Sir William Strang for Great Britain, and Ambassador Fyodor T. Gusev for the Soviet Union. The American representative was meagerly briefed and poorly informed. Winant, on December 19, 1944, sent Hopkins a telegram, seen in the State Department archives in Washington, which read: "I am grateful for the radio as I am largely dependent upon it for actions taken in the United States that affect foreign policy here." Winant's deputy on the commission was George F. Kennan, counselor of Embassy and political advisor to the Ambassador. When Kennan left, Philip E. Mosely, a specialist in Soviet and Balkan affairs and a linguist, took his place.

Kennan writes that at the first EAC working session on January 14, 1944, "The British, who were well prepared, at once laid on the table a draft [German] surrender instrument and detailed proposal for future zones of occupation in Germany. . . . We Americans, of course, had no instructions on either subject—or, for that matter, on any other. We forwarded the British proposals to Washington and waited for a reaction.

"Several weeks went by. No word from Washington. Repeated telegraphic appeals for instructions went unanswered. Our British colleagues became restive, we ourselves acutely embarrassed.

"On February 18 the Soviet delegate put forward his government reaction to the British initiative. The Russians submitted their own alternative draft of the surrender terms. The British proposals on zones of occupation, on the other hand, they accepted practically *in toto*. We Americans still had no instructions."[17]

Strang, a careful observer who stayed on the job from January, 1944, to August, 1945—the Kennan and Mosely periods—dissected the American dilemma in a 1956 book. "As for the Americans," he wrote, "there

15. Hull, p. 1621.
16. Stimson and Bundy, p. 581.
17. George F. Kennan, *Memoirs 1925–1950*, pp. 164–168.

were people in authority in Washington who did not like the Commission. The military authorities, with their war-time predominance (to which there was no parallel in London) were displeased by this invasion [by the State Department] of what they regarded as their preserve. . . ."[18]

In London Churchill dominated the military. In Washington Roosevelt and the military, in tandem, dominated the civilian foreign-policy structure.

It was impossible for the British and Soviet delegates not to notice the helplessness of their uninstructed American colleagues for whom the width of the Atlantic exceeded the distance to the moon. Finally, on March 8, 1944, a curt message came to the bewildered Americans. It originated with the U.S. Joint Chiefs of Staff and consisted, as Kennan remembered it, of one sentence which would have assigned to the United States zone 51 percent of the population and 43 percent of the territory of Germany, thereby limiting the Soviet zone to a much smaller area than did the British proposal, accepted by Moscow, and pushing the western frontier of the Soviet zone eastward.

Kennan realized that the Soviets were unlikely to take less than had already been granted them. He accordingly decided to repair to Washington where, since the State Department could not offer any assistance (the matter was in the hands of the military), the young, conscientious worrier-diplomat decided to seek out the President, whom he had interviewed earlier on another important though less vexatious problem. "Once again," Kennan writes, "the President received me graciously. But I had difficulty, this time, getting through to him what it was I had come to see him about. He was now already locked into his celebrated conflict with the British over which of us would have the northern, and which the southern, of the contemplated two Western zones. This was what was on his mind, and this is what he wanted to talk about. When I finally managed to convey to him that it was a confusion relating primarily to the boundary of the *Soviet* zone that I had in my mind, he was quite surprised. When I explained to him the nature of the confusion and showed him the instruction we had received in London, he laughed gaily and said, just as I had expected him to say, 'Why that's something I once drew on the back of an envelope.' I asked him whether he would himself see to the removal of the confusion, or whether there was something more I should do about it. He said I could relax—he would see to it that the mixup was straightened out."

On May 1, 1944, instructions were sent to Winant to approve the boundaries of the Soviet zone as already agreed by the British and the Soviets and as they are to this day.[19] However, no final settlement on the zones

18. Lord Strang, *Home and Abroad,* p. 208.
19. Kennan, pp. 169–171.

took place until 1945, and that on account of F.D.R.'s preference for the northwestern zone. Winant wrote the President on January 28, 1945, that his, the Ambassador's, "holding to your instructions to insist on the northwestern zone was responsible for the delay in reaching agreement on zones."[20]

The wisdom of zones is a doubtful one. It was questioned before the agreement. When Eisenhower was in Washington in January, 1944, prior to taking command of the cross-Channel invasion of Europe (Overlord), "I thought and suggested," he recalled after his terms in the White House, "that the whole occupation [of Germany] would be more smoothly conducted if we could avoid the establishment of national zones; I believed that quadripartite government over the entire area as a single entity would give no nation an opportunity to be troublesome. But even then the President was apparently committed, with Great Britain and the Soviets, to the occupation of Germany by national zones."[21]

In Berlin in 1946 I had an interview with General Lucius D. Clay, U.S. commander in Germany, on September 21, dined in his home on September 23 with him and Mrs. Clay à trois, and saw him again in his office on October 2. On each occasion Clay expressed the hope of achieving for Germany "an Austrian solution" under which the four zones of occupation, French, Russian, British, and American, were administered by one Austrian government. This would supersede the then already existing division of Germany into an East Germany under a communist regime and the three western noncommunist regimes. "If Moscow," Clay said, "wanted ten billion dollars for this unification of Germany, the money would be well spent." I suggested that 18 million East Germans, not to speak of the territory whereon they existed, were worth more to Stalin, even in Russia's straitened state, than America's billions.[22] The damage had been done at Tehran in November-December, 1943, and confirmed thereafter by the EAC in London and by others elsewhere. The damage was the decision in principle to dismember. From it flowed the absence of a national government, Soviet power implanted in the heart of Europe, exacerbated Russo-American rivalry, and the suppurating sore of Berlin.

In the admiral's cabin aboard the U.S.S. *Iowa* at 2 P.M. on November 19, 1943, President Roosevelt, en route to Tehran, met with the Joint Chiefs of Staff to discuss strategy and Germany. The President said "we should go as far as Berlin. The Soviets could then take the territory to the east thereof. The United States should have Berlin. . . . There would definitely be a race for Berlin. We may have to put the United States divisions into

20. Dwight D. Eisenhower, "My Views on Berlin," *Saturday Evening Post,* December 9, 1961.
21. *Ibid.*
22. Louis Fischer, *This Is Our World,* pp. 53–54.

Berlin as soon as possible. . . . Mr. Hopkins suggested that we be ready to put an airborne division into Berlin two hours after the collapse of Germany."[23]

This showed a proper appreciation of the importance of Berlin. Yet neither the President nor any associate took steps to invest Berlin when the opportunity presented itself. Churchill insisted on driving to Berlin —and to Prague. The U.S. government paid no heed. There was no race to get to Berlin. Instead the American army sat on its haunches or moved in the wrong direction. Its commanders in the field made the decisions. They did so for humanitarian reasons and because they ignored the political consequences of their military orders. Rumor and Nazi boasts also affected the outcome.

At the same meeting on the *Iowa* with the Joint Chiefs of Staff, President Roosevelt asked for a National Geographic Society map of Europe on which he drew in pencil his proposed line of demarcation of the American zone in Germany. It included Berlin and the port of Stettin on the Baltic Sea as well as Bremen and Hamburg.[24]

With Stettin in the American zone it would not have been incorporated into postwar Poland and, this is less certain, Poland might have enjoyed greater freedom from Russia. With Berlin in the American zone many German lives would have been saved, no ugly wall would now divide the city in twain, and innumerable bitter confrontations between the U.S.A. and the U.S.S.R. from then until today would have been avoided.

But Roosevelt proposed and permitted generals to dispose of the fate of Germany and Europe. The events that unfolded between the autumn of 1944 and May, 1945, make a tragic tale. Not until the end of the war, when American, British, and Soviet armies had conquered all of Germany, was the future of that country and of Berlin determined. Throughout this long waiting period Churchill, conscious of Russia's designs, pressed for the longest possible western lunges eastward. The American military innocently refused.

23. *Foreign Relations of the United States. Diplomatic Papers. The Conferences at Cairo and Tehran 1943.* From the minutes kept by the Joint Chiefs. Pp. 248–255.

24. The map was handed to General George C. Marshall and is reproduced in Maurice Matloff, *Strategic Planning for Coalition Warfare, 1943–1944,* opposite p. 341. This map is probably "the back of an envelope" Roosevelt mentioned to Kennan on April 3, 1944.

XXI SECRETARY MORGENTHAU
AND MR. WHITE

During the second world war President Roosevelt evolved an attitude toward Russia and a policy toward Germany in defeat. Each seemed to have independent status. The effect of the treatment of Germany on Soviet power in Europe appears never to have been assessed in the White House. But it was obvious to some of the President's advisors outside the Executive Mansion.

Roosevelt often encouraged high officials unrelated to the State Department to dabble in formulating foreign policy. Foreign affairs, to be sure, impinge upon many branches of government: Commerce, the Treasury, Agriculture. And, of course, the military. When they differed, as was inevitable, Roosevelt exercised his constitutional prerogative to decide.

Henry Morgenthau, Jr., a friend and neighbor of Roosevelt in the New York countryside, was notably active in putting his favored ideas on foreign affairs before the President. Assistant Secretary of the Treasury Harry Dexter White assiduously aided Morgenthau in this effort. Mr. White manifested an unremitting concern for the welfare of Soviet Russia irrespective of her foreign policy. He at times acted in Moscow's interest at the expense of the West. On August 13, 1940, for instance, he sent President Roosevelt a plan for a "three-way arrangement with China via Russia." The Kremlin then supported Hitler against Britain and, *ipso facto,* against America. Helping China with Russia as intermediary would have placed China at Stalin's mercy and given Germany the same easy access to Chinese resources as she had to Russian.

Mr. White went still further in his partisanship of Russia when he drafted an 18-page memorandum for Secretary Morgenthau in May, 1941, again during the period of Soviet-Nazi collaboration. Its startling terms would "Permit Russia to purchase up to $300 million a year in the United States of any kind of raw or finished material she may wish—with certain exceptions." Further, the White plan would "Permit Russia to maintain up to 5,000 technical men in the United States as students or experts in our industries" and "Permit Russia to maintain fifty military and naval attachés [every one a spy] who shall be permitted to participate in our military and naval maneuvers." Mr. White's memorandum suggested extending a $500 million 10-year credit to the Soviet government and giving Russia most-favored-nation treatment.

The Morgenthau-White team apparently believed in the unlimited ability of the omnipotent dollar to shape major decisions of other nations. On November 17, 1941, twenty days before Pearl Harbor, Morgenthau offered President Roosevelt a memorandum entitled "An Approach to the Problem of Eliminating Tension with Japan and Insuring the Defeat of Germany."

Once America went to war, Germany became Morgenthau's, and White's, intimate concern. On August 13, 1944, the eve of the second Quebec Conference, both men and Ambassador Winant met in Foreign Secretary Eden's London home for an afternoon's discussion. Robert Sherwood came in later. Mr. White made these notes: Eden told the company that the dismemberment of Germany had been decided upon at the Tehran Conference. He promised to show Morgenthau a copy of the minutes which he kept in his office. Eden then explained that British opinion on Germany was divided. One group, to which he belonged, wanted harsh treatment of Germany, including dismemberment, and measures to prevent Germany from becoming a "strong economic power." A second wished to restore Germany as an important country which would stem the advance of communism in Europe. Eden held this policy to be dangerous. A third group stood somewhere between the first two. Eden "hesitatingly admitted that Churchill was probably in that third group."

[At Quebec, in September, 1944, nevertheless, Churchill sided with Morgenthau while Eden opposed Churchill's stand.]

Secretary Morgenthau submitted a proposal dated January 1, 1945, to President Roosevelt for a $10 billion loan to Russia. Assistant Secretary White elaborated ten days later on a $10 billion reconstruction credit to Russia.[1]

Morgenthau's policy toward Germany was a purely emotional and easily comprehensible reaction to Nazi atrocities against Jews and others. Mr. White, who, as he himself testified before the House Un-American Activities Committee on August 13, 1948, "participated in a major way in the formulation" of the Morgenthau Plan, probably shared his chief's sentiments. But he combined this with a patent partisanship of Soviet Russia. He understood international balance-of-power politics which operates like a seesaw: when one end, in this case Germany, is down, the other end, Russia, is likely to be up. Stalin never forgot this simple law. There is no sign that Roosevelt bore it in mind at Tehran or Yalta or in the months between. After the war the imbalance resulting

1. All facts and quotations are from the Harry Dexter White Papers in the Manuscript Room of the Firestone Library of Princeton University.

from wartime decisions and actions created a situation in which the West felt it had to bring its end up. Russia naturally tried to keep her end up.

Roosevelt followed a Wilsonian, or perhaps American, thought pattern. President Woodrow Wilson said in his January 22, 1917, address to the U.S. Senate, "There must be not only a balance of power, but a community of power; not organized rivalries, but an organized common peace." He proposed "some definite concert of power which will make it virtually impossible that any such catastrophe should ever overwhelm us again."

This was the expression of a high ideal. Roosevelt, too, aspired to a definite peace-perpetuating concert of power consisting, as he conceived it, of the U.S., the U.K., the U.S.S.R., and China, chiefly of the U.S. and the U.S.S.R. Wilson, however, said the peace he wanted must rest on "right" and on "the just settlement of vexed questions of territory or of racial and national allegiance." Example: "a united, independent and autonomous Poland." Franklin D. Roosevelt, by contrast, identified not a "community of power" but his two-superpower peace with right, and in the process of wooing the other superpower created a complex of vexed questions of territory and settled none at Yalta or elsewhere.

After Yalta the President diplomatically and without explanation reduced the Treasury's role in foreign affairs to a passive one. He wrote Secretary Stettinius on February 28, 1945, that all nonmilitary decisions taken at Yalta were to be implemented by the State Department in consultation, if necessary, with officials in other branches of the government "on matters touching their respective fields." He confirmed this in a letter to Secretary Morgenthau on March 12: the Secretary of State will carry out all Yalta decisions and inform the Treasury of anything that affected it.[2] Secretary Morgenthau nonetheless persisted in pressing his Plan upon Roosevelt and Stettinius.[3]

Harry Dexter White was accused by two self-confessed Soviet spies—Elizabeth Bentley and Whittaker Chambers—of having been a member of a Soviet spy ring that infested the Treasury. Mr. White thereupon volunteered to testify before the House Un-American Activities Committee and rebut the charges. He appeared on August 13, 1948, and spent several hours on the stand. That day he took the train to New York and saw a physician who told him to go home and stay in bed. The next day he went by train to Fitzwilliam, New Hampshire. A doctor was called. Two physicians attended him on August 15. An electrocardiogram showed definite heart trouble. (Mr. White had been confined to bed from September to December, 1947, as a result of a heart attack.) On August

2. President's Map Room Papers. Crimea Conference folder 3–45. Seen at Hyde Park.
3. *Ibid.*

16 Dr. George E. Emerson, his physician, visited him twice. That afternoon he died after Dr. Emerson left. Dr. Emerson is reported in the Boston *Globe* of November 15, 1953, as having said, "There is nothing to this suicide talk. I don't believe he could have died from an overdose of digitalis."[4]

The story of Harry Dexter White's suicide is not proven. It was possible. The same can be said of his membership in a Soviet spy ring. The Bentley-Chambers testimony on White and others is riddled with inaccuracies and contradictions. This does not mean that Harry Dexter White did not, from violent hatred of Nazi Germany or soft sympathy with the Soviet Union, endeavor shortsightedly to help communist-ruled Russia. For so intelligent a person as White to have proposed, during the Soviet-Nazi 1940 honeymoon, to bring fifty Russian military and naval attachés into the United States, when even the friendliest nation rarely keeps more than five or six, indicates that emotional commitments can eclipse common sense.

XXII STALIN'S STRATEGY

In the beginning is knowledge. And if knowledge is unattainable or uncertain, the least to be expected of government leaders and opinion makers is a meticulous study and analysis of problems, trends, historic background, and current policies. In dealing with Stalin, President Roosevelt allowed his own good hopes and rose-colored spectacles to color his views. He misread Russia.

On July 7, 1942, Roosevelt sent Churchill a telegram: "We have got always to bear in mind the personality of our ally [Stalin] and the very difficult and dangerous situation that confronts him. No one can be expected to approach the war from a world point of view whose country has been invaded. I think we should try to put ourselves in his place."[1]

This highly laudable reminder to Churchill meets the primary requirement of human communication: identification with the recipient. It was neglected during much of the second world war. Stalin was no riddle or enigma or puzzle. His expansionist aspirations, documented in

4. Nathan I. White, *Harry Dexter White, Loyal American*, pp. 71–72. Nathan was the brother of Harry. Bessie (White) Bloom, the sister of both, had the book published privately in 1956, the year after Nathan died.

1. Secret telegram seen at the Franklin D. Roosevelt Library in Hyde Park.

the Soviet-Nazi pact and secret protocol of August 23, 1939, were restated to Foreign Secretary Eden in December, 1941, and adumbrated at Tehran in November, 1943. Stalin broadcast a few of them to the Soviet public on May 1, 1944.[2]

The element of time is a major factor in politics. Ignoring it leads governments into egregious blunders. A policy that is wise and beneficent today may turn injurious and ludicrous a year hence or three years hence. This seems simple enough yet often one necessary deed is exalted into a doctrine for all seasons. Men's actions easily become addictions. When Roosevelt dispatched that wire to Churchill on July 7, 1942, the Soviet Union was bleeding profusely and staggering under Nazi blows. Aid, encouragement, and sympathy were justified. The omnipresent fear of Stalin making another deal with Hitler and the profound conviction that Russia's assistance was needed to speed the defeat of Japan further conduced to a policy of give-and-no-take toward the Soviets. But by 1944 Russia and her allies were winning the war and Stalin would have been a fool to parley with the Nazis. He had, moreover, committed his country to participation in the war against Japan—obviously for the territorial reward he expected. Above all, the Russian government had displayed clear symptoms of a nineteenth-century malady: imperialism.

There was not much anybody could do about it in 1942 or 1943 or early in 1944 except to utter verbal protests—and they rarely deter. One step was available to the West: to let Germany and Russia fight and ruin one another while the Anglo-Americans brought Japan low. Few urged this and none listened. Europe was the nub of the war. No Allied government wished to accomplish communist Russia's destruction. The Soviets were "our gallant allies."

That began to change in 1944.

President Roosevelt realized from the beginning that a pro-Soviet policy had to be rooted in a friendly attitude of the American citizenry toward the Soviet Union. He was a master propagandist. He knew that many Americans, notably Catholics, were alienated by the Kremlin's antireligious stance. Thinking to attack the problem at its source, F.D.R. wrote His Holiness the Pope on September 3, 1941—before America entered the war but when she was already helping Russia: "In so far as I am informed, churches in Russia are open. I believe there is a real possibility that Russia may as a result of the present conflict recognize freedom of religion in Russia, although, of course, without recognition of any official intervention on the part of the church in educational or political matters within Russia. I feel that if this can be accomplished it will put

2. Joseph Stalin, *The Great Patriotic War of the Soviet Union*, p. 125.

the possibility of the restoration of real religious liberty on a much better footing than religious freedom is in Germany today."[3]

During the war the U.S. government encouraged and helped Joseph E. Davies, former ambassador to the Kremlin, to write a nonsense book about the Soviet Union entitled *Mission to Moscow,* subsequently made into a widely distributed motion picture. Stalin's "brown eye," he wrote, "is exceedingly kindly and gentle. A child would like to sit in his lap and a dog would sidle up to him. It is difficult to associate his personality and this impression of kindness with these purges and shootings of the Red Army generals, and so forth. His friends say and Ambassador Troyanovsky [Soviet envoy to Washington] assures me, that it had to be done to protect themselves against Germany—and that some day the outside world will know 'their side.' "

"Their side" would be known through the publication of proof of collusion between the executed marshals, generals, and other officers—an estimated 15,000 to 30,000—and Germany. The United States and the Soviet Union captured carloads of secret German documents when they conquered Germany. Shelves of books filled with these documents have been published. None casts one ray of guilt on the Red military. Soviet prosecutors interrogated the Nazi leaders at the Nuremberg War Criminals trials. No questions were put to them about the Soviet generals and marshals. But Davies justified the Kremlin's murders and spread his absurd judgments throughout the United States: "The story which was unfolded in these [Moscow] trials disclosed a record of Fifth Column and subversive activities in Russia under a conspiracy agreement with the German and Japanese governments that were amazing." No evidence. Only confessions extorted by torture or by promises of clemency, which were broken, and promises to spare the defendant's family, which were usually kept.

On the Soviet political system Davies had this to say: "The fact of dictatorship is apologized for here. It is justified on the ground that it is a realistic expedient, resorted to only to protect the masses of the people until they can themselves rule under a system where ideologically the individual and not the state shall be supreme." Comment would be superfluous.

Ambassador Davies was a gullible small-town lawyer. But Walter Duranty, "King of Reporters," as Bernard Shaw called him, a worldly cynic, veteran Moscow correspondent of the *New York Times,* told his influential readership that "the Bolshevik Revolution has ostensibly—and perhaps genuinely—renounced its international aspect" and "reverted from

3. *Wartime Correspondence Between President Roosevelt and Pope Pius XII,* p. 61.

the methods of pure Marxism . . . to capitalism, in the matter, that is, of stimulus . . ." Relations with the West, therefore, can be "peaceful and mutually advantageous." [4]

Other staff members of the *New York Times* assured America's nervous petty bourgeoisie that the Kremlin no longer aimed to undermine marriage or the family or the foreign capitalist system. On the contrary, Stalin favored Russian nationalism, discouraged divorce, and had lost interest in revolutions abroad.[5]

Even General Douglas MacArthur, never known for pro-Soviet views, greeted the Red Army on February 23, 1942, its twenty-fourth birthday, with a characteristic flourish: "the hopes of civilization," he telegraphed from beleaguered Bataan, "rest on the worthy banners of the courageous Russian Army." It was driving the Germans back into Germany "by a smashing counterattack. . . . The scale and grandeur of this effort marks it as the greatest military achievement in all history."[6]

This somewhat extravagant statement and many others by high officials made friends for Russia. Stalin contrived to reduce their number. A "Memorandum for the President" prepared by the State Department began with a reference to "Increased public *confusion* and *disillusionment*" which it attributed to events in Greece, Italy, and Poland, where England and Russia seemed to be carving out spheres of influence in contravention of the Atlantic Charter. It also noted lack of unity among America, Britain, and Russia, and disappointment with the effectiveness of American diplomacy despite the "vast national contribution to winning the war." Churchill was blamed more than Stalin for the fact that "confidence in our British and Russian allies has declined," but the December, 1944, survey "revealed" that the American public remained more trustful of the possibilities of postwar cooperation with Britain than with Russia. This may have been based on ideas about the cultural affinities between the English-speaking nations or, just as likely, on the expectation that England's weakness would benefit American diplomacy. The survey also reflected a widespread sense that other countries were taking advantage of the United States. The President and the government in general were, in the opinion of an increasing percentage of those polled, not taking care of American interests.[7]

The public pulse fluctuates feverishly. Most people did not pierce the thick curtain that conceals the intricacies of world affairs. Another Big Three conference, its significance highly touted, its final communiqué

---

4. *New York Times,* July 30, 1944.
5. Anne O'Hare McCormick, July 10, 1944; W. H. Lawrence, July 16, 1944.
6. Robert E. Sherwood, *Roosevelt and Hopkins. An Intimate History,* p. 407.
7. PSF. Stettinius Folder 2–44. Copy supplied by the Franklin D. Roosevelt Library.

proclaiming heavenly unity and pie for all, might temporarily reverse mercurial sentiment. But Russia's actions in Poland, particularly her failure to come to the aid of the Warsaw insurrection, internecine strife in Greece, and political unrest in Italy did conjure up an image, sometimes nebulous, sometimes acute, always disturbing, of a Europe which had again become the arena of the kind of jockeying for power that brought on the second world war. Americans—because they have not been invaded or threatened with invasion—habitually think they are fighting a war for more than victory and more than self, that the war is a war to end wars, a war to eliminate the causes of war or to exterminate a great evil. This, though naïve, is deeply seated in the viscera. Hence the malaise and disappointment in the second half of 1944, first within the State Department and then in a widening circle beyond it.

The President and those nearest him remained undaunted. Fleet Admiral William D. Leahy, Chief of Staff to Roosevelt, on whom F.D.R. leaned as heavily as he did on Hopkins, wrote a letter on May 16, 1944, which was attached to the material the President took to Yalta. Any world conflict in the foreseeable future, Leahy stated, "will find Britain and Russia in opposite camps." In that event, the admiral predicted, the United States would defend Britain but could not defeat Russia. Nor could Russia defeat America. Therefore the best policy was friendship among the three major allies.[8]

No doubt. But friendship is not a one-way road.

The fear of a third world war as the second drew to a close was unjustified. But it indicated that out of the bowels of a struggle to destroy one menace a new menace was being born. Both menaces had their origin in totalitarian regimes, one brown and the other red. One wrote race on its banner, the other revolution. Both subjugated foreign nations. Despite repeated avowals by Stalin and his lieutenants that Moscow would not change the social systems of the countries it occupied, Russia did in fact establish a chain of "people's democracies" on her western and southern frontiers.

The term "people's democracy" is tautological. Democracy is rule by the people. In the people's democracies dictators from the beginning ruled the people. Moscow ruled the dictators. This is not extraordinary. It would have been surprising if Stalin had done otherwise.

The logic of imperialism does not permit a colony to have more freedom or a higher standard of living than the so-called motherland. The East European countries, never models of liberty or prosperity, therefore had to be leveled downward to Russian standards. This was the "revolution" Stalin exported to the satellites from 1944 to 1947. What was good

---

8. Seen at the Franklin D. Roosevelt Library.

enough for Russia was good enough for Russia's vassals. The "revolution" consisted in exploiting workers, collectivizing peasants, chaining intellectuals, enthroning bureaucrats, and turning east five times daily to Moscow-Mecca for divine guidance. On the eve of an era in which India and most of Asia and all but a few countries in Africa were liberated from western imperialism, the Russia that preached Leninist anti-imperialism made ready to erect the earth's largest surviving empire. Inevitably, some have sought release. Stalin's heirs held them with steel, fire, threats, and bribes, all poorly wrapped in the transparent tissue of ideology. As the British, French, Dutch, Belgian, U.S., and other capitalist imperialists did not venture abroad in order to bring the benefits of Christian civilization to the peoples of Asia, Africa, and Latin America, so no one will long be misled by Russia's protestations of wishing to confer the blessings of socialism upon her benighted neighbors. This is a red herring. Stalin could annex, therefore he annexed. Territory has a strong lure, especially when a possibility exists that somebody else might take it. The cost to the Soviet people has been high.

Empires antedated capitalism, but because the great empires of modern times were capitalistic, imperialism has been identified with capitalism. However, Lenin's warning that a victorious proletarian revolution might try "to ride on somebody else's back"—the central characteristic of imperialism—leaves room for only one of two conclusions: either socialism, too, can be imperialistic or the proletarian revolution failed to establish socialism. Since Russia, with her money economy, wage system, economic inequality, and burgeoning rather than withering state, conforms more to state capitalism than to socialism, it seems that in the second half of the twentieth century only two countries, capitalist Portugal and state-capitalist Russia, think they need colonial possessions.

The first world war was the crucible of the Bolshevik revolution. The second was the crucible of the Bolshevik empire. As the Red Army pursued the Wehrmacht beyond the Soviet frontier, Russia laid her hand on new lands. British and American armed forces drove the Germans from Italy, France, Holland, Belgium, Denmark, and Norway yet did not annex them or rob them of territory. Where the Russian army penetrated Russian power remained.

Stalin was too clever to impose communist rule precipitately. At home he had climbed to the pinnacle of the power pyramid by deliberate installments. Applying the same gradualism he had destroyed the human obstacles encountered on his way up. Coups and revolutions were alien to his nature. The presence in the new lands of the Red Army and of the Soviet secret police which accompanied it secured Russian rule. Foisting native communists on the doomed nations was an infinitely more delicate task and would have to be performed in stages. The communists were a minuscule minority not only of the population but of political activists. Most of them, exiles in Russia for many years, were foreigners in their country and considered traitors to it. Another Big Three conference, moreover, impended, where Stalin expected agreement and concessions. He did not intend to relinquish what his fighting men had conquered nor did he wish to face Roosevelt and Churchill with irritating accomplished facts.

Nevertheless, a few key positions had to be seized immediately. Primary was the Ministry of Interior, synonym of secret police, which would, as necessity arose, or if it did not, arrest, torture, try, transport to Russia or kill opponents of communist domination. Stalin believed in first manning the dungeons and building from there to the roof.

When, accordingly, the Yalta or Crimean Conference convened in February, 1945, much had been decided—Germany would be divided and Russia would have her satellites and join in fighting Japan. Yalta made less history than is generally believed. It did serve the useful purpose of making Stalin's goals unmistakably clear. Roosevelt's eyes were opened just before he died.

BIBLIOGRAPHY

BOOKS

Armstrong, Hamilton Fish. *Tito and Goliath.* New York: The Macmillan Co., 1951.

Baldwin, Hanson W. *Battles Lost and Won. Great Campaigns of World War II.* New York: Harper & Row, 1966.

———. *Great Mistakes of the War.* New York: Harper & Brothers, 1949.

Blum, John Morton. *Years of Urgency 1938–1941. From the Morgenthau Diaries.* Boston: Houghton Mifflin Co., 1965.

Bor-Komorowski, T. *The Secret Army.* London: Victor Gollancz, Ltd., 1950.

Browder, Earl. *Teheran. Our Path in War and Peace.* New York: International Publishers, 1944.

Browder, Robert Paul. *The Origins of Soviet-American Diplomacy.* Princeton, N.J.: Princeton University Press, 1953.

Bryant, Sir Arthur. *The Turn of the Tide. A History of the War Years Based on the Diaries of Field-Marshal Lord Alanbrooke, Chief of the Imperial General Staff.* Garden City, N.Y.: Doubleday & Co., Inc., 1957.

Bullock, Alan. *Hitler. A Study in Tyranny.* New York: Harper & Row, 1962.

Butler, J. R. M. (Ed.). *History of the Second World War. Grand Strategy.* Vol. II. *September 1939-June 1941.* London: United Kingdom Military Series, Her Majesty's Stationery Office, 1957. Vol. III. Gwyer, J. M. A., and Butler, J. R. M. *June 1941-August 1942. London:* United Kingdom Military Series, Her Majesty's Stationery Office, 1964. Vol. V. *Ehrman, John. August 1943-September 1944.* London: United Kingdom Military Series, Her Majesty's Stationery Office, 1964. Vol. VI. Ehrman, John. *October 1944-August 1945.* London: United Kingdom Military Series, Her Majesty's Stationery Office, 1956.

Bychowski, Gustav. *Dictators and Disciples. From Caesar to Stalin. A Psychoanalytic Interpretation of History.* New York: International Universities Press, 1948.

Channon, Sir Henry. *Chips. The Diaries of Sir Henry Channon.* Edited by Robert Rhodes James. London: Weidenfeld and Nicolson, 1967.

Chuikov, Vasili I. *The End of the Third Reich.* Translated from the Russian by Ruth Kisch. London: MacGibbon & Kee, Ltd., 1967.

———. *The Fall of Berlin.* New York: Holt, Rinehart and Winston, 1967.

217

Churchill, Winston S. *Great Contemporaries.* New York: G. P. Putnam's Sons, 1937.

———. *The Second World War. Closing the Ring.* Boston: Houghton Mifflin Co., 1951.

———. *The Second World War. The Grand Alliance.* Boston: Houghton Mifflin Co., 1950.

———. *The Second World War. The Hinge of Fate.* Boston: Houghton Mifflin Co., 1950.

———. *The Second World War. Triumph and Tragedy.* Boston: Houghton Mifflin Co., 1953.

Clark, Alan. *Barbarossa. The Russian-German Conflict. 1941–45.* New York: William Morrow and Co., 1965.

Cline, Ray S. *Washington Command Post: the Operations Division.* Washington, D.C.: War Department, Office of the Chief of Military History, Department of the Army, 1951.

Collins, Larry, and Lapierre, Dominique. *Is Paris Burning?* New York: Simon and Schuster, 1965.

Custine, de. *The Journals of the Marquis de Custine. Journey for Our Time.* Edited and translated by Phyllis Penn Kohler. New York: Pellegrini & Cudahy, 1951.

Czapski, Joseph. *The Inhuman Land.* Translated from the French by Gerard Hopkins. New York: Sheed & Ward, Inc., 1952.

———. *Unmenschliche Erde.* Cologne: Kiepenheur & Witsch, 1967.

Dallin, Alexander (Ed.). *Soviet Conduct in World Affairs.* New York: Columbia University Press, 1960.

Dallin, David J. *Soviet Russia's Foreign Policy. 1939–1942.* New Haven: Yale University Press, 1942.

Deakin, F. W. *The Brutal Friendship. Mussolini, Hitler and the Fall of Italian Fascism.* New York: Harper & Row, 1962.

Deakin, F. W., and Storry, G. R. *The Case of Richard Sorge.* New York: Harper & Row, 1966.

Deane, John R. *The Strange Alliance. The Story of Our Efforts at Wartime Co-Operation with Russia.* New York: The Viking Press, 1947.

Dedijer, Vladimir. *Tito.* New York: Simon and Schuster, 1953.

Djilas, Milovan. *Conversations with Stalin.* Translated from the Serbo-Croat by Michael B. Petrovich. New York: Harcourt, Brace & World, Inc., 1962.

Eden, Anthony. *The Memoirs of Anthony Eden, Earl of Avon. Facing the Dictators.* Boston: Houghton Mifflin Co., 1962.

———. *The Memoirs of Anthony Eden, Earl of Avon. Full Circle.* Boston: Houghton Mifflin Co., 1960.

———. *The Memoirs of Anthony Eden, Earl of Avon. The Reckoning.* Boston: Houghton Mifflin Co., 1965.

Ehrman, John. *See* Butler, J. R. M. (Ed.), *History of the Second World War. Grand Strategy.*

Eisenhower, Dwight D. *Crusade in Europe.* New York: Doubleday & Co., Inc., 1952.

Erickson, John. *The Soviet High Command. A Military-Political History 1918–1941.* London: St Martin's Press, 1962.

Feis, Herbert. *Churchill * Roosevelt * Stalin. The War They Waged and the Peace They Sought.* Princeton, N.J.: Princeton University Press, 1957.

Fischer, George. *Soviet Opposition to Stalin. A Case Study in World War II.* Cambridge, Mass.: Harvard University Press, 1952.

Fischer, Louis. *The Great Challenge*. New York: Duell, Sloan and Pearce, 1946.
————. *Men and Politics, An Autobiography*. Rev. ed. New York: Harper & Row, 1966.
————. *Russia's Road from Peace to War. Soviet Foreign Relations 1917–1941*. New York: Harper & Row, 1969.
————. *This Is Our World*. New York: Harper & Brothers, 1956.
Fleming, D. F. *The Cold War and Its Origins. 1917–1960*. Vol. I. *1917–1950*. Garden City, N.Y.: Doubleday & Company, Inc., 1961. Vol. II. *1950–1960*. Garden City, N.Y.: Doubleday & Company, Inc., 1961.
Fontaine, André. *Histoire de la Guerre Froide*. Vol. I. *de la Révolution d'octobre à la Guerre de Corée. 1917–1950*. Paris: Fayard, 1965.
Garthoff, Raymond L. *Soviet Strategy in the Nuclear Age*. New York: Frederick A. Praeger, 1958.
General Sikorski Historical Institute (Eds.). *Documents on Polish-Soviet Relations 1939–1945*. Vol. I. *1939–1943*. London: Heinemann, 1961. Vol. II. *1943–1945*. London: Heinemann, 1967.
Greenfield, Kent Roberts (Ed.). *Command Decisions*. Prepared by the Office of the Chief of Military History, Department of the Army. New York: Harcourt, Brace and Co., 1959.
Halperin, Ernst. *The Triumphant Heretic. Tito's Struggle against Stalin*. London: Heinemann, 1958.
Hamrell, Sven, and Widstrand, Carl Gösta. *The Soviet Bloc, China and Africa*. Uppsala: The Scandinavian Institute of African Studies, 1964.
Hannak, Jacques. *Karl Renner und seine Zeit. Versuch einer Biographie*. Vienna: Europa Verlag Wien, 1965.
Hansen, Reimer. *Das Ende des Dritten Reiches. Die deutsche Kapitulation 1945*. Stuttgart: Ernst Klett Verlag, 1966.
Heath, F. W. *A Churchill Anthology*. London: Odhams Press Limited, 1962.
Higgins, Trumbull. *Hitler and Russia. The Third Reich in a Two-Front War. 1937–1943*. New York: The Macmillan Co., 1966.
————. *Winston Churchill and the Second Front*. New York: Oxford University Press, 1957.
Hildebrandt, Rainer. *wir sind die letzten. Aus dem leben des Winderstandskämpfers Albrecht Haushofer und Seiner Freunde*. Berlin: Michael-Verlag Neuwied. No date.
Horelick, Arnold L., and Rush, Myron. *Strategic Power and Soviet Foreign Policy*. Chicago & London: University of Chicago Press, 1965.
Hull, Cordell. *The Memoirs of Cordell Hull*. Vols. I and II. New York: The Macmillan Co., 1948.
Institute of Marxism-Leninism of the Soviet Communist Party. *Istoria Velikoi Otechestvennoi Voiny Sovetskovo Soyuza 1941–1945*. (The History of the Great Fatherland War of the Soviet Union 1941–1945). Vol. I. (The Preparation and Unleashing of the War by the Imperialist Powers). Deborin, G. A. (Ed. in chief); Zastavenko, G. F.; Lekomtsev, R. Z.; Semenov, N. A.; Tamonov, F. I.; Shuktomov, P. I.; Ekshtein, A. E. Moscow: Military Publishers of the Ministry of Defense of the Soviet Union, 1960. Vol. 2. (The Repulse by the Soviet People of the Treacherous Attack of Fascist Germany against the U.S.S.R. The Creation of Conditions for a Basic Change in the War. June 1941–November 1942). Fokin, N. A. (Ed. in chief); Belikov, A. M.; Yemelianov, A. P.; Melchin, A. I.; Popov, V. I.; Skotnikov, Y. A.; Spirin, L. M.; Tamo-

nov, F. I. Moscow: Military Publishers of the Ministry of Defense of the Soviet Union, 1961. Vol. 3 (A Basic Change in the Course of the Great Fatherland War. November 1942-December 1943). Petrov, Y. P. (Ed. in chief); Abaeva, L. N.; Grushko, V. I.; Yershov, A. G.; Samoilo, N. A.; Soldatenko, E. I.; Spasskii, A. A.; Utkin, G. M.; Churbanov, L. G. Moscow: Military Publishers of the Ministry of Defense of the Soviet Union, 1961. Vol. 4. (The Expulsion of the Enemy from the Territories of the Soviet Union and the Beginning of the Liberation of the Peoples of Europe from the Fascist Yoke. 1944). Minasian, M. M. (Ed. in chief); Bogdanov, P. P.; Dolgii, M. S.; Krestinkova, N. V.; Prokofev, E. A.; Tavrovskaia, G. M.; Traktuev, M. I.; Sharev, M. A.; Shuktomov, P. I. Moscow; Military Publishers of the Ministry of Defense of the Soviet Union, 1962. Vol. 5. (The Victorious Conclusion of the War against Fascist Germany. The Defeat of Imperialistic Japan. 1945). Roshchin, S. I. (Ed. in chief); Bogush, E. U.; Bulycheva, G. I.; Zhabkin, I. M.; Zhelanov, V. N.; Klimov, I. D.; Seregin, V. P.; Soldatenko, E. I. Moscow: Military Publishers of the Ministry of Defense of the Soviet Union, 1963. Vol. 6 (The Results of the Great Fatherland War). Vasilenko, V. A. (Ed. in chief); Voronin, V. V.; Gurevich, S. M.; Deborin, G. A.; Zalesskii, T. K.; Zastavenko, G. F.; Zverev, V. A.; Popova, V. I.; Raskatmy, M. Y.; Redko, Y. A.; Semenov, N. A.; Seregin, V. P.; Skurichiin, M. D. Moscow: Military Publishers of the Ministry of Defense of the Soviet Union, 1965.

International Military Tribunal. *Trial of the Major War Criminals. Official Text in the English Language.* Vol. XVII. *Proceedings 25 June 1946-8 July 1946.* Nuremberg, 1948.

Israilian, V. L. *Diplomatiticheskaia Istoriia Velikoi Otechestvennoi Voiny 1941– 1945* (Diplomatic History of the Great Fatherland War 1941–1945). Moscow: Publishing House of the Institute of International Relations, 1959.

Jakobson, Max. *Finnish Neutrality. A Study of Finnish Foreign Policy Since the Second World War.* New York: Frederick A. Praeger, 1969.

Kardelj, Edvard. *After Five Years.* New York: Yugoslav Information Center, 1953.
———. *Socialism and War.* Belgrade: Beogradski Graficki Zavod, 1960.

Kennan, George F. *Memoirs 1925–1950.* Boston: Atlantic Monthly Press, 1967.

Kertész, Stephen D. *Diplomacy in a Whirlpool. Hungary between Nazi Germany and Soviet Russia.* Notre Dame, Ind.: University of Notre Dame Press, 1953.

Knapp, Wilfrid. *A History of War and Peace 1939–1965.* New York: Oxford University Press, 1967.

Kolko, Gabriel. *The Politics of War. The World and United States Foreign Policy, 1943–1945.* New York: Random House, 1968.

Kolkowicz, Roman. *The Soviet Military and the Communist Party.* Princeton, N.J.: Princeton University Press, 1967.

Laqueur, Walter Z. *The Soviet Union and the Middle East.* New York: Frederick A. Praeger, 1959.

Leahy, Fleet Admiral William D. *I Was There. The Personal Story of the Chief of Staff to Presidents Roosevelt and Truman Based on His Notes and Diaries Made at the Time.* New York: McGraw-Hill Book Co., Inc., 1950.

Macintosh, J. M. *Strategy and Tactics of Soviet Foreign Policy.* London: Oxford University Press, 1962.

Mackiewicz, Josef. *Katyn-ungesühntes Verbrechen.* Zurich: Thomas Verlag, 1949.

Maclean, Fitzroy. *Eastern Approaches.* London: Jonathan Cape, 1949.

Macmillan, Harold. *The Blast of War. 1939–1945.* New York: Harper & Row, 1967.

McLane, Charles B. *Soviet Strategies in Southeast Asia. An Exploration of Eastern Policy under Lenin and Stalin.* Princeton, N.J.: Princeton University Press, 1966.

Maisky, Ivan. *Vospominania Sovietskovo Posla, Voina 1939–1943.* Moscow: 1965.

———. *Memoirs of a Soviet Ambassador, The War 1939–1943.* Translated by Andrew Rothstein. London: Hutchinson, 1967.

Matloff, Maurice. *Strategic Planning for Coalition Warfare 1943–1944.* Washington, D.C.: Office of the Chief of Military History, Department of the Army, 1959.

Matloff, Maurice, and Snell, Edwin M. *United States Army in World War II. Strategic Planning for Coalition Warfare. 1941–1942.* Washington, D.C.: Office of the Chief of Military History, Department of the Army, 1953. *1943–1944.* Washington, D.C.: Office of the Chief of Military History, Department of the Army, 1959.

Mikolajczyk, Stanislaw. *The Pattern of Soviet Domination.* London: Sampson, Low, Marston & Co., Ltd., 1948.

———. *The Rape of Poland: The Pattern of Soviet Aggression.* New York: McGraw-Hill, 1948.

Monfort, Henri de. *Le Massacre de Katyn. Crime Russe ou Crime Allemand?* Paris: La Table Ronde, 1966.

Moran, Lord. *Churchill. Taken from the Diaries of Lord Moran. The Struggle for Survival 1940–1945.* Boston: Houghton Mifflin Co., 1966.

Morgan, Sir Frederick (Cossac). *Overture to Overlord.* New York: Doubleday & Co., Inc., 1950.

Mosely, Philip E. *The Kremlin and World Politics. Studies in Soviet Policy and Action.* New York: Vintage Books, 1960.

Murphy, Robert. *Diplomat among Warriors.* New York: Doubleday & Co., Inc., 1964.

Neal, Fred Warner. *Titoism in Action. The Reforms in Yugoslavia.* Berkeley and Los Angeles: University of California Press, 1958.

Neumann, William L. *After Victory: Churchill, Roosevelt, Stalin and the Making of the Peace.* New York: Harper & Row, 1967.

Penkovskiy, Oleg. *The Penkovskiy Papers.* Translated by Peter Deriabin. Garden City, N.Y.: Doubleday & Co., Inc., 1965.

Perkins, Frances. *The Roosevelt I Knew.* New York: Viking Press, 1946.

Phillipps, G. D. R. *Russia, Japan and Mongolia.* London: Frederick Muller, Ltd., 1942.

Ponomarev, B. N.; Gromyko, A. A., and Khostov, V. M. (Eds.). *Istoria Vneshnei Politiki SSSR 1917–1966* (The History of the Foreign Policy of the U.S.S.R. 1917–1966). *Chast Pervaya 1917–1945.* (Part I, 1917–1945.) Moscow: Nauka Publisher, 1966.

Reale, Eugenio, avec Duclos, Jacques. *Au Banc des Accusés à la Réunion Constitutive du Kominform à Szklarska Poreba (22–27 Septembre 1947).* Translated from the Italian by Pierre Bonuzzi. Paris: Librairie Plon, 1947.

Reischauer, Edwin O., and Fairbank, John K. *East Asia. The Great Tradition.* Boston: Houghton Mifflin Co., 1958.

Renouvin, Pierre. *World War II and Its Origins. International Relations, 1929–1945.* Translated by Rémy Inglis Hall. New York: Harper & Row, 1969.

Rock, Vincent P. *A Strategy of Interdependence. A Program for the Control of Conflict Between the United States and the Soviet Union.* New York: Charles Scribner's Sons, 1964.

Roosevelt, Eleanor. *The Autobiography of Eleanor Roosevelt.* New York: Harper & Brothers, 1961.

Roosevelt, Elliott. *As He Saw It.* New York: Duell, Sloan and Pearce, 1946.

Rostow, W. W. in collaboration with Alfred Levin. *The Dynamics of Soviet Society.* New York: W. W. Norton & Co., 1967.

Rozek, Edward J. *Allied Wartime Diplomacy. A Pattern in Poland.* New York: John Wiley & Sons, Inc., 1958.

Rozhdestvenskii, P., and Shkarenkova, G. *Spravochnik Propagandista—Mezhdunarodnika* (Reference Book for the Propagandist on International Affairs). Moscow: Publisher of Political Literature, 1967.

Ryan, Cornelius. *The Longest Day. June 6, 1944.* New York: Simon and Schuster, 1959.

Salisbury, Harrison E. *The 900 Days. The Siege of Leningrad.* New York: Harper & Row, 1969.

Sanakoyev, S. P., and Tsibulevsky, B. L. (Eds.). *Tegeran, Yalta, Potsdam. A Collection of Documents.* Moscow, 1967.

Schellenberg, Walter. *The Labyrinth. Memoirs of Walter Schellenberg.* New York: Harper & Brothers, 1956.

Scheurig, Bodo. *Freies Deutschland. Das Nationalkomitee und der Bund Deutscher Offiziere in der Sowjetunion 1943–1945.* Munich: Nymphenburger Verlagshandlung, 1960.

Sherwood, Robert E. *Roosevelt and Hopkins. An Intimate History.* New York: Harper & Brothers, 1948.

Shirer, William L. *The Rise and Fall of the Third Reich. A History of Nazi Germany.* New York: Simon and Schuster, 1960.

Slessor, Sir John. *The Central Blue: The Autobiography of Sir John Slessor, Marshal of the RAF.* New York: Frederick A. Praeger, 1957.

Smith, Gaddis. *American Diplomacy during the Second World War, 1941–1945.* New York: John Wiley and Sons, 1965.

Sokolovsky, Marshal V. D. (Ed.). *Military Strategy. Soviet Doctrine and Concepts.* New York: Frederick A. Praeger, 1963.

———.*Soviet Foreign Policy During the Patriotic War. Documents and Materials.* Translated from the Russian by Andrew Rothstein. Vol. I. *June 22, 1941– December 31, 1943.* London: Hutchinson & Co. (Publishers), Ltd. No date. Vol. II. *January 1, 1944–December 31, 1944.* London: Hutchinson & Co. (Publishers), Ltd. No date.

Stahl, Zdzislaw. *The Crime of Katyn. Facts and Documents.* With a foreword by Gen. Wladyslaw Anders. London: Polish Cultural Foundation, 1965.

Stalin, Marshal Joseph. *On the Great Patriotic War of the Soviet Union. Speeches, Orders of the Day, and Answers to Foreign Press Correspondents.* London: Hutchinson & Co., 1944.

———. *The Great Patriotic War of the Soviet Union.* New York: International Publishers, 1945.

Standley, Admiral William H., and Ageton, Rear Admiral Arthur A. *Admiral Ambassador to Russia.* Chicago: Henry Regnery Co., 1955.

Stettinius, Edward R. Jr. *Roosevelt and the Russians. The Yalta Conference.* Walter Johnson (Ed.). Garden City, N.Y.: Doubleday & Co., 1949.

Stimson, Henry L., and Bundy, McGeorge. *On Active Service in Peace and War.* New York: Harper & Brothers, 1948.

Strang, Lord. *Home and Abroad.* London: Andre Deutsch Limited, 1956.

The Tehran Conference. The Three-Power Declaration Concerning Iran. Decem-
ber 1943. Iran: The Ministry of Foreign Affairs, 1943.

Toscano, Mario. *The History of Treaties and International Politics. I. An Intro-*
duction to the History of Treaties and International Politics: The Documen-
tary and Memoir Sources. Baltimore: Johns Hopkins Press, 1966.

Trotsky, Leon. *Trotsky's Diary in Exile 1935.* Translated from the Russian by
Elena Zarudnaya. Cambridge, Mass.: Harvard University Press, 1959.

Ulam, Adam B. *Titoism and the Cominform.* Cambridge, Mass.: Harvard University Press, 1952.

Umiastowski, R. *Poland, Russia and Great Britain 1941–1945.* London: Hollis &
Carter, 1946.

U.S. Congress. House Select Committee. *The Katyn Forest Massacre. Hearings.*
Washington, D.C.: U.S. Government Printing Office, 1951. Part 4 *(London,*
England). Washington, D.C.: U.S. Government Printing Office, 1952. Part 6.
Washington, D.C.: U.S. Government Printing Office, 1952.

U.S. Department of State. *Bulletin.* Vol. V. Numbers 106–131. July 5–December 27,
1941. Washington, D.C.: U.S. Government Printing Office, 1942.

———. *Documents on German Foreign Policy.* Series D. *(1937–1945).* Vol. XIII. *The*
War Years. June 23–December 11, 1941.

———. *Foreign Relations of the United States. Diplomatic Papers. The Confer-*
ences at Cairo and Tehran 1943. Washington, D.C.: U.S. Government Printing Office, 1961. *Foreign Relations of the United States. Diplomatic Papers.*
1942. Vol. III. *Europe.* Washington, D.C.: U.S. Government Printing Office,
1961. *Foreign Relations of the United States. Diplomatic Papers. 1944.* Vol.
V. *The Near East, South Asia, and Africa. The Far East.* Washington, D.C.:
U.S. Government Printing Office, 1965.

———. *Nazi-Soviet Relations, 1939–1941. Documents from the Archives of the*
German Foreign Office. Raymond James Sontag and James Stuart Beddie
(Eds.). Washington, D.C.: U.S. Government Printing Office, 1948.

U.S. Senate Committee on the Judiciary, 87th Congress. James O. Eastland, Chairman. *Yugoslav Communism. A Critical Study.* Washington, D.C.: U.S. Government Printing Office, 1961.

U.S. War Department. *Biennial Report of the Chief of Staff of the United States*
Army to the Secretary of War, July 1, 1943 to June 30, 1945. Washington,
D.C.: War Department, 1945.

U.S.S.R. Ministry of External Affairs. *Perepiska Predsedatelia Sovieta Ministrov*
SSSR S Presidentami SSHA I Premier-Ministrami Velikobritanii Vo Vremia
Velikoi Otchestvennoi Voiny 1941–1945. Tom Pervii, Perepiska Y. Cherchil-
lem I K. Ettli (Iul 1941–Noyabr 1945) (Correspondence of the Chairman of
the Council of Ministers of the U.S.S.R. with the Presidents of the U.S.A. and
the Prime Ministers of Great Britain during the Great Fatherland War 1941–
1945. Vol. I. Correspondence with W. Churchill and C. Attlee) (July 1941–
November 1945). Moscow, 1958. Vol. II. Correspondence with F. Roosevelt
and H. Truman (August 1941–December 1945). Moscow, 1958.

———. *Correspondence between the Chairman of the Council of Ministers of the*
U.S.S.R. and the Presidents of the U.S.A. and the Prime Ministers of Great
Britain during the Great Patriotic War of 1941–1945. Vol. I. *Correspondence*
with Winston S. Churchill and Clement R. Attlee (July 1941–November
1945). Moscow: Foreign Languages Publishing House, 1957. Vol. II. *Corre-*
spondence with Franklin D. Roosevelt and Harry S. Truman (August 1941–
December 1945). Moscow: Foreign Languages Publishing House, 1957.

Voznesensky, Nikolai A. *The Economy of the USSR During World War II.* Washington, D.C.: Public Affairs Press, 1948.

Wartime Correspondence between President Roosevelt and Pope Pius XII. New York: The Macmillan Co., 1947.

Watt, D.C. *Britain Looks to Germany. British Opinion and Policy Towards Germany Since 1945.* London: Oswald Wolff, 1965.

Weber, Hermann. *Die Kommunistische Internationale. Eine Dokumentation.* Hanover: J. H. W. Dietz Nachf. GmbH, 1966.

Welles, Sumner. *The Time for Decision.* New York: Harper & Brothers, 1944.

———. *Where Are We Heading?* New York: Harper & Brothers, 1946.

Werth, Alexander. *Russia at War 1941–1945.* New York: E. P. Dutton & Co., Inc., 1964.

White, Nathan I. *Harry Dexter White, Loyal American.* Waban, Mass.: Published by Bessie (White) Bloom, 1956.

Wilmot, Chester. *The Struggle for Europe.* New York: Harper & Brothers, 1952.

Winant, John Gilbert. *Letter from Grosvenor Square. An Account of a Stewardship.* Boston: Houghton Mifflin Co., 1947.

Woodward, E. L., and Butler, Rohan (Eds.). *Documents on British Foreign Policy. 1919–1939.* Third Series. *1938–1939.* Vol. I. *1938.* London: Her Majesty's Stationery Office, 1949. Vol. II. *1938.* London: Her Majesty's Stationery Office, 1949. Vol. III. *1938–9.* London: Her Majesty's Stationery Office, 1950. Vol. IV. *1939.* London: Her Majesty's Stationery Office, 1951. Vol. V. *1939.* London: Her Majesty's Stationery Office, 1952. Vol. VI. *1939.* London: Her Majesty's Stationery Office, 1953. Vol. VII. *1939.* London: Her Majesty's Stationery Office, 1954. Vol. VIII. *1938–9.* London: Her Majesty's Stationery Office, 1955.

Woodward, Sir Llewellyn. *British Foreign Policy in the Second World War.* London: Her Majesty's Stationery Office, 1962.

Young, Kenneth. *Churchill and Beaverbrook. A Study in Friendship and Politics.* London: Eyre & Spottiswoode, 1966.

Zawodny, J.K. *Death in the Forest. The Story of the Katyn Forest Massacre.* Notre Dame, Ind.: University of Notre Dame Press, 1962.

PAMPHLETS AND ARTICLES

McVey, Ruth T. *The Soviet View of the Indonesian Revolution.* Ithaca, N.Y.: Cornell University, Southeast Asia Program, Modern Indonesia Project, 1957. (Interim report, 83 pp.)

Piyade, Mosha. *About the Legend that the Yugoslav Uprising Owed Its Existence to Soviet Assistance.* London, 1950. Pamphlet, 24 pp.

Yugoslavia Central Committee of the Communist Party. *The Soviet-Yugoslav Dispute. Text of the Published Correspondence.* London and New York: Royal Institute of International Affairs, 1948. Pamphlet, 79 pp.

INDEX

72 73 74 75 10 9 8 7 6 5 4 3 2 1